The Christian Structure of Politics

The Christian Structure of Politics

On the *De Regno* of Thomas Aquinas

William McCormick, SJ

The Catholic University of America Press
Washington, D.C.

Copyright © 2022
The Catholic University of America Press
All rights reserved

Cataloging-in-Publication Data available
from the Library of Congress
ISBN 978-0-8132-3709-1

For my mother

CONTENTS

Acknowledgments	ix
A Note on the Text	xiii
Introduction: Christianity and Politics	1
1. The Aristotelian State of Nature	23
2. The Augustinian Earthly City	61
3. The Reward of the King	99
4. The Politics of Revelation	151
5. The Christian Structure of Politics	205
Conclusion: On Actions and Words	255
Bibliography	261
Index	269

ACKNOWLEDGMENTS

This book is the fruit of friendship, and I am happy to open it with an expression of gratitude for those friendships. This project originated as a dissertation, and I remain most grateful to my dissertation committee: J. Budziszewski, Benjamin Gregg, Russell Hittinger, Rob Koons, Devin Stauffer, and the late Father James Schall, SJ. For their kindness and guidance at Texas, I also thank Zoltan Barany, Cathy Boone, Dan Brinks, Erik Dempsey, Al Martinich, Rob Moser, Lorraine Pangle, Thomas Pangle, and Kurt Weyland.

College mentors and friends nurtured in me a deep love and reverence for texts in the best Chicago tradition, a reverence that I hope comes across in this text. There are too many people to thank, but I wish to single out Nathan Tarcov, Danielle Allen, Constantin Fasolt, Leon Kass, Thomas Levergood, Jacob T. Levy, John P. McCormick, Emily Nacol, Patricia Nordeen, Father Patrick Rugen, and the late Father Michael Yakaitis. I owe a special debt to Jennie Ikuta, who has been a constant friend throughout this project.

This project took final form during my Jesuit regency at Saint Louis University, and I owe great thanks to many friends and colleagues there: Sharilyn Bazile, Greg Beabout, Jeff Bishop, J. D. Bowen, Ellen Carnaghan, Sarah Cate, Bob Cropf, Chris Duncan, Ali Fisunoglu, Chad Flanders, Jim Gilsinan, Ruth Groff, Morgan Hazelton, Grant Kaplan, Nori Katagiri, Mary Lapusan, Michelle Lorenzini, Wynne Moskop, Matt Nanes, Scott Ragland, Steve Rogers, Eric Royer, Julie Hanlon Rubio, Eleonore Stump, Emmanuel Uwalaka, Ken Warren, and Penny Weiss.

Acknowledgments

Since Chicago, many friends and colleagues guided me through the manuscript process in Austin, Cambridge, the Bronx, and Saint Louis, including Serena Arancibia, Ayca Arkilic, Michael and Janice Breidenbach, Matt and Elodie Buehler, Cody and Cat Carter, Thomas D'Andrea, Sean and Maria Ferguson, Peter and Allison Harris, Austin Hart and Laura Field, Anthony Hayden, Doug Kries, Pete Lucier, Jeff, Lisa and Brittany Mohr, Cary Nederman, Laura Rabinowitz, Paul Rogers, Kevin and DeAnn Stuart, Nick Tampio, Mark and Mijke Verbitsky, and Danny Wasserman.

My debt to the Society of Jesus is incalculable. I particularly wish to thank my brothers who have assisted me in making this book a reality: Andrea Bianchini, Matt Cortese, Brendan Gottschall, Jim Kennedy, Michael Mohr, Ian Peoples, Juan Ruiz, Aric Serrano, Lucas Sharma, and Bill Woody. I also thank my formatores and superiors: Mark Thibodeaux, Joe Sands, Joe O'Keefe, Dan Daly, Mark Lewis, Doug Marcoullier, Ron Mercier, and Tom Greene. I thank the many Jesuit scholars who have helped form me, including: Mike Barber, Matthew Baugh, Matt Carnes, Chris Collins, Chris Cullen, Bart Geger, Joe Koterski, Fred Kammer, Tom Krettek, Joe Lienhard, Dave Meconi, John O'Malley, John Padberg, Bill Rehg, Tom Reese, Michael Rozier, and Steve Schoenig. Brian Davies, OP, and Aidan Nichols, OP, deserve thanks in the Dominican section. Finally, I give God thanks for the life and memory of Fathers Jim Schall, SJ, and Joe Koterski, SJ.

I want to express my deep gratitude to my family, immediate and extended. My parents, Bill and Loreita, and siblings, Ann Marie and Matthew, have put up with only God knows what and have done so with great love, patience, and cheer. My extended family has throughout my life offered love and prayers that have brought me to where I am today.

Acknowledgments

I thank my students at Texas and SLU for showing me how teaching is but another form of learning. I thank John Martino and the staff at the Catholic University of America Press for guiding me through the publication process.

A NOTE ON THE TEXT

All translations of *De Regno* are mine, from the Latin of Dondaine's critical edition in consultation with the English translation of Eschmann and the French of Roguet.[1] Although Eschmann's edition is excellent, relying on Gerald B. Phelan's 1935 translation, at times I depart from it in favor of more direct renderings of the Latin. This directness at times comes at the price of elegance. Book and chapter numberings follow Eschmann and Dondaine.[2] A Roman numeral followed by an Arabic numeral indicate book and chapter, for example, "I.4" denotes book I, chapter 4. Subsequent stand-alone Arabic numerals indicate a paragraph number, for example, (59) cites paragraph 59.

Students of *De Regno* will note a diversity of book and chapter arrangements across editions of the work, adding yet another impediment to its study. I follow the arrangement of Dondaine and Eschmann. Some editions, including those of the *Corpus Thomisticum* and Divine Providence Press, differ from those of Eschmann and Dondaine in dividing I.1 into I.1 and I.2; combining I.11 and I.12; treating II.1–4 as I.13–16; and treating II.5–8 as II.1–4. Thus, in the Eschmann and Dondaine editions, Ptolemy of Lucca's continuation of the work of Thomas Aquinas begins at II.9, whereas in the *Corpus Thomisticum*, the Ptolemaic elaboration begins at II.5.

1. Roguet's French is Aquinas, *Du Gouvernement Royal*; Eschmann's revision of Phelan's English translation is *On Kingship*, trans. I. Th. Eschmann, OP (Toronto: Pontifical Institute of Mediaeval Studies, 1949).

2. Eschmann, *On Kingship*, introduction, xiv; cf. Dondaine, *De regno ad Regem Cypri*, préface, 443.

The Christian Structure of Politics

Introduction

Christianity and Politics

This book is a small foray into a big question: what is the relationship between Christianity and politics? A critical question for Western culture, and all cultures influenced by the West, the subject is historically vast, theoretically complex, and inevitably polemical. My book, *The Christian Structure of Politics: On the De Regno of Thomas Aquinas*, brings this fraught question into focus through a reading of Thomas Aquinas's *De Regno*.

In *The Christian Structure of Politics,* I argue that Aquinas offers an answer to our question. Christianity, he argues, shows politics to be at once natural to humans but also the site of some of humanity's most unnatural activities. In affirming politics as natural but affected by the Fall, he presents political rule as noble but difficult, a governance that must take its task as seriously as it must respect the spiritual government that transcends it.

To illuminate this Christian message for politics, Aquinas articulates a Gelasianism at whose core is a dualism, which is to say the affirmation of the existence and integrity of the two powers, and the "primacy of the spiritual" over the temporal power.[1] The interplay between dualism and primacy makes *De Regno* an incredible intervention on the role of Christianity in public life,

---

1. This dualism is, of course, quite different from that of Cartesian metaphysics.

a statement made possible by Aquinas's subtle blend of Aristotle and Augustine. Aquinas affords criteria for the evaluation of political communities and their relationship to the transcendent in any time and place through five principles: Gelasianism; the rejection of civil religion and theocracy; Thomistic naturalism; ambivalence to particular regimes; and political pedagogy.

While many thinkers before and after Aquinas present the relation between Christianity and political authority as a contest between institutions, as in the very phrase "church and state," I show that Aquinas provides a teleological framework by which to bypass these often-sterile jurisdictional debates and a prudential framework by which to integrate his theory flexibly within a variety of regimes. Aquinas thereby charts a middle path between contending theories of his time, and gives political practice the benefit of theological principles and practical reflection.

In so doing, Aquinas develops some of the most startling ideas and themes in the history of Christian political thought: a devastating critique of civil religion based on a theology of history found nowhere else in Aquinas's works; the methodical desacralization of monarchy; an analogy between divine and human governance that distinguishes as much as unites the two regimes; the reward of the king as the end of man; a distinction between mild tyranny and "an excess of tyranny," with an implicit admission that mild tyranny is common; a Christian revision of the classical virtue of magnanimity; and, of most direct importance for his royal reader, the Christian ruler as *minister Dei* under the church. *De Regno* turns out to be no ordinary *speculum*.

The Christian Structure of Politics: Why It Matters

The value of such a study, however, may not be obvious. While religion remains a powerful force in global politics, what can a medieval text teach us about such contemporary events?

The end of the Cold War brought neither the halcyon days of liberalism nor the demise of religion. Religion has therefore made itself especially conspicuous in debates over the fate of liberal democracy. In the United States, for example, many evangelical Protestants defended President Donald Trump's policies as the long-awaited recovery of America's providential role in history as a "City upon a Hill," a rollback of the secular modernity that has frustrated the true end of the United States and the institutions through which it functions. Many liberal Catholics and mainline Protestants, on the other hand, denounce those same policies as diametrically opposed to the humanistic secularism inspired by the Gospel, while at the same time agreeing with the evangelical claim that U.S. political institutions need to be restored to their original, good purpose.[2] Still other religious citizens, such as conservative Catholics, have become disillusioned with contemporary liberal politics, and disagree that such reform of liberal democracy is possible, advocating for various "options" as alternatives to liberal democracy. They have thus abandoned "Whiggish" narratives about the complementarity between Catholicism and America advocated by thinkers like John Courtney Murray and Richard

---

2. Examples include Jim Wallis, *God's Politics: Why the Right Gets It Wrong and the Left Doesn't Get It* (San Francisco: HarperSanFrancisco, 2006); Michael Wear, *Reclaiming Hope: Lessons Learned in the Obama White House About the Future of Faith in America* (New York: Thomas Nelson, 2017); and Michael Sean Winters, *Left at the Altar: How the Democrats Lost the Catholics and How the Catholics Can Save the Democrats* (New York: Basic Books, 2008).

John Neuhaus.³ The precise nature of these alternatives to liberal democracy remains hazy, however, and even more so the path of action from liberal democracy to those distant horizons.⁴

What has evaded analysis is the extent to which such political thought and behavior draws on the full range of possibilities of Christian politics. Prima facie, many Christians seem caught between two extremes: throwing their full weight into a concrete political regime, or rejecting and fleeing politics in the hope of a new utopia. Surely there are other alternatives, ones guided by something more substantive than a simple embrace or rejection of contemporary politics.

These doubts about liberal modernity, it is safe to hazard, are not internal merely to Christianity: even authorities profoundly sympathetic to liberalism, like German philosopher Jürgen Habermas, harbor deep reservations about the nature of liberal modernity. But what is the way forward? And are students of the Christian political tradition in a position to contribute to that search?

My core contention in this book is to make plausible, if not prove, that the past can reveal possibilities for the present. I hope in this study of *De Regno* to expand our political imagination by uncovering possibilities that have been shrouded by the centuries. For some, this will mean realizing that politics as practiced in 2020—or 1950 or 1970, for that matter—is not the only possible way to understand or conduct politics.⁵ On the contrary, "the past can reveal possibilities for the present," the task of which it is

---

3. Perhaps best expressed in Murray's claim that "the Religion Clause of our First Amendment 'codified' the freedom of the Church," quoted in Richard W. Garnett, "The Freedom of the Church," *Journal of Catholic Social Thought* 4, no. 1 (2007): 63.

4. Examples of this attitude include Patrick Deneen, *Why Liberalism Failed* (New Haven, Conn.: Yale University Press, 2018) and Rod Dreher, *The Benedict Option* (New York: Sentinel, 2017).

5. I allude to Levin's thesis about the favored golden ages of U.S. liberals and conservatives: Yuval Levin, *The Fractured Republic* (New York: Basic Books, 2016), 13–30.

the scholar to uncover.[6] As Plato's sojourn in Syracuse reminds us, however, it is of course up to the politically active themselves to determine how such treasures can guide and even transform political practice.

For such inspiration, I propose to turn to Aquinas's *De Regno*, or "On Kingship." While Aquinas has long been a crucial figure in Christian thought, his political thought has always been understudied, generally limited to cursory glances at small sections of the *Summa Theologica* or his *Commentary on the "Sentences."* That neglect is unfortunate, as *De Regno* is one of the most fascinating medieval texts on politics. Aquinas's only stand-alone political work, *De Regno* is profoundly practical in its orientation, showing Aquinas at his most sensitive to the interplay between political reflection and the concrete world of politics. Debunking tired clichés about medieval political thought's subjection to superficial Aristotelianism and ill-fitting methods from theology, *De Regno* presents a model of dialogue between political and ecclesiastical authority that preserves prudent and tolerant politics. That model, moreover, has more than antiquarian interest, and it can serve as a valuable guide for how to think about contemporary religion and politics.

De Regno offers an invaluable and unique perspective on Aquinas's political theory. Four facts about *De Regno* supply sufficient reason for studying it in the light of our original questions: *De Regno* is a neglected text; it is a practical work; the few disputes that have arisen over its interpretation center around whether it is philosophical or theological; and it borrows heavily from both Aristotle and Augustine.

First, the neglect of *De Regno*. For good reason, the *Secunda*

---

6. Quentin Skinner, *Liberty Before Liberalism*, Canto Classics (Cambridge: Cambridge University Press, 2012), 112–20. On Skinner, I follow Jacob T. Levy, *Rationalism, Pluralism, and Freedom* (Oxford: Oxford University Press, 2017), 5–6.

Pars of the *Summa Theologica* has pride of place among texts of Aquinas's political thought. Indeed, as we shall see, there is much to be gained in turning to the *Summa* and other works of Aquinas in a study of *De Regno*. It cannot be denied, however, that a *ressourcement* attitude toward the study of Aquinas, which is to say to read Aquinas rather than his interpreters, has considerable merit. Because *De Regno* has been historically neglected, we can short-circuit a great many debates over the structure and meaning of the *Summa Theologica* that have bogged down countless interpreters.[7] Moreover, I argue that a study of a relatively "new" work of Aquinas can reinvigorate debate on his other politically relevant works, not only his *Questions on Law* in the *Prima Secundae* but also his commentaries on Aristotle's *Nicomachean Ethics* and *Politics*, as well as his scriptural commentaries, for example, on the Letter to the Romans.[8] Such study will give us a more dynamic picture of Aquinas's political thought.

If such neglect is a reason to study *De Regno*, then *a fortiori* it is a reason to study the full text, eschewing the piece-meal approach that has characterized most scholarship on it thus far. Just because scholars have neglected *De Regno*, it would be irresponsible to proof-text it simply for its complementarity with other Thomistic texts. I hope to show that *a priori* decisions not to take *De Regno* seriously as an important source of insights on politics do not withstand a careful consideration of the text itself.

Second, *De Regno* is a practical work. It is also Aquinas's longest

---

7. A remarkable feat along these lines is Fulvio Di Blasi, *God and the Natural Law: A Rereading of Thomas Aquinas* (South Bend, Ind.: St. Augustine's Press, 2006).

8. See Marc D. Guerra, "Beyond Natural Law Talk: Politics and Prudence in St. Thomas Aquinas's *On Kingship*," *Perspectives on Politics* 31, no. 1 (2002): 9–14, for the place of the *Questions on Law* in Aquinas's political thought and Jacques Maritain, *An Essay on Christian Philosophy*, trans. Edward H. Flannery (New York: Philosophical Library, 1955), 62–5 on the commentaries.

political work and, in fact, his only freestanding one.⁹ *De Regno*, again, is a letter written to a prince.¹⁰ If this is a letter to a prince, how ought it to be read? What would this prince derive from reading it? Aquinas might not have known much about this king or his kingdom, but certainly he knew that he was writing a letter meant to be of practical value for a Norman war baron attempting to show up his royal prerogative, not an abstract delineation of theoretical principles for theology students at the University of Paris. For this reason, I suspect that *De Regno* will be a particularly valuable example of how Aquinas takes his theological teachings to be relevant in practical affairs. If he would teach the prince toward a better regime, what kind of reform does Aquinas envision? How does it accommodate political actors already *in situ*? And how does Aquinas make his teachings agreeable to someone he could not assume to be particularly intelligent or virtuous? Thus, what makes *De Regno* so attractive for our purposes is that one sees in it Aquinas wrestling with several practical tensions in political life that any polity will have to address. I hope to make this case particularly in regard to his nuanced treatment of tyranny.

Of course, to call it "practical" is one thing; it is quite another to ask whether it is practical theology or philosophy. This has been a flashpoint in discussion about *De Regno*. As one of many *specula principis* (mirrors of prince) written in the medieval ages, *De Regno* has often been invoked in the defense of various programs, sometimes proto-Gallican, sometimes avowedly hierocratic.¹¹ Yet

---

9. The *Commentary on the "Politics"* is famously incomplete, and while Aquinas's *Commentary on the "Ethics"* is a rich and varied practical work, Aquinas does not therein consider the regime as explicitly as he does in *De Regno*. Aquinas's *Letter to the Duchess of Brabant* is something like a freestanding political work, although it focuses on the narrow question of religious toleration.

10. I. Th. Eschmann, OP, introduction to *On Kingship*, by Thomas Aquinas, trans. I. Th. Eschmann (Toronto: Pontifical Institute of Mediaeval Studies, 1949), xxx–xxxi.

11. Ironically, one of the first works to cite *De Regno* came as a defense of Philip the

the few twentieth-century studies on it have taken pains to emphasize that *De Regno* cannot be read as "an independent treatise on political philosophy," or even deny that it has a political teaching.¹² This conversation tends to conflate "theological" with "speculative" and "philosophical" with "practical." If *De Regno* does turn out to be primarily theological, these arguments assume, then, it has no substantial bearing on politics.¹³ But the assumption that theology has no practical relevance is unwarranted. Moreover, no full reading of *De Regno* has been undertaken, and the tantalizing passages on the relationship between the political and ecclesial communities (church and state) have been studied largely in isolation from the overall text.¹⁴ I will show that this discussion of the relationship between philosophy and theology is useful for our understanding of *De Regno* and the nature of practical philosophy within Aquinas's work.

Lastly, I turn to *De Regno* because of its relevance to understanding Aquinas's knowledge and use of Aristotle and Augustine. As is well-attested, Aristotle and Augustine influenced Aquinas's thought perhaps more than anyone short of the Holy Spirit.¹⁵ To

---

Fair's campaign against the papacy, in John of Paris' *De potestate regia et papali*. John of Paris, also known as Quidort, argues that political and religious matters are not only formally but materially distinct, and that the church lacks any temporal authority, even indirectly, as it bears upon the spiritual. See John of Paris, *De Potestate Regia et Papali*, trans. Arthur P. Monahan (New York: Columbia University Press, 1974).

12. Mark F. Jordan, "*De Regno* and the Place of Political Thinking in Thomas Aquinas," *Medioevo* 18 (1992): 163.

13. Aquinas says at *ST* I, q.1, a. 4 that *sacra doctrina* is primarily speculative, not practical, but it is practical insofar as it touches on practical activity from the perspective of God.

14. See, for instance, Laurence Fitzgerald, OP, "St. Thomas Aquinas and the Two Powers," *Angelicum* 56 (1979): 515–56, and Leonard E. Boyle, OP, "The De Regno and the Two Powers," in *Facing History: A Different Thomas Aquinas* (Louvain-la-Neuve: Collège Cardinal Mercier, 2000), 3–12.

15. Servais Pinckaers, OP, *The Sources of Christian Ethics*, trans. Mary Thomas Noble, OP (Washington, D.C.: The Catholic University of America Press, 1995), 134, 174.

state the question crudely, how can one harmonize two competing political teachings, one of which elevates politics above convention and sophistry to the virtue and reason of nature, and the other of which sees in nature corruption and evil? In a work such as *De Regno*, in which Aquinas purports to treat of the regime, we will want to be attentive to when and how Aquinas reconciles these seemingly contradictory strands of his intellectual heritage.

To be tediously clear: I do not question that Aquinas throughout his *opera* masterfully harmonizes the insights of Aristotle and Augustine. Nor do I assert a facile and ultimately false dichotomy between these two great thinkers. I do assert, however, that any thinker working with these figures must account for their differences. Aquinas typically does so, moreover, in texts of a more speculative nature than *De Regno*, works intended for more speculatively inclined audiences. Insofar as *De Regno* is more practical than, say, the *Summa Theologica*, and written as a *speculum* for a prince rather than as a textbook for a Dominican theology student, we should not prejudge how Aquinas will choose to raise and reconcile the positions of Aristotle and Augustine on matters of common interest to both. Rather, we should attend carefully to the movement by which Aquinas brings their respective positions to light.

Moreover, if Eschmann and Dondaine determine correctly that Aquinas wrote *De Regno* during his early encounter with Aristotle's *Politics*, then we should be particularly grateful for this unique insight into Aquinas's own understanding of how to understand politics as both natural and marked by grace and sin. As we will see, *De Regno* clearly signals both ways of viewing the political activity of man.

De Regno: Text, Context, Transmission, and Reception

This book is a work of political theory, which always materially depends upon historical scholarship to make sense of the texts it studies, including their context, transmission, and reception. In the case of *De Regno*, the task of recovering a vision of Thomistic politics has not been aided by the complex textual history of *De Regno*. Yet despite the air of uncertainty surrounding *De Regno* in contemporary scholarship, we know more about the text than one might think. In this section, I will briefly consider some critical issues surrounding its reception: the textual tradition and authorship; the date; the integrity of the text; and the teaching of the work. The magisterial account of *De Regno* comes from H.-F. Dondaine's preface to the Leonine edition, the critical edition of Aquinas's work, so called because of its initiative by Pope Leo XIII. Dondaine relies heavily on I. Th. Eschmann, who, in turn, draws from A. O'Rahilly and J. Échard.[16]

As Dondaine has it, three textual traditions have transmitted *De Regno*: the text of Thomas Aquinas that we know today as *De Regno*; a larger work believed to be devised by one of Aquinas's students; and a shorter version. The first tradition we know of from at least eleven manuscripts from the thirteenth and fourteenth centuries. As Dondaine notes, the copies present the same text with no "notable differences," taking us to the end of

---

16. H.-F. Dondaine, préface to *De regno ad Regem Cypri*, by Thomas Aquinas, ed. H.-F. Dondaine, OP, in *Sancti Thomae de Aquino opera omnia*, vol. 42, *Opuscula* III (Roma: Editori di San Tommaso, 1979), 419–44; Alfred O'Rahilly, "Notes on St. Thomas. IV. *De Regimine Principum*. V. Tolomeo of Lucca, the Continuator of the '*De Regimine Principum*,'" *Irish Ecclesiastical Record* 31 (1928): 396–410; and Jacques Quetif, OP, and Jacques Échard, OP, *Scriptores Ordinis Praedicatorum* (Paris, 1719).

De Regno II.8.[17] These manuscripts explicitly identify the work as one of Saint Thomas Aquinas. To this day, no serious doubts remain about Aquinas's authorship of *De Regno*, the evidence for which Eschmann calls "very imposing indeed."[18]

By the fourteenth century, two other traditions emerged: a shorter text and a longer one. The shorter text ends at II.6. Eschmann and Dondaine both argue that the stop appears to be a mistake on the part of the copyist.[19]

The third textual tradition supplies much of the controversy surrounding *De Regno*, which for most of its history has been known only through, or in spite of, its concealment within a larger text known as *De Regimine Principum*.[20] While leaving *De Regno* I-II.8 intact, *De Regimine Principum* adds sixty-two new chapters, including eight chapters to book II and two wholly new books, III and IV.[21] These additional chapters differ significantly from the style and teaching of *De Regno*, which prompted prominent students of Aquinas to question its authenticity by the fifteenth century.[22] Most scholars believe that this elaboration was worked out by a student of Aquinas, Ptolemy of Lucca.[23] There need not

17. Dondaine, *De regno ad Regem Cypri*, préface, 421, n. 151.
18. Eschmann, *On Kingship*, introduction, xxii. See also Antony Black, *Political Thought in Europe, 1250–1450* (Cambridge: Cambridge University Press, 1992), 22.
19. Dondaine, *De regno ad Regem Cypri*, préface, 438, cf. 441. Eschmann cites O'Rahilly extensively on the shorter version (Eschmann, introduction, 73).
20. Dondaine, *De regno ad Regem Cypri*, préface; Eschmann, introduction, ix–xii; Jean-Pierre Torrell, *Saint Thomas Aquinas: The Person and His Work*, vol. I, trans. Robert Royal (Washington, D.C.: The Catholic University of America Press, 2005), 14. But see I. Th. Eschmann, "St. Thomas Aquinas on the Two Powers," *Mediaeval Studies* 20, no. 1 (1958): 204–5.
21. For a fuller history and analysis of this text, see James M. Blythe, introduction to *On the Government of Rulers: De Regimine Principum*, by Ptolemy of Lucca, trans. James M. Blythe (Philadelphia: University of Pennsylvania Press, 1997), 1–59.
22. Dondaine, *De regno ad Regem Cypri*, préface, 422; Blythe, *On the Government of Rulers*, introduction, 3–5.
23. O'Rahilly, "Notes on St. Thomas," 408.

have been anything sinister in Ptolemy's intentions: medieval authors regularly embellished and completed others' works, with a greater concern for avoiding the *horror vacui* than for preserving the integrity of a text as it was received.[24]

For our purposes, it suffices to say that Aquinas's contribution ends in book II. Échard brought clarity to this issue in an eighteenth-century bibliography of Dominican writings,[25] arguing that Aquinas's text ends in the middle of book II, after which begins that of some other author. Échard thus confirms the witness of the earliest manuscripts. As Dondaine concludes, "At the end of this overview, the testimony of the collections of opuscules of the 13th and 14th centuries remains intact."[26]

The date of *De Regno* has remained elusive. Eschmann dates *De Regno* from between 1260 and 1265.[27] He argues this on the basis of the text itself, which he thinks betrays a superficial acquaintance with Aristotle's *Politics*. Thus, he argues, Aquinas would have written *De Regno* after William of Moerbeke's Latin translation of the *Politics* of Aristotle (~1260) but before his more mature reflections on Aristotle, including the *Prima Secundae* (~1265). Dondaine, invoking Grabmann, doubts that we can establish the date of the text's composition with any certainty but notes that Eschmann's dates should be adjusted to between 1260 and 1271 in the light of Gauthier's research.[28]

The organization and teaching of the text have also been at issue, raising questions about genre and audience. Eschmann describes *De Regno* as a "collection of fragments," a judgment the

---

24. Eschmann, *On Kingship*, introduction, ix–x, xiii–xiv, xxv.
25. Dondaine, *De regno ad Regem Cypri*, préface, 422–23; Eschmann, *On Kingship*, introduction, xxii–xxv.
26. Dondaine, *De regno ad Regem Cypri*, préface, 423.
27. Eschmann, *On Kingship*, introduction, xviii–xxx.
28. Dondaine, *De regno ad Regem Cypri*, préface, 424–25.

cooler Dondaine declines to endorse.²⁹ There are indeed places in *De Regno* that appear to have gaps or lacunae in the text, particularly on the prevention of tyranny (I.6), and the analogy between human and divine government (II.3). Further, there are parts of the text that are perhaps misplaced, as with the reward of the king (I.7–11). Finally, there are places in which Aquinas seems to depart from his later teaching, including on the two powers and the best regime. Such apparent departures later led Eschmann to profound doubts about *De Regno*.³⁰ While this is an overreaction on Eschmann's part, it is true that the text of *De Regno* presents difficulties that must be squarely faced by the careful reader.

Assessing the nature and severity of these gaps and contradictions in *De Regno*, however, requires more attention to the text than Eschmann or subsequent scholars have given it, a deficiency I aim to remedy in this work, particularly by addressing such interpretive concerns, which require attention to audience and genre. When assessing the structure and content of *De Regno*, some scholars, most notably Eschmann, treat *De Regno* as a treatise of political theology. By all accounts, however, *De Regno* is a *speculum principis*: a pedagogical text meant for the intellectual and moral edification of a politically active leader.³¹ Aquinas probably wrote *De Regno* for a Cypriot king to encourage the Cypriot royal house to look favorably on the expanding Dominican presence in

---

29. Eschmann, *On Kingship*, introduction, xxi; Dondaine, *De regno ad Regem Cypri*, préface, 423.

30. Eschmann, "St. Thomas Aquinas on the Two Powers," 204–5; cf. John Finnis, *Aquinas: Moral, Political, and Legal Theory* (Oxford: Clarendon Press, 1998), 254. Here, Eschmann adverts to his earlier doubts about *De Regno*'s structure and lacunae as though he viewed them even then as grounds for questioning Aquinas's authorship, although that doubt is not obvious to the reader of the 1949 introduction. Boyle responded to Eschmann by demonstrating grounds for reconciling these two texts but misses the heart of Eschmann's trepidation (Boyle, OP, "The De Regno and the Two Powers").

31. Dondaine, *De regno ad Regem Cypri*, préface, 423.

the Levant, that is, to become a strategic maritime base for the expansion of Western Christendom. The composition of *De Regno*, therefore, was itself a political act.[32]

The nature of that genre has implications for how we read the text. It can be no easy task determining the relevance of genre for the interpretation of *De Regno*, but one example will highlight the importance and benefits of doing so. One of Eschmann's major concerns about *De Regno* is the introduction, or *prooemium*, in which Aquinas promises to discuss two subjects: the "origin of kingship" (*regni originem*) and "the things which pertain to the office of a king" (*ea quae ad regis officium pertinent*). Yet Aquinas does not execute this plan, Eschmann argues, because the last chapters of book I concern not the origin of kingship but rather its reward. The reward of the king is a practical rather than a theoretical consideration, Eschmann argues, and thus, it belongs in book II, with "the things which pertain to the office of the king."

What can we make of this claim? Prima facie, Eschmann could have a case, although we might wonder if we simply lack a text between I.6 and I.7 that justifies this organization.[33] But one could also ask if Eschmann's rigid separation between theory and practice obscures Aquinas's purpose in writing *De Regno*. As a letter written for a king, would we not expect Aquinas to link closely the king's reward with the preconditions for its attainment? In this vein, Roguet and Chenu both suggest that *De Regno* needs to be read as a moral education for a prince.[34]

Eschmann ignores an obvious question: if this is a letter to a

---

32. Eschmann, *On Kingship*, introduction, xxx–xxxi; Geoffrey F. Hill, *The Frankish Period*, vol. 2 of *A History of Cyprus* (Cambridge: Cambridge University Press, 1948), 305, n. 2.

33. Jordan, "*De Regno* and the Place of Political Thinking in Thomas Aquinas," 161–62.

34. Thomas Aquinas, *Du Gouvernement Royal*, trans. Claude Roguet (Paris: Librairie du Dauphin, 1931), vii; Marie-Dominique Chenu, OP, book review, *Bulletin thomiste* (1928): 198, quoted in Dondaine, *De regno ad Regem Cypri*, préface, 423.

prince, how ought it to be read? Aquinas might not have known this king personally, but certainly he knew that he was writing a letter meant to be of practical value for a Norman baron, not an abstract delineation of theoretical principles for advanced theology students at the University of Paris.

Mark Jordan's work sharpens the question of genre. As does Dondaine, Jordan rejects Eschmann's description of the work as "a collection of fragments" and takes issue with Eschmann's interpretative strategy for *De Regno*, making it clear that *De Regno* cannot be read as "an independent treatise on political philosophy."[35] Jordan goes on to speculate as to the reasons for Aquinas "abandoning *De regno* in favor of more adequate structures for ethical teaching."[36] Jordan seems to assume that a work that is not a treatise cannot contain important political teachings, a claim against which I will later argue, and as such, he concludes with the suggestion that "Thomas thinks about political matters only within the larger project of a Christian morality ... [and] never intended to construct a political theology."[37] Granting its possibility, we might yet wonder if the content of the text itself has as much to say about its moral or theological context as any putative abandonment. After all, if this genre is inadequate to Aquinas's aims, why is that the case? This is not an obvious claim. The most famous *speculum*, Machiavelli's *The Prince*, is one of the most original books on politics, and is itself, in fact, a tremendous innovation on the mirror of the princes genre. Yet no one argues that Machiavelli failed because he did not meet the conventions of the *speculum*.[38]

Moreover, what precisely was the aim of Aquinas that he

35. Jordan, "*De Regno* and the Place of Political Thinking in Thomas Aquinas," 163.
36. Jordan, "*De Regno* and the Place of Political Thinking in Thomas Aquinas," 163.
37. Jordan, "*De Regno* and the Place of Political Thinking in Thomas Aquinas," 167–68.
38. Allen Gilbert, *Machiavelli's* Prince *and its Forerunners,* The Prince *as a Typical Book* De Regimine Principum (Durham, N.C.: Duke University Press, 1938).

found himself unable to fulfill through *De Regno*? We cannot assume that it is the same as that of his other works, precisely because no other works in his oeuvre are quite like *De Regno*, and I do think Jordan would undoubtedly agree with these last points. I do accept his chief thesis: *De Regno* is not a theoretical treatise, and if we are to learn from it, we must not treat it as one.

In view of the investigations of Dondaine, Eschmann, and others, the deliverances of more recent scholarship are disappointing. *De Regno*'s career has not been much brighter for the light shed on it.[39]

John Finnis, in his *Aquinas: Moral, Political, and Legal Theory*, speaks of *De Regno* with respect to the common good and tyrannicide.[40] While in his treatment of tyrannicide Finnis is advised in his use of the text and warns against taking it as Aquinas's final word on the subject, he abandons this restraint in his discussion of the common good. He rejects the teaching of *De Regno* and questions the authenticity of the text because it does not comport with his own controversial interpretation of Aquinas on the common good.[41]

Mary M. Keys takes an admirably cautious approach with *De Regno*, noting that the work seems to speak more of preventing tyranny than constructing a just regime.[42] This last claim is par-

---

39. Since its rescue from *De Regimine Principum*, *De Regno* has been included in a few sourcebooks of medieval political thought. See Ralph Lerner and Muhsin Mahdi, *Medieval Political Philosophy: A Sourcebook* (Ithaca, N.Y.: Cornell University Press, 1972); John O'Donovan and Joan Lockwood O'Donovan, *From Irenaeus to Grotius: A Sourcebook in Christian Political Thought* (Grand Rapids, Mich.: Wm. B. Eerdmans, 1999); and *Thomas Aquinas On Law, Morality and Politics*, trans. Richard J. Regan, 2nd ed. (Indianapolis, Ind.: Hackett Publishing Company, 2002).

40. Finnis, *Aquinas*, 228–31, 287–88.

41. Finnis, *Aquinas*, 228. See Michael Pakaluk, "Is the Common Good of Political Society Limited and Instrumental?" *The Review of Metaphysics* 55, no. 1 (2001): 57–94, and Matthew D. Wright, "The Aim of Law and the Nature of Political Community: An Assessment of Finnis on Aquinas," *The American Journal of Jurisprudence* 54 (2009): 133–60.

42. See Mary M. Keys, *Aquinas, Aristotle, and the Promise of the Common Good* (Cambridge: Cambridge University Press, 2006), 164.

ticularly rich in insights, for if, as Jordan suspects, this work has as much to say about politics' relation to ethics as about politics itself, then perhaps this preoccupation with tyranny relates to what Aquinas sees as the ethical basis and limitations of political rule. Keys thus may be quite right that *De Regno* does not expressly concern the best regime, but why this should be so could prove most revealing. This question alone shows us how little we yet know about *De Regno* and the stakes in understanding who Aquinas took himself to be writing for and with what purpose.

To be sure, *De Regno* is a peculiar text written for a particular audience with which we must exercise great caution.[43] *De Regno* requires a treatment that examines its meaning through the entirety of its structure, is open to the possibility that it is not congruent with all of Aquinas's other works, and that allows that *De Regno* might not even be the same sort of genre as those other works. If that is the case, then it will have to be read on its own terms, as I now propose to do.

Two scholars deserve mention as guides for that kind of reading: Cary Nederman and Robert Kraynak. Nederman has written perceptively on the influence of Aristotle, Cicero, and Augustine in medieval political thought. Specifically, he argues that Cicero's ideas often helped medieval thinkers reconcile "natural sociability and human sin" and thus puts at the center of our analysis the question of reconciling classical political philosophy with Christian revelation.[44] This question of "Athens and Jerusalem" will be crucial to the interpretation of *De Regno*.

Robert Kraynak's *Christian Faith and Modern Democracy* presents a compelling interpretation of Christian political

---

43. Marc D. Guerra. "Beyond Natural Law Talk: Politics and Prudence in St. Thomas Aquinas's *On Kingship*," 9–10.

44. Cary J. Nederman, "Nature, Sin and the Origins of Society: The Ciceronian Tradition in Medieval Political Thought," *Journal of the History of Ideas* 49, no. 1 (1988): 4–6.

thought that conforms to the central message of *De Regno*. Here I will advert to two of his claims that help illuminate our reading of *De Regno*. First, although Christian political thought has historically recognized monarchy as the best regime, other regime forms are legitimate, as well.[45] This means we should be cautious about medieval ideologies of sacral kingship as well as the modern fascination with democracy. The second point is what I am pleased to call the "Kraynak Dilemma": political regimes need the legitimacy of the church more than the church needs legitimacy from those regimes. While Aquinas will embrace the relative autonomy of the political order, at least as important to him is the freedom of the church from any untoward temporal influence. As this *libertas Ecclesiae* is a concern that animates Christian thought today, an attention to Aquinas's treatment of it reveals the value of *De Regno* for our own time, and, indeed, for the future.

The Plan of This Book

In what remains of this introduction, I lay out the plan of this book. It will rely on textual exegesis, which will follow the structure of *De Regno* and expose concepts and themes central to the text. My hope is that the exegesis will be valuable even if my interpretations are not always so. Given that no study could cover the full range of subjects in *De Regno*, my interpretative concerns will inevitably guide how I approach the text and what I choose to exposit on. While this framework will require some patience on the part of the reader, I again note that *De Regno* is written as a *speculum principis* for the education of the reader. a critical dimension

---

45. Robert Kraynak, *Christian Faith and Modern Democracy* (Notre Dame, Ind.: University of Notre Dame Press, 2001), xiii.

of its interpretation must be how Aquinas chooses to unfold his teaching through the genre of the *speculum*.

I do not seek in the present study to replace the invaluable historical scholarship of Eschmann or Dondaine. Their work has an enduring value on which others should build, as I aim to do. My main purpose, rather, is to lay out an interpretation that opens up the vision of politics in *De Regno*, for this book is first and foremost a work of political theory. Historians inform my work, and I will advert to their scholarship as necessary, but I am chiefly interested in Aquinas's argument, not his context. I am not interested in *De Regno* primarily because it is a medieval book but because it has something to say to us today.

In the introduction, I have laid out the argument of the book, the reception of *De Regno,* and the intellectual history with which I engage.

In chapter 1, "The Aristotelian State of Nature," I demonstrate that Aquinas advances an Aristotelian presentation of politics in the early chapters of *De Regno*. Contrary to interpretations of *De Regno* that see it as solely focused on tyranny, I articulate how, for Aquinas, politics is natural to man, that the best regime is rational and fulfilling of human ends, and that monarchy is the best regime according to scripture, metaphysics, and history. I further argue that Aquinas's presentation of monarchy as the best regime reveals important strategies for how he engages the ideology of monarchy and how he employs the *speculum principum* genre.

In chapter 2, "The Augustinian Earthly City," I explore one of the most fascinating and controversial parts of *De Regno*: Aquinas's meditations on tyranny. While many scholars have noted *De Regno*'s surprising focus on tyranny, I read this section in its context in a *speculum*, arguing that Aquinas emphasizes the dangers of tyranny not to reject the possibility of rational politics but rather to underline the necessity of virtuous politics and to moderate the expectations for those politics. That argument for virtue, in fact, strengthens the argument for monarchy as the best regime. I then show how, this task accomplished, he can subsequently distinguish between an "excesses of tyranny" and "mild tyranny" to suggest that the latter is common but tolerable. Finally, I argue that Aquinas does not fail to explain how to prevent tyranny, as scholars have suggested, but rather shifts his reader's focus from institutional mechanisms, which he argues will always eventually fail, to the question of the virtue of the ruler and of his subjects. This Augustinian vision of politics raises important questions about the more "Aristotelian" presentation with which Aquinas opens *De Regno*, and so I next articulate the nature of the tension between these two visions of politics. I end chapter 2 by drawing out a question: why does Aquinas juxtapose these two visions of politics?

Chapter 3, "The Reward of the King," presents the central section of *De Regno*, which I claim resolves the tension between the Augustinian and Aristotelian dynamics of the text. Aquinas achieves this resolution, I argue, by reorienting the discussion of politics to account for the ends of the human person, ends which are beyond the capacity of political activity to fulfill completely. I first show how Aquinas places his arguments in a teleological framework: ostensibly seeking the just reward of the king, he, in fact, argues that all earthly ends are insufficient as reward of the king, and that beatitude as the proper end of man is the only such reward. I then show how this teleological framework resolves the tension between the Aristotelian and Augustinian facets of the early part of *De Regno*. I close by arguing how Aquinas's careful attention to the monarchical ideologies of his day allows him in this section to focus on political communities in general, and it is thus the first place in *De Regno* where Aquinas abstracts from and deemphasizes monarchy.

In chapter 4, "The Politics of Revelation," I analyze book II of *De Regno*, perhaps the most interesting but least-studied portion of *De Regno*. I argue that only in book II does Aquinas explicitly articulate the God-king metaphor that he invokes in the first pages of *De Regno* and that pervades medieval political thought. I show that the earthly king is God-in-his-kingdom only in a limited sense, and, indeed, Aquinas desacralizes kingship in a fashion highly unique for his time. That desacralization is a two-part move, I argue. First, Aquinas adumbrates a distinction between creation and governance: while God undertakes both activities, only the latter is proper to the king. Second, Aquinas presents a historical account of civil religion, one by which kings and all humans come to see that governance and not creation is proper to temporal rule, and therefore that the spiritual authority is both distinct from and superior to temporal authority. This desacralization secure, Aquinas can revisit the task of founding a kingdom in II.5–8.

In chapter 5, "The Christian Structure of Politics," I turn to the church/state teaching of *De Regno*. While *De Regno* offers little explicit guidance on this matter, I draw out five principles of church/state relations from my analysis of *De Regno* and compare them to the teaching of two medieval thinkers, John of Paris and Giles of Rome, who represent Aristotelian and Augustinian traditions, respectively. From this comparison, I argue that these three thinkers, Aquinas, John, and Giles, present theoretically distinct options for understanding the relationship between Christianity and politics, with Aquinas proposing a *via media* between the Aristotelian and Augustinian schools of his time. From this set of options, I am able to relate Aquinas to early modern political thought, namely social contract theory. While contractarianism is not the whole of modern political thought, it forms a crucial and influential role in our political imaginations even today. For this reason, I rely on Jacob Levy's work, which places contractarianism within the horizon of modern liberalism. I then compare Aquinas's theory to contractarianism's liberal twin, pluralism. I conclude that Aquinas's Gelasian dualism largely concords with pluralism's understanding of the political and social function of religious bodies vis-a-vis the state, but that significant metaphysical and ethical differences distinguish this dualism from modern pluralism.

In the conclusion, "On Actions and Words," I argue that the questions raised by *De Regno* continue to resonate into late modernity. Indeed, I show that Aquinas has much to contribute to the various Christian critiques of contemporary liberalism that have flourished in the early twenty-first century. For while Aquinas might seem to favor the "integralism" invoked by critics and supporters of the notion, the picture of politics advanced by Aquinas in *De Regno* differs in crucial respects from the caricature of "integralism." This epilogue is thus in part a vindication of Robert Kraynak's central theses in *Christian Faith and Modern Democracy*. I argue that the five principles outlined in chapter 5 of my book can aid those who seek critical engagement with and the reform of liberal modernity.

In the end, I will count this project a success if I enkindle in the reader a desire to enter into the "innermost soul" of *De Regno*, which Eschmann warmly describes as "the profoundest and clearest formula of the mediaeval City of God."[46] *De Regno* offers no recipes for perfecting politics on earth but rather illuminates the challenge and gift of Christianity to politics as profound and perennial. That challenge and gift is no less powerful in our own time.

46. Eschmann, *On Kingship*, introduction, xxxix.

CHAPTER I

The Aristotelian State of Nature

De Regno I.1–2

While early sections of *De Regno* have puzzled scholars for their focus on tyranny, this preoccupation with tyranny is not immediately evident, arising only in I.3. Aquinas, in, fact begins *De Regno* with a rational and naturalistic account of the origins of politics and a regime typology, one that culminates in a forceful elevation of monarchy as the best regime. Drawing from sources as diverse as the Bible and Aristotle, Cicero and Augustine, Aquinas does not consign politics to the reign of tyrants but rather paints a hopeful, rational picture of a politics that is just and peaceful.

In this chapter, I consider the promise of the beginning of *De Regno*: the *prooemium* and I.1–2. After studying Aquinas's proposed plan of proceeding, I discuss his regime analysis and his elevation of monarchy as the best regime. Aquinas's account of political naturalism in I.1–2 sets up a number of tensions that only later sections of *De Regno* will resolve, particularly concerning Aquinas's bold claims about the excellence of monarchy, the relative influence of Augustine and Aristotle on Aquinas, and the absence of theological concepts like sin, the Fall, and the church. Those tensions are resolved to reveal the ways in which politics is both natural and corrupted by sin, a dramatic tension set in the context of the two forms of government: temporal and spiritual authority.

Why Aquinas Writes: The *Prooemium*

Aquinas begins *De Regno* with a brief address to the king of Cyprus, which opens with the phrase "*Cogitanti mihi*." These words, meaning "in thinking to myself" or "reflecting," were a stock phrase of *specula* and echo Cicero's famous *De Oratore*, a central theme of which is the rare coincidence of the political power of oratory and philosophical wisdom.[1] Aquinas states that he intends the work to be a gift "worthy of [your] royal highness and befitting my profession and duty." This gift turns out to be a book on kingship, both its purpose, "*in quo et regni originem*," and the duties attached to it, "*et ea quae ad regis officium pertinent*." As the gift of an erudite theologian, Aquinas's prospective sources for the work are not surprising: "the authority of Holy Scripture, the teachings of the philosophers, and examples of illustrious princes."[2]

As a letter to a king, *De Regno* is an example of the *specula principum*, or "mirrors of princes," genre, along with Xenophon's *Education of Cyrus*, Machiavelli's *Prince*, and Erasmus's *Education of a Christian Prince*. *Specula* were widely prevalent in the medieval and early modern period and flourished in large part because monarchy flourished: as monarchy was the dominant regime form of this period, political reflection in this epoch characteristically took the form of advice to kings.[3] Thus, it is not surprising that

---

1. Lynn Thorndyke and Pearl Kibre, *A Catalogue of Incipits of Mediaeval Scientific Writings in Latin* (Cambridge, Mass.: The Mediaeval Academy of America, 1937), 105.

2. Dondaine notes the variant *dogma* for *dogmata* [teachings]. In both cases, of course, Aquinas is using a venerable Greek work. Dondaine, *De regno ad Regem Cypri*, préface, 449.

3. Francis Oakley, *Empty Bottles of Gentilism: Kingship and Divinity in Late Antiquity and the Early Middle Ages (to 1050)*, vol. 1 of *The Emergence of Western Political Thought in the Latin Middle Ages* (New Haven, Conn.: Yale University Press, 2010), 177–78, 134.

monarchy turns out to be of central concern in *De Regno*: the text is of a *genre* addressed to kings and predicated on monarchical ideologies of the times. Given its widespread extension, medieval monarchy was as varied and textured as democracy is today.[4] The *speculum* genre reflects that variation. *Specula* range tremendously in originality and sophistication, from the rigidly formulaic to the strikingly original. Sometimes very practical or highly theoretical, parochial, or sensitive to broad transnational dynamics like the struggle between the papacy and empire, they also vary tremendously in their substance, encompassing hierocratic as well as regalist positions.[5]

Granting the incredible diversity of the *genre*, identifying *De Regno* as a *speculum principum* still perhaps does not tell us much about the work, but we can at least consider two of its aspects: audience and content. The audience of a *speculum* is a king. As such, we expect much of what Aquinas says about politics to be refracted through the prism of monarchy, but that context need not necessarily limit Aquinas. Perhaps his remarks about monarchy are subtly critical of monarchy, or even redefine the scope and end of kingship as conventionally understood by someone like Aquinas's reader. Moreover, since kingship was the dominant way of thinking about political authority in his time, perhaps Aquinas took monarchy as exemplary of political authority more generally, as indeed the word *princeps* could be a generic term for any kind of single ruler.[6] Here is where we would want to know more about Aquinas's sophistication with Aristotle, for were Aquinas at least familiar with classical teachings on the diversity of regime forms

---

4. Black, *Political Thought in Europe*, 136.
5. I. P. Bejczy and Cary J. Nederman, *Princely Virtues in the Middle Ages, 1200–1500*, Disputatio (Belgium: Brepols, 2007), 3–4, 7–8.
6. Black, *Political Thought in Europe*, 141; Bejczy and Nederman, *Princely Virtues*, 1.

and the naturalness of political authority, he would have a theoretically robust basis on which to contextualize monarchy within political life more broadly.

But for whom was Aquinas writing? While there has been controversy as to which king of Cyprus Aquinas penned *De Regno*, all three possible addressees shared similar features that would be material to a *speculum*.[7] They were from a French comital family elevated to royalty in the Levant through the Crusades. They were at the forefront of state-building, and in the name of Christianity against Islam. They were French kings, moreover, warriors from a country that long considered itself the guardian of the Catholic Church. Whichever king Aquinas addressed, he was a Christian king fighting against deadly political adversaries he would have considered to be illegitimate and unjust Muslim tyrants. Thus, issues of justice, faith, and military power would be at the center of his governance. Given the complex web of politics and religion at stake here, it will not surprise us that sacral kingship and civil religion turn out to be important topics in *De Regno*.

As for content, *specula* were often concerned with the personal virtues of the monarchy. Authors commonly framed that virtue in relation to God, even if that framing was more flattering than substantive.[8] Given Aquinas's penchant for schematizing human knowledge in relation to God, perhaps in *De Regno*, he developed that *genre* convention to argue for something about the king's relationship to God beyond just the personal virtues of the king. In the *Summa Theologica*, for example, he describes human law in terms of a "participation" or sharing in divine law. As Foucault notes, Aquinas seems to make a similar claim in *De Regno*, sketch-

---

7. Dondaine, *De regno ad Regem Cypri*, préface, 424.
8. Black, *Political Thought*, 137; Oakley, *Empty Bottles*, 178; and Bejczy and Nederman, *Princely Virtues*, 1–3.

ing a kind of analogy between God's government of the universe and human governance of kingdoms.⁹

These possibilities make more intriguing the closing of the address. Aquinas ends the *prooemium* by asking for the help of God, whom he calls "King of kings and Lord of lords, through whom [all] kings reign, God, great Lord and great King above all gods."¹⁰ While Aquinas begins the *prooemium* with an attestation to this earthly king's majesty, he ends with a forceful reminder of the majesty of the King of all kings, God. In other words, if Aquinas means for this work to help this particular king understand his office precisely insofar as he is an example of kings in general, Aquinas also reminds the royal reader that God is king of kings in a way that no earthly king can be. Instead, this organization reflects Aquinas's method of guiding his reader from the uncritical and self-interested ideology of monarchy to a more nuanced understanding of his royal role as mediated by the travails of politics and the glory of rewards beyond riches and fame.

The Naturalness of Political Authority: I.1

What is a king? (*quid nomine regis intelligendum sit*?) This question opens chapter 1. As we learn in this chapter, the paradigmatic king is the directive principle of a community leading it to its common good. This chapter thus concerns the need for political authority among humans. As Aquinas addresses the argument to his princely reader, we may wonder if he distinguishes between general political authority and monarchy as one form of political authority. Given the close association of arguments for

---

9. Michel Foucault, *Security, Territory, Population: Lectures at the Collège de France, 1977–1978*, trans. Graham Burchell (New York: Picador, 2007), 232–34.

10. There are echoes in this line of several Bible verses, as Eschmann and Dondaine note, including Deuteronomy 10:17, Proverbs 8:15, and Psalm 94:3 (Dondaine, *De regno ad Regem Cypri*, préface, 449).

the naturalness of politics with Aristotle, we will also have to examine how far the argument of this chapter conforms to that of Aristotle.

All things ordered to an end, Aquinas begins, require some directive principle to guide them there "directly" (I.1.3). The human person is an intelligent agent and clearly acts in light of an end "to which his whole life and all his actions are ordered." Thus, he needs a directive principle to lead him toward that end, but as humans are intelligent creatures, this directive principle is simply reason. Indeed, the "light of reason" is "implanted naturally" in each person: it guides humans toward their end (I.1.4). This light of reason would be sufficient were men meant to live alone, each person ruling himself as a king under God, the highest king (*summo rege*). But humans are, in fact, an *animal sociale et politicum*, according to a teaching that defines much of classical political philosophy, and they naturally live in groups.[11] Aquinas then goes on to explain how man's social and political character is a necessity of his nature.

Aquinas thinks three characteristics make the sociality of the human person evident: his lack of natural defense, his lack of instincts, and his faculty of speech (I.1.5–7). All three involve explicit comparisons with other animals, for humans are animals. Unlike other animals, however, man lacks teeth, horns, and other natural attributes for defense, nor does he have hair for covering or an immediate supply of food. Unlike other animals, man has no "inborn skill" by which he discerns readily what is useful or poisonous for him (I.1.6). Man therefore cooperates with other men to remedy these lacks. What man lacks in the physical realm

---

11. Dondaine notes the testimony of Seneca, Macrobius, and Aristotle, with Avicenna on *De Anima* informing much that follows (Dondaine, *De regno ad Regem Cypri*, préface, 449). The strong influence of Avicenna Eschmann insists on (Eschmann, *On Kingship*, introduction, 4, n. 3).

he compensates for in his intellectual attributes, qualities he completes with and through other men. For although man lacks physical attributes for his survival, he has reason, "by the use of which he could procure all these things for himself by the work of his hands." And while he lacks instinctual knowledge of what is particularly good and harmful for him, he does have "a natural knowledge of the things which are essential for his life."

As for speech, which he can use far more articulately than animals can, this is a great boon to his gregariousness (I.1.7). Language is instrumental to the cooperation whose need arises from these two lacks, but speech also seems to be itself a proof of his sociality: "by which one man can fully express his conceptions [*conceptum*] to others." And, indeed, Aquinas argues that humans are more communicative than any other gregarious animal (I.1.7).[12] He illustrates this point with his first scriptural reference of book I, quoting Solomon that "It is better that there be two than one, for they have the advantage of their company [*emolumentum mutue societatis*]," (Eccl 4:9).

Since man does not live alone, Aquinas has argued, men in community need something to lead them to their end. But what is this new directive principle? To what end does it lead them? Moreover, what precisely is its relation to the reason that guides each man? Having adduced these reasons for man's sociality, Aquinas goes on to state:

If, then, it is natural for man to live in the society of many, it is necessary that there exist among men some means by which the group may be governed. For where there are many men together and each one is looking after his own interest, the multitude would be broken up and scattered

---

12. Dondaine sees in these arguments about language a reference to Aristotle's *History of Animals*, although, again, for Eschmann, it is Avicennan (Dondaine, *De regno ad Regem Cypri*, Préface, 450).

[*in diversa dispergeretur*] unless there were also an agency to take care of what appertains to the commonweal (I.1.8).

While Aquinas accepts that the human person is naturally social and political, he emphasizes that this communal ordering is not spontaneous: it must be directed by someone. Such relations are an achievement in a way that man being oxygen-breathing by nature is not: they must be developed and attained. Aquinas concludes I.1.8 with another quotation of Solomon: "Where there is no governor, the people shall be scattered [*dissipatibur populus*]" (Prov 11:14).[13] The community, like a body, must be held together.

To explain his quotation of Solomon, Aquinas turns to metaphysics: "Indeed it is reasonable that this should happen, for what is proper [*proprium*] and what is common [*commune*] are not identical" (I.1.9).[14] The "proper" is what is particular to the individual; the common is shared across individuals. Aquinas recasts this distinction between the "proper" and the "common" into one of cause and effect: the different effects proper to individuals are due to a diversity of causes. A common good requires a common cause. Instituting and preserving the common good, then, would require identifying that cause which produces similar effects in all individuals "over and above that which impels towards the proper good of each individual." Aquinas can immediately say one thing about this cause: it is one. As he explains it, "in all things that are ordered towards one end, one thing is found to rule the rest." As the soul rules the body and the rational part of the soul rules the other parts, so the first mover in the universe moves subsequent

---

13. Eschmann translates *dissipatibur* as "shall fall," which, while not wrong, fails to capture the passivity suggested by the Latin, as with *dispergeretur* of the previous sentence.

14. Eschmann here directs the reader to *ST* I.96.4, presumably because therein Aquinas distinguishes and relates the proper end of man and the common good and argues that even in the state of innocence, man as a social animal would require some sort of authority to direct his activities to the common good (Eschmann, *On Kingship*, introduction, 6, n. 8).

The Aristotelian State of Nature 31

bodies, and the heart moves the body. "There must be, therefore, in every multitude some government [*regitivum*]" (I.1.9).[15]

I.1.9 raises at least two questions. First, what function is this metaphysics playing in the argument of I.1? Second, is it an argument in favor of specifically monarchical authority? As for the first question, it is notable that Aquinas ends rather than begins I.1 with arguments from metaphysics, which he uses, in other words, to confirm and illustrate what he has already argued. In other works, for instance, Aquinas speaks of the principle of social unity among persons as rather weak, as a "unity of order."[16]

Furthermore, to the extent that Aquinas does employ metaphysics in I.1, that use concerns not only efficient but also final causality. This observation has consequences for how we understand Aquinas's intellectual debts, as we shall see. Some scholars, including Oakley and perhaps Eschmann, have argued that Aquinas emphasizes the role of political authority in the order of efficient causality in *De Regno* I, having little to nothing to say about political authority's bearing on final causality. Such an emphasis on efficient causality in accounts of political authority would reflect a Ciceronian heritage, whereas an emphasis on final causality would suggest a more Aristotelian influence.[17] Yet while at I.1.8 Aquinas indeed argues that political authority must gather up and constitute a reluctant scattering of humans into a community, his metaphysics makes clear here that political authority also bears upon final causality: the authority must direct the community to its end.

---

15. Or "governing power," as Eschmann has it.
16. *Summa Contra Gentiles*, III, 69; *De Ver*. 11.1; *De Ver*. 5.8 ad 12; and *In Sent*. II.1.1.5. Cf. Michael Baur, "Aquinas on Law and Natural Law," in *The Oxford Handbook of Aquinas*, ed. Brian Davies and Eleanor Stump (Oxford: Oxford University Press, 2011), 238–54.
17. Francis Oakley, *The Mortgage of the Past: Reshaping the Ancient Political Inheritance (1050–1300)*, vol. 2 of *The Emergence of Western Political Thought in the Latin Middle Ages* (New Haven, Conn.: Yale University Press, 2012), 80.

The second question raised is whether Aquinas's arguments for the necessity of political authority necessarily mandate monarchy. The reader of *De Regno* might be led to think so by phrases like "in all things that are ordered towards one end, one thing is found to rule the rest." As we will see, however, Aquinas thinks that multiple rulers can act in a unitary fashion, such that this "one thing" might, in fact, be a council of aristocrats or an assembly of citizens. And terms like *princeps* were often used generically in Aquinas's time for rulers in general. Yet it cannot be denied that later portions of *De Regno* are at least superficially strongly promonarchy. If it turns out that a monarch best fulfills the function of "one thing" that can "rule the rest," which is to say that monarchy gives greatest expression to the metaphysical architecture of political authority, then perhaps Aquinas's arguments for the naturalness of politics are more metaphysical than we thought.

Taking in the full span of I.1, we see that Aquinas has in it justified political authority in general, but does this argument conform to that of Aristotle? And how does this account compare to arguments for political naturalism in his other works? These are related questions, as some see a movement from more primitive claims in *De Regno* to more Aristotelian arguments in his later works.

For many commentators, Aquinas's arguments in *De Regno* I.1 are uncontroversially Aristotelian and therefore in accord with his commentary on Aristotle's *Politics*. Black argues, for instance, that in *De Regno*, Aquinas "rehearsed with little development" Aristotle's thought on the origin of politics.[18] Yet a whole body of scholarship has arisen to argue that students of Aquinas's politics and ethics have overestimated Aristotle's influence on him.[19]

---

18. Black, *Political Thought*, 22. See also Blythe, *On the Government of Rulers*, introduction, 39–59.

19. Dondaine would presumably fall in this camp, with his scanty references to Cicero in his footnotes.

The Aristotelian State of Nature 33

That scholarship has particularly questioned the Aristotelian provenance of medieval political naturalism: the idea that "man is by nature a social and political creature." As Nederman explains, this idea came from a multiplicity of sources, including Cicero. When medieval thinkers took up Aristotle's thoughts on political naturalism, it was not because the concept was new to them, but rather because it was old: a vigorous twelfth-century investigation into nature predisposed them to adopt Aristotle's language of the naturalness of politics.[20] Indeed, the argument of *De Regno* is naturalistic even compared to Aquinas's later arguments, such that, for Eschmann, *De Regno* I.1 smacks more of Avicenna than of Aristotle.[21]

Nevertheless, it is worth questioning whether *De Regno* I.1 is unproblematically Aristotelian. Let us consider, then, whether *De Regno* I.1 arises from Ciceronian rather than from Aristotelian sources. Nederman argues that Cicero's ideas often stood as a *via media* between Augustine and Aristotle.[22] Medieval Christian thinkers needed such a *via media* because, while they embraced political naturalism, they also had to account for the Fall, the "profoundly anti-social" effects of which made political life more difficult. These thinkers had to "cope," in other words, with "natural sociability and human sin."[23] On Nederman's account, Cicero balanced the need to show both that man is political in his pristine state and that man as fallen does not always act in accord with his political nature. Most notably, Cicero argues that speech and reason incline man toward political community, but they do not coerce him toward it: "man's associative nature" is not "sufficient

---

20. Oakley, *The Mortgage of the Past*, 74–81.
21. Eschmann, *On Kingship*, introduction, 4, n. 2. Dondaine directs us to Aquinas's use of Avicenna in *Contra impugnantes* V (Dondaine, *De regno ad Regem Cypri*, préface, 449).
22. Nederman, "Nature, Sin and the Origins of Society," 4–6.
23. Nederman, "Nature, Sin and the Origins of Society," 4.

to inspire and incite the creation of a community," but requires the strong hand of political leadership.[24] On this account, Cicero therefore privileges the efficient causality of the founder in the rise of human community.

Is this account true for *De Regno*? The evidence is mixed. On the one hand, our reading of *De Regno* I.1 underlines that Aquinas indeed shares Cicero's preoccupations with speech and reason. And while Aquinas agrees with Aristotle's claim that the city arises out of necessity, a teaching to which Cicero also subscribes, Aquinas, at least in *De Regno*, is somewhat more circumspect about how the city also secures human excellence. We also saw that I.1.8 can be read as an account of political authority with a Ciceronian emphasis on efficient rather than final causality.

On the other hand, Aquinas affirms man's political nature: "it is natural for man, more than for any other animal, to be a social and political animal, to live in a group" (I.1.4). He further orients *De Regno* I.1 with regard to man's end, as we saw at I.1.3, the first chapter after the *prooemium*. And the centrality of man's end is redoubled through Aquinas's emphasis on the importance of political authority for final causality in the paragraphs that open (I.1.3) and close (I.1.9) the chapter, and thus frame the section (I.1.8) that would seem to privilege efficient causality. Aquinas thus brings to bear an "Aristotelian teleological orientation" on *De Regno*.[25]

Further, if Cicero should be taken as a help in integrating the Fall into Christian political thought, it is revealing that Aquinas nowhere refers to the Fall in I.1, nor does he mention sin, grace, the church, or any other theme obviously connected to the problem of the Fall and the coercive political authority often said to issue from it in the Augustinian tradition. Rather, Aquinas evinces

---

24. Nederman, "Nature, Sin and the Origins of Society," 5.
25. Oakley, *The Mortgage of the Past*, 113.

a great faith in reason and its ability to organize human society from a basis in human nature apparently intact after the Fall. The need to reconcile Aristotle and Augustine, in other words, does not even arise. On the evidence of I.1, then, Aquinas conforms more to Aristotelian than to Ciceronian political naturalism in *De Regno*. And if he is employing Cicero, Aquinas would not seem to be doing so out of a need to balance the traditions inspired by Aristotle and Augustine.

We should note that for Nederman, as for others, Aquinas stands firmly in the Aristotelian camp, and probably had no need of Cicero to bridge Aristotle with Augustine.[26] But we nonetheless should ask our own Nederman question of how Aquinas reconciles Aristotle and Augustine. After all, the question of reconciling Aristotle and Augustine is the question of reconciling classical political naturalism with Christian doctrine on man's sinful nature, a theme that Aquinas could not avoid. And even a cursory consideration of Aquinas's other works suggest that this is a preoccupation for Aquinas. He argues for political naturalism in several other places, particularly *Summa Theologica* I.96, his *Commentary on the Sentences*, and, of course, in his commentary on Aristotle's *Politics*. He does so, moreover, with frequent appeals to Aristotle and Augustine. Indeed, Aquinas notably appeals to St Augustine in a most unlikely setting: an explanation of why there would be political authority even without the Fall (*ST* I.96.4). Black argues that Aquinas "dovetailed" Augustine and Aristotle, employing Augustine's distinction between free and servile authority, but also moving beyond Cicero's teaching through distinctly Aristotelian arguments.[27] Examining how Aquinas tackles this challenge in *De Regno* will tell us much about the place of this

26. Nederman, "Nature, Sin and the Origins of Society," 5.
27. Black, *Political Thought*, 22–24.

text in Aquinas's work. Perhaps early sections of *De Regno* betray ambiguous traces of Ciceronian political naturalism that conflict with or evolve into more explicitly Aristotelian forms of naturalism later in the work. I.1 justifies political authority on rational and naturalistic grounds, perhaps setting the stage for a defense of monarchy. While it presents some evidence of Cicero, it betrays a greater debt to Aristotle, and, moreover, raises the question of the relationship between Aristotle and Augustine.

We can thus address the compatibility of *De Regno* I.1 with Aquinas's other texts. There is no question that in other places Aquinas's presentation of the origins of political community are more clearly in line with that of Aristotle. I would thus defer to Eschmann's claim that *De Regno* I.1 betrays the influence of Avicenna. It is possible that, either because of his ignorance of Aristotle or his misreading of Avicenna, Aquinas takes Avicenna's argument to be wholly adequate when he composed *De Regno*.

Another possibility, however, is that Aquinas is presenting a simple argument about the origins of community at *De Regno* I.1. and sees no need here to venture into the question of excellence. In other words, perhaps Aquinas does not understand the argument of Avicenna to be closed to elaboration and extension by that of Aristotle. Along these lines, it is highly relevant that in one of the texts Eschmann flags as departing from *De Regno* I.1, Aquinas's *Commentary on the* "Ethics," Aquinas cites Avicenna in I.1 as part of an argument that humans come together in community both for necessities and for excellence. Perhaps Aquinas took Avicenna's argument to be insufficient for a full account of the origins of political community, but nevertheless propaedeutic to that fuller account.

It is possible, again, that *De Regno* I.1 does not present Aquinas's full argument, and that we must continue reading *De Regno* to compare it fruitfully with other Thomistic texts. Indeed, we saw that I.1 contains no reference to important political concepts for Christians, especially the Augustinian tradition: the Fall, the church, and the law. As *De Regno* unfolds, we will have to consider if and how such themes emerge.

The *Liber* and the *Servus*

In the second half of I.1, Aquinas takes up questions concerning regime typology and the self-sufficient community.[28] Along the way, he invokes distinctively Augustinian and Aristotelian categories that begin to frame answers to our questions regarding I.1.

Having established in the early part of I.1 that human society requires government, Aquinas asks how that government ought to act in governing the multitude. As with all things, the multitude can be led in a right way and a wrong way: "[a] thing is rightly directed when it is led towards a befitting end; wrongly when it is led towards an unbefitting end," (I.1.10).[29] But what is a "befitting end?" To answer this question, Aquinas elaborates another distinction:

Now the end which befits a multitude of free men [*multitudini liberorum*] is different from that which befits a multitude of slaves [*servorum*], for the free man is for his own sake [*sui causa est*], while the slave is for the sake of another [*alterius est*]. If, therefore, a multitude of free men is ordered by the ruler towards the common good of the multitude, that regime will be right and just, as is suitable to free men. If, on the other hand, a regime aims, not at the common good of the multitude, but at the private good of the ruler, it will be an unjust and perverse regime (I.1.10).

---

28. Some editions of *De Regno* end I.1 here. I follow Eschmann and Dondaine in treating the first sixteen paragraphs of the text as I.1 (Dondaine, *De regno ad Regem Cypri*, préface, 443; Eschmann, *On Kingship*, introduction, xiv). This chapter division reflects both the early manuscript tradition and the thematic ordering of the early chapters (Eschmann, introduction, xxi).

29. Dondaine notes here the influence of *Politics* III (Dondaine, *De regno ad Regem Cypri*, préface, 450).

Aquinas differentiates between the *liber* and the *servus*, or the free man and the slave. The free man is or exists for his own sake (*sui causa*); the slave exists for that of another (*alterius*). The contrast with the slave suggested here is illuminating, for the slave acts for the good of another: he is an instrument. The *liber* is not an instrument of another. As his own cause, he directs himself to his proper goods. The word *causa*, after all, ought to remind us of Aquinas's discussion only a paragraph before about the diverse causes that lead to the different proper effects of individuals and the one cause that brings them together toward a common good. Aquinas does not speak here only of the *finis liberis* but the *finis multitudini liberorum*, the end of a "multitude" of free men.

In drawing this distinction between *liber* and *servus*, Aquinas appeals to both Aristotle and Augustine.[30] While the phrases might evoke Aristotle's discussion of natural slavery, Aquinas does not here seem to be invoking any such doctrine here. Rather, he draws the phrase *"liber est causa sui"* from Aristotle's *Metaphysics*. While the phrase appears in several other places in Aquinas's *opera*, this reference in *De Regno* is perhaps Aquinas's earliest citation of it.[31] He seems to employ the distinction between *liber and servus* to draw out something about the *causa sui* and his "befitting end": the *causa sui* acts for his own sake, and out of a freedom ultimately grounded in reason.[32] For the *liber* to be governed justly, then, he must be governed in such a way that he can act for his

---

30. See Paul J. Weithman, "Augustine and Aquinas on Original Sin and the Function of Political Authority," *Journal of the History of Philosophy* 30, no. 3 (1992): 360–64.

31. This reference in *De Regno*, for instance, would seem to precede most of the others, including the *Summa Contra Gentiles* (II, 48), the *Summa Theologica* (I.83.1 ad 3), and his *Commentary on the "Metaphysics."*

32. See Lord's n. 31 in Aristotle, *Politics*, 2nd ed., trans. Carnes Lord (Chicago: University of Chicago Press, 2013), 11; cf. Jamie Anne Spiering, "*Liber est Causa Sui*: Thomas Aquinas and the Maxim "The Free is the Cause of Itself," *Review of Metaphysics* 65 (December 2011): 375–76.

own sake and so that the common good of a multitude of *libri* are also governed for their own sake. If the *liber* is not governed with a view toward these goods, then that governance is unjust.

This use of Aristotle finds support in how Aquinas appeals to Augustine in the same passage. As Black notes, Aquinas often calls upon Augustine's authority by making distinctions to which Augustine appears indifferent, and often when Augustine and Aquinas would seem not to agree.[33] As at *Summa Theologica* I.96, Aquinas distinguishes between rule over slaves, which Augustine (and Aquinas) justifies as the wages of sin, and political rule over free men, which Aquinas (but not always Augustine) thinks still obtains in a postlapsarian state. Thus, Aquinas can acknowledge Augustine's teaching on the coercive power of politics as a fruit of sin in principle and yet maintain that politics as such is natural to man and is even now in salvation history a domain of his *libertas* and of just government. While Aquinas does not directly appeal to the Fall here, he does with this *liber* versus *servus* distinction exclude Augustine's tragic view of politics from being the only way to view politics, and so limits the impact of the Fall on Christian political thought. This passage thus confirms Black's claim that Aquinas subtly dovetails Aristotle and Augustine.

This notion of justice allows Aquinas to preserve the traditional distinction between just and unjust regimes. As Aquinas continues, he argues that the "right and just regime" will ensue when a "multitude of free men is ordered by the ruler to the common good of the multitude," (I.1.10). The "unjust and perverse regime" arises when a rule aims at "the private [*privatum*] good of the ruler." Rule aiming at the private good of the prince is unjust: it is the very definition of tyranny. Aquinas quotes Ezekiel's warning to the tyrant: "Woe to the shepherds that feed themselves: should

---

33. Black, *Political Thought*, 23–24.

not the flocks be fed by the shepherd?" (Ezek 34:2). As the shepherd seeks the good of his flock, so the ruler seeks the good of his people. Earlier, Aquinas contrasted the *bonum proprium* of the individual with the *bonum commune* of the community. The tyrant does not seek his own proper good but rather his own private good. Here again, Aquinas adds color to the *liber* or *causa sui*. The "proper" good of the *liber* accords with the common good of the multitude. The "private" good of the tyrant, however, detracts from that common good.[34]

The Augustinian tradition rears its head again here. In distinguishing between the proper good of the *liber* and the private good of the tyrant, Aquinas accepts the reality of injustice and gestures at Augustine's privative theory of evil: the tyrant's injustice is a privation of the common good in book XII of *The City of God*. Yet Aquinas does not identify such privative injustice to show that justice is impossible but rather to show that it is the exception. He qualifies the private nature of the tyrant's good to distinguish it from what is proper to any member of a regime.

Aquinas then proceeds to a division of regimes: the three unjust (I.1.11) and the three just (I.1.12). Both just and unjust rule can be executed by one, a few, or many.[35] Aquinas begins with a description of unjust governments, the most notable dimension of which is his emphasis on force: the tyrant "oppresses by might"; oligarchs "oppress the people by means of their wealth"; and the democrats "by force of numbers oppress the rich." Aquinas accents this point in his proposed etymology of "tyrant": "such a ruler is called a tyrant—a word derived from strength—because he oppresses by might instead of ruling by justice. Thus, among

---

34. *Privatum* occurs in *De Regno* three times in connection with the good of the tyrant (I.1.10; I.4.24, and I.4.26), although it is later used to refer to the private person who seeks to kill the tyrant on his own authority (VII.47–48).

35. Eschmann, *On Kingship*, introduction, 7, n. 16.

the ancients, all powerful men were called tyrants" (I.1.11).[36] Aquinas notably relates oligarchy and democracy back to tyranny as he describes them: "the few ... differ from the tyrant only by the fact that they are more than one," and in democracy, "the whole people will be as one tyrant." Every unjust regime, Aquinas seems to underline, is rooted in tyranny's violent opposition to justice.

Aquinas next outlines the just governments: polity, aristocracy, and monarchy. After defining polity in military terms, following Aristotle's claim in the *Politics* (1279b1–3) that a great body of men can only hope for a kind of military virtue, and then his description of aristocracy as "noble governance," Aquinas presents monarchy: "And if a just government is in the hands of one man alone, he is properly called a king. Wherefore the Lord says through Ezekiel: "My servant, David, shall be king over them and all of them shall have one shepherd" (I.1.12). To underline this point, Aquinas concludes this regime typology with a summary: "the idea of king [*ratione regis*] implies that he be one who has charge[*praesit*], and that he be a shepherd, seeking the common good [*bonum commune*] of the multitude and not his own" (I.1.13).[37]

This regime division is not particularly novel, betraying a basic knowledge of Aristotle's *Politics*.[38] As Eschmann rightly notes, Aristotle lays out two regime divisions: one on the basis of number and one on the basis of the qualifications or virtue of the rulers.[39] Here, Aquinas follows the first teaching of Aristotle on the basis

---

36. Eschmann, *On Kingship*, introduction, 8, n. 17; see James M. Blythe, *Ideal Government and the Mixed Constitution in the Middle Ages* (Princeton, N.J.: Princeton University Press, 2014), 30.

37. The verb *praesum* could be rendered in several ways. Eschmann renders it "who is chief."

38. Eschmann notes the influence of *Politics* III.6–7, as well as *Nicomachean Ethics* VIII (Eschmann, *On Kingship*, introduction, 7, nn. 13 and 16; cf. Dondaine, *De regno ad Regem Cypri*, préface, 450).

39. *Politics* 1271a27 et seq. and *Politics* 1279b38, respectively.

of number, although in other works he embraces Aristotle's discussion of the virtue of rulers. Aquinas will later have much to say about the virtue of the ruling element of a regime.[40]

And while Aquinas predictably departs from Aristotle in employing scripture, Aquinas curiously reserves such citations for kingship alone of the three just regimes. Aquinas quotes scripture to illustrate monarchy and notes that God calls David, the biblical king par excellence, *servus meus*. He further cites by name Solomon, another vaunted biblical king, throughout the chapter.[41] Indeed, Aquinas speaks of polity and aristocracy in classical terms, and only of kingship in biblical language, when, for example, he might have turned to the Hebrew commonwealth as an example of polity, as he would later do in the *Summa Theologica*.[42] That Aquinas then ends this regime typology at I.1.13 with a definition of kingship, which he reiterates at the end of the chapter (I.1.16), only underlines the centrality of monarchy for this account. Perhaps this is because Aquinas writes for a king, but perhaps also because he anticipates his apology for monarchy as the best regime, as well as his analogy between divine and human monarchy in book II.[43]

Aquinas concludes I.1 by inquiring into the kind of community over which government should rule. The *societas perfecta* is that which supplies fully the necessities of life, for it is these necessities that lead man to live in community in the first place (I.1.14).

40. Eschmann, *On Kingship*, introduction, 7, n. 16.
41. I.7, 8, I.15. Aquinas's scriptural references in *De Regno* deserve further study than we can give them here. In the case of Solomon, however, it seems that Aquinas uses scripture to confirm what he has already argued through history and philosophy, bringing the authority and example of Solomon to bear for the benefit of Aquinas's royal reader.
42. *ST* I-II.105.
43. Here begins Dondaine's and Eschmann's concern that *De Regno* does not comport with the *Summa Theologica* on the best regime (Dondaine, *De regno ad Regem Cypri*, préface, 424; Eschmann, *On Kingship*, introduction, xvi–xviii).

The Aristotelian State of Nature   43

Recalling Nederman's arguments about Cicero's influence on medieval political naturalism, we note that Aquinas does not spell out here the connection between political naturalism and man's full flourishing or virtue, something he is at pains to do later in the *Summa Theologica*.[44] The family provides a certain sufficiency for "nourishment" and raising children, Aquinas argues in *De Regno*, and the neighborhood, or *vicus*, a measure of economic sufficiency.[45] But the city (*civitas*) is the *perfecta communitas* as the full expression of that sufficiency: "it exists with regard to all the necessities of life" (I.1.14). The *civitas* in his account is perfect because of its ability to provide necessities, but with the subsequent line, Aquinas adds: "Still more self-sufficiency is found in a *provincia* because of the need of fighting together and of mutual help against enemies" (I.1.14).

This text betrays an Aristotelian and an Augustinian dimension. The Aristotelian *polis*, rendered *civitas* in Latin, had a flexible, generic meaning for thinkers of Aquinas's time, one that accommodated a variety of political forms in medieval Europe under the umbrella of empire and papacy. As for the *prooemium*, Eschmann notes: "Nothing is very definite about this notion except that, at any rate, a province is part of a greater and more comprehensive whole."[46] Indeed, in invoking the *provincia*, Aquinas could be pointing to the Cypriot's dominion as a part of a greater Norman confederation or as a part of Christendom.

As Nederman underlines, however, it is somewhat alarming that many medieval thinkers equate the *polis* with far-larger

---

44. See *ST* I-II.90 and Thomas Aquinas, *Commentary on the "Nicomachean Ethics,"* trans. C. I. Litzinger, OP (Chicago: Henry Regnery Company, 1964), lect. 1.
45. See Aristotle, *Politics* 1252b12–16, and Eschmann, *On Kingship*, introduction, 9, n. 22.
46. Eschmann, *On Kingship*, introduction, 10, n. 23.

kingdoms and empires.[47] At best, that practice confirms Black's thesis that Aristotle served more as a source of language than of novel ideas in medieval political thought. At worst, it raises questions about the facility of medieval thinkers with ancient political thought. The medieval elevation of the *provincia* as a self-sufficient community, for example, seems to ignore all the reasons why the *civitas* or *polis* was thought to be the perfect community, namely its ability to inculcate virtue in its citizens. Casting the *provincia* as a perfect society, in other words, risks mischaracterizing the kind of human ends the perfect community ought to seek. Aquinas's conflation of the *civitas* and the *provincia* reflects that ambiguity.

To be sure, Aquinas does recognize an important difference between the *civitas* and the *provincia*: the latter's ability to defend itself. Aquinas attributes the superiority of the *provincia* to its ability to respond to the "*necessitatem compugnationis.*" This emphasis on military strength would resonate with Aquinas's royal reader, whose kingdom originated in the Christian Crusades against Islam. Indeed, Cyprus' role in the fight for recovering the Holy Land would seem to be the very epitome of the kingship that serves God, recalling the earlier *servus meus* title God assigns to David. Aquinas has suggested, moreover, that the highest excellence of the polity was a kind of military one, a military excellence that is, in fact, the great advantage of the *provincia* above the city.

If a *provincia* were large enough to secure itself through military defense, however, it would not retain the character of a polis as classically conceived.[48] One might wonder from this account of

---

47. Cary J. Nederman, "Aristotelianism and the Origins of 'Political Science' in the Twelfth Century," *Journal of the History of Ideas* 52, no. 2 (1991): 185–86. For a profound treatment of the distinction between polis, empire, and church, see Pierre Manent, *Metamorphoses of the City*, trans. Marc LePain (Cambridge, Mass.: Harvard University Press, 2013).

48. Aristotle, *Politics* 1276a27–30; Aristotle, *Nicomachean Ethics*, trans. Robert C. Bartlett and Susan D. Collins (Chicago: University of Chicago Press, 2011), 1170b34–35.

the *provincia*, then, if Aquinas does not have in mind, or even does not fully understand, Aristotle's teaching on human flourishing. One could argue, of course, that Aristotle as well as Aquinas accept the diversity of regimes: that at times the need for a strong military legitimately takes priority over the city's need to be virtuous. Perhaps the Cypriot's situation demands that his community seek survival before it can then progress to excellence, yet Aquinas curiously betrays no evidence here that he is choosing a lower political end over a higher one.

Aquinas's recourse to and comfort with military force and self-defense as part of the perfect society could also reveal his debt to the Augustinian tradition and is, indeed, one of the strongest traces of Augustine in the text thus far. While Aquinas has distinguished carefully between the rational, just regime and the violent, unjust regime, in his depiction of the *provincia*, he admits that violence cannot be eradicated from the politics of even the most just regime. Not only must the just regime provide for its own necessities, it must also protect itself against hostile enemies. If man seeks in community what he cannot have in solitary life (I.1.4–6), then it would seem from Aquinas's arguments about the *provincia* that he stays in that community on account of another consideration: protection from men in other societies. This emphasis on human antisociality and violence would, of course, resonate not only with the Cypriot king but also with students of the Augustinian tradition.

If Aquinas does invoke this tradition, then we must again ask Nederman's question about the relationship of Aristotle and Augustine, for, recalling Aquinas's claim that the free man acts for his own sake, it is striking that the life of the *liber* should become so dependent on the military might of his society. For then the *liber* would possess a *libertas* from bodily evils rather than a *libertas* toward human rational fulfilment. Yet Aquinas never makes these connections, and thus far seems untroubled by their implications. Indeed, I.1 leaves unclear whether Aquinas adequately grapples with Aristotle's political naturalism. And so, while it is tempting to dismiss Aquinas's treatment of the *provincia* as a bow to historical change since the time of Aristotle, too much is at stake to treat these matters glibly.

Aquinas closes this treatment of the self-sufficient community, as he closed his regime typology, by relating it to kingship: "It is plain, therefore, from what has been said, that a king is one who rules the people of one city or province, and rules them for the common good. Wherefore Solomon says (Eccl. 5:8): "The king rules over all the land subject to him" (I.1.15).

Surveying I.1, Aquinas's regime typology has accorded monarchy a central place, not least with his biblical language, although he has not yet broached the question of the best regime. He has described kingship alone of the possible regime forms as a service to God, and he has cited Solomon three times as not only a dispenser of wisdom for kings but also as an example of a king obedient to God. Aquinas might be so framing kingship out of a rhetorical strategy. Given that this is a *speculum principum*, perhaps Aquinas relates kingship to divine rule because of his audience. The rulers of any regime need to be servants of God, on that account, but Aquinas wishes to highlight this dynamic especially for his royal audience. Given how little Aquinas has written of the other regimes, one wishes he had spelled out what the monarch's divine service implies for the other just regimes. Can they participate in this ministry to God by degree?

One has to wonder if kingship is somehow more closely related than other regimes to God. Given Aquinas's earlier metaphysical arguments (I.1.9) that everything must be ruled by one, and, moreover, his references to the king as serving beneath God the king in the *prooemium*, we will not be surprised to see Aquinas develop an account of monarchy rooted in an analogy between God-in-His-Creation and the king-in-his-kingdom in book II. The question of God's relation to the king might remind us of our earlier questions about the relation of the king to man, or rather the analogy between the king ruling the multitude as reason rules each man. Granting that humans in community need something to lead them to their end, what precisely is its relation to the reason that guides each man? And does the relationship between God and king give us any answers to that question? At the very least, we can note that while *De Regno* I.1 gave us a rational defense of political authority, it has also confirmed or enhanced that argument with biblical warrants. There have as yet, however, been no references to the church or the Fall.

Along with monarchy, *De Regno* I.1 further addresses Aquinas's subscription to Aristotle's political naturalism. If he indeed believes that the *civitas* is the perfect community because it provides mere necessities, and that the *provincia* is still more self-sufficient for its military advantage, then Aquinas has indeed been content to promote a Ciceronian version of political naturalism, rather than an Aristotelian one that would advance human excellence as the ultimate *arche* and *telos* of human community.

Yet if Cicero allows Christian political thought to take seriously both human flourishing and the Fall, we must again observe that Aquinas invokes Cicero without any explicit reference to the Fall. Perhaps a discussion of sin and the Fall is forthcoming.

The Best Regime: I.2

Both Aquinas's general justification for political authority and his regime typology have privileged monarchy over other regimes, but without arguing for monarchy as the best regime. In I.2, Aquinas proposes to address the question of the best regime directly: "it is necessary to seek after what provides better for a province or city: whether to be ruled by many or one" (I.2.16). "This question may be considered first," Aquinas writes, "from the end of government [*ex ipso fine regiminis*]."

It is not clear why Aquinas omits "the few" when he lays out a regime typology of rule by one, the few, and the many. Perhaps Aquinas means to give reasons for the excellence of a certain regime that hinge on the distinction between "one" and "more than one." The subsequent line is also intriguing, as the *finis regiminis* is precisely what we wanted explained further in I.1: what is this *bonum commune* for the author of *De Regno*? What follows is revealing: "Now the good and safety of a multitude formed into a society lies in the preservation of its unity, which is called peace. If this is removed, the benefit of social life is lost and, moreover, the multitude in its disagreement becomes burdensome to itself (I.2.17)." Something of this teaching emerged in I.1: a ruling element is necessary to impel the diverse elements of a society toward a single effect (I.1.9), but Aquinas did not there describe this unity as peace. What follows is similarly intriguing: the ruler must then procure the unity of peace (*pacis unitatem*). What is this end of peace, and how is peace a kind of unity? According to Eschmann, William of Moerbeke used the Latin *pax* in his translation of the *Nicomachean Ethics* to translate Aristotle's εὐνομία. While *pax* might not be the most apt translation of εὐνομία, meaning something more literally like "good laws," it is not clear from *De Regno* that it leads Aquinas astray. After all, Aquinas calls not just *pax* the end of governance but also *unitas pacis*, which surely implies something like a well-ordered regime of laws.[49] The phrase *uni-*

---

49. Aristotle, *Nicomachean Ethics* 1112b14; Aquinas, *Commentary on the "Nicomachean*

tas pacis may also have resonated with Aquinas's own thinking, as he frequently describes human communities as a unity of order, or *unitas ordinis*, as we noted above.⁵⁰ As Russell Hittinger notes, such an order sees "individual persons as members of a unity of order that transcends the sum of the parts," but this unity does not reduce them to "absolutely one." Aquinas thus avoids two extremes: "One extreme depicts society as a kind of superindividual having a single mind or a single body like a biological organism. The other extreme is to think of a society as a purely accidental unity ensuing upon the choices and actions of individuals who follow their own preferences."⁵¹ In invoking the phrase *unitas pacis*, Aquinas suggests that the king ought to order his people toward peace as a genuine *societas*.

Aquinas continues by arguing that the ruler may not "deliberate whether he shall establish peace in the multitude subject to him" any more than the physician may deliberate as to securing the health of a sick man. He then states the classic definition of prudence: "for no one should deliberate [*consiliari*] about an end which he is obliged to seek, but only about the means [*de hiis*] to attain that end." Returning to the teaching of the latter part of I.1, Aquinas argues that "the more efficacious a government is in keeping the unity of peace, the more useful it will be. For we call that more useful which leads more directly to the end." This brings Aquinas to his conclusion: "Now it is manifest that what is itself one can more efficaciously bring about unity than several." What

---

Ethics," III.8: 474, as noted in Eschmann, *On Kingship*, introduction, 11, n. 2; and Dondaine, *De regno ad Regem Cypri*, préface, 451.

50. Aquinas, *Summa Contra Gentiles*, III, 69; *De Ver.* 11.1; *De Ver.* 5.8 ad 12; and *In Sent.* II.1.1.5.

51. Russell Hittinger, "The Coherence of the Four Basic Principles of Catholic Social Doctrine: An Interpretation," Pontifical Academy of Social Sciences, XVIII Plenary Session (Città Del Vaticano), May 2, 2008, 80–81.

is itself one can better than many bring about unity. Thus, the rule of one is more useful than the rule of many.

Aquinas's second argument for the superiority of monarchy is simple: other regimes become better through imitating it. Aquinas then argues that "several persons could by no means preserve the stability of the community if they totally [*omnino*] disagreed" (I.2.18). Aquinas chooses *omnino* for a reason: to rule at all they must have some modicum of agreement, and to rule well, they must be substantially united. However, they then draw closer to being one. Even the rule of many, then, must imitate the rule of one. "Therefore one rules better than many approaching one."

Aquinas then gives a third reason in favor of monarchy as the best regime: it is according to nature. What is in accord with nature is best, "for in all things nature does what is best [*optimum*]" (I.2.19). But governance in nature is always by one. Now humans in making things according to art imitate nature: a "work of art is better according as it attains a closer likeness to what is in nature." Therefore, human community, in imitating nature, ought to conform to this rule by one.

Having endorsed the monarchical standard of nature, Aquinas gives examples of this monarchical principle: the heart moves the organs; reason is chief of the powers of the soul; a beehive has one bee king; and in the universe there is one God, maker and ruler of all things (I.2.19). Aquinas has already cited a few of these examples in I.1.9, but he now appends a lesson to them: "Every multitude is derived from one."[52] This is a startling statement, because Aquinas's argument all along has been that the multitude exists and must be held together by the ruler. In what sense is the multitude derived from the one ruler?

The examples Aquinas gives of nature's monarchical tendency

---

52. Eschmann renders *"ab uno"* as "unity."

are stock examples in medieval and ancient politics, and perhaps some would be familiar to the Cypriot. While they are all examples of monarchy in nature, however, they do not evince the same kind of unity derived from one. That need not concern us or the king, save that this ambiguity complicates Aquinas's statements on the king and God, ambiguities that Aquinas will seek to resolve in book II. The heart might move all of the other organs, but it is nonetheless an organ, one among many.[53] The heart as the principle of the body's activity would be internal to that very activity. Similarly, the bee king is but one bee of many, as reason is but one of the powers of the soul. God, however, stands outside creation. God as the creator and mover of the cosmos is external or outside of that activity as the foundation of its being, so the heart and God stand in radically different positions vis-à-vis their subjects.

The human king seems to rule more like the heart, reason, or the bee king than like God, because the king is an internal or inherent part of the unity he shapes. On the other hand, we know that the king will rule with reason, something the heart and bee lack, and he has some kind of freedom to choose his proximate ends and the means through which he pursues them. The heart and bee lack this, as well. In that sense, then, the king seems to rule more like God than like the bee and heart. Yet the king is not quite like God, because he did not create what he rules and lacks perfect knowledge of and providence over it.[54] And while

---

53. In Aquinas's *Commentary on Aristotle's "Metaphysics,"* probably written several years after *De Regno*, Aquinas argues that for Aristotle the heart is the principle of the body because "all of the soul's powers are diffused throughout the body by means" of it, not because of the conventional opinion according to which the heart is merely the principle of motion in the body (*Metaphysics* V.1:755).

54. The heart does not rule over the other organs in every sense; that would make it like the horseman in Plato's Republic, who commands the bridlemaker despotically (Republic X). Cf. *ST* I.83.3 ad 2; *ST* I-II.56.4 ad 3.

man does rule himself in reason, we have been left to wonder how rational the king's rule of the multitude can be, and *a fortiori* how precisely God's rule will be exemplary for human rule.

Aquinas has confirmed the importance of political naturalism for *De Regno*, even if the respective roles of Aristotle and Cicero are obscure. Aquinas's examples from nature have led us, however, to ask where exactly to place humans within the universe. In what way should man imitate nature? In what sense should the king imitate God? Particularly given Aquinas's comparisons of human monarchy to divine rule in I.1. and I.2., we can hope that Aquinas will have more to say on this subject in book II.

The concluding paragraph of I.2 claims the evidence of experience as proof of the superiority of monarchy to rule by the many. It is worth quoting in full:

> This is also evident from experience. For provinces or cities that are not ruled by one are torn with dissensions and tossed about [*fluctuant*] without peace, so that the complaint seems to be fulfilled which the Lord uttered through the Prophet [Jer 12:10]: "Many pastors have destroyed my vineyard." On the other hand, provinces and cities which are ruled under one king enjoy peace, flourish in justice, and delight in prosperity [*affluentia rerum*]. Hence, the Lord by His prophets promises to His people as a great reward that He will give them one head and that "one Prince will be in the midst of them" [Ez 34:24, Jer 30:21] (I.2.20).

These are curious quotations. One might have expected Aquinas to present historical examples of good and bad human rulers. Instead, he gives an example of the "many pastors" of Israel who allowed the Babylonians to ravage Israel, and then the hope of a good *princeps* as some kind of reward or gift for an unspecified reason. In this case, the *princeps* would be the effect rather than the cause of a good society. Moreover, if this *princeps* bears a Christological mark, then the evidence Aquinas gives us of the "experience" of terrestrial cities would, in fact, be a promise in the supernatural order.

The complexity of Aquinas's examples does not end there, for he is also invoking a history that is not entirely favorable to monarchy. The Old Testament at times excoriates monarchy as a rejection of God's rule, given that for Israel, "God is the king," not "the king is a God."[55] In many places, the prophets and chroniclers lament the weakness of a monarchy that cannot fulfill God's promise of a united Israel.[56] And the supreme example of biblical kingship, David, who has already been cited as God's *servus*, is himself no moral exemplar. We have yet to see if Aquinas will address this complicated testimony on kingship, and indeed if at any point in *De Regno* advert to the limitations of monarchy.

One could respond, however, that thus far Aquinas has had little to say in general about scripture in *De Regno* and has not employed scripture probatively. While Aquinas outlines three sources in the *prooemium* as scripture, philosophy, and history, here Aquinas quotes scripture to illustrate and confirm his argument from history, rather than invoke the power of revelation to justify monarchy as the best regime. Thus, Aquinas does not undermine the rational and naturalistic foundations of I.1 by these references to the Bible. We can thus far reject as too simple claims that Aquinas's political thought by necessity must be a political theology.[57]

At the beginning of this chapter, we noted that Aquinas inquires into the rule of only the one and the many but not the few. We have now seen a few reasons to justify that move. First, the argument for the need for effectual unity applies as much to the few

---

55. Moshe Halbertal and Stephen Holmes, *The Beginning of Politics* (Princeton, N.J.: Princeton University Press, 2017), 5.
56. Kraynak, *Christian Faith and Modern Democracy*, 46–52; Halbertal and Holmes, *The Beginning of Politics*, 6–7.
57. Jordan, "*De Regno* and the Place of Political Thinking in Thomas Aquinas," 151–68.

as to the many: Aquinas thinks that any number of rulers greater than one must unite as one. The argument *secundum naturam* is also a strike against the few as much as against the many, as he clearly spells out at I.2.18. And the argument from experience, Aquinas makes quite clear, is also directed against any regime forms "which are not ruled by one person."

Given that *De Regno* is a *speculum,* there also may be pedagogical reasons for why Aquinas focuses on the distinction between the one and the many. Perhaps Aquinas desires to show that monarchy is superior to the category nonmonarchy. Such arguments in favor of monarchy would obviously sit well with Aquinas's royal reader. Additionally, many medieval monarchies were "constitutional": they involved other political authorities, even if the monarch made the final decisions on many matters.[58] So if the Cypriot king's regime involves others besides himself, as Eschmann suggests, it might not be politic to abuse rule by the few.[59] After all, Aquinas has argued that rulers who cannot agree amongst themselves can achieve little. And this is a persistent threat among such regimes, Aquinas suggests, insofar as they must strive to be effectually one if not factually one. Without accusing Aquinas of dissimulation, then, it is clear that he has been able to paint monarchy in a most favorable light in the second half of I.1. This is a bit different from his more complex tone in the *prooemium*.

However reasonable these strategies, we cannot ignore that Aquinas has been markedly promonarchy throughout these early sections of *De Regno*. While his writings have been used to justify every regime as best, on the whole, Aquinas's *opera* strikes one as

---

58. See Fritz Kern, *Kingship and Law in the Middle Ages*, trans. S. B. Chrimes (Oxford: Blackwell, 1939); Geoffrey Barraclough, *The Origins of Modern Germany* (Oxford: Blackwell, 1947); and Robert Folz, *The Concept of Empire in Western Europe from the Fifth to the Fourteenth Century*, trans. Sheila Ann Ogilvie (London: Edward Arnold, 1969).

59. Eschmann, *On Kingship*, introduction, xxxvi–vii.

in favor of the mixed regime as best.⁶⁰ And even in his strongest formulations of the best regime, as Kraynak argues persuasively of much of the Christian political tradition in general, Aquinas typically is more assiduous in maintaining the classical teaching that there are a multiplicity of legitimate regimes whose instantiation in a given community is a prudential consideration.

To be sure, Aquinas has not denied that there is a multiplicity of just regimes: polity and aristocracy are also legitimate regime forms. Yet Aquinas's approach in I.2 seems a robust endorsement of monarchy, with little room for the prudential application of aristocracy or polity that I.1 might have seemed to leave open. If monarchy is metaphysically superior to other regimes, and is indeed apparently the only one sanctioned by and conforming to God, how can any other regime be legitimate?

I would like to consider five possible reasons for Aquinas's staunchly promonarchy position in *De Regno*: Aquinas's time period, his personal experience, his reading of Aristotle, his audience, and, finally, the possibility that, in fact, Aquinas is not promonarchy in *De Regno*. If Aquinas did indeed embrace monarchy rather uncritically in *De Regno* I.1–2, perhaps this is because he was still under the influence of rather uncritical notions of monarchy. The first three reasons assume as much.

One line of argument might claim that Aquinas's robust support for monarchy in *De Regno* speaks to his time period: Aquinas is simply bowing to the prevailing ideology of his time. While this might seem an insulting insinuation, it is important to realize the strength of monarchical ideologies in Aquinas's time, indeed, in most premodern times. As Oakley notes, a variety of influences made it almost impossible to imagine any sort of regime besides

---

60. Blythe, *Ideal Government*, 40–41; *ST* I-II.105.1.

monarchy at many points in history.⁶¹ Christians were not exempt from this orientation toward monarchy.⁶² Just as few twenty-first-century citizens can imagine living in anything other than some kind of democracy, so perhaps Aquinas has a difficult time compassing any regime besides monarchy. This argument would thus not necessarily impugn Aquinas's intelligence, but it does propose a limitation to his political imagination.

Indeed, perhaps Aquinas is, in fact, predisposed from personal experience to embrace monarchy. Not only did he live in a time period immersed in monarchy, but he grew up in a noble home with deep ties to monarchy. As Dyson recounts, both of Aquinas's parents were born into comital families and "related to the Emperors Henry VI and Frederick II, and to the Kings of Aragon, France, and Castile." His uncle was the abbot of Monte Cassino, where Aquinas began as an oblate.⁶³ Aquinas was no stranger to power.

If Aquinas did indeed grow up in such a setting, he may very well have been comfortable with the notion of monarchy as the best regime. As a man who knew something of the politics of his time, the idea of dilating on regime forms besides monarchy might have seemed irresponsibly hypothetical or even frivolous. And, since Aquinas is writing for a prince, he could assume he was writing for someone who shared such views. One might plausibly if cynically maintain, however, that Aquinas's personal experience in royal circles was, in fact, a strong argument *contra* monarchy for him. After all, Aquinas did not himself embrace the life of his family but ran away to join the Dominicans. He was also later prevailed on to arbitrate bitter disputes within his family.

These arguments about Aquinas's time period and personal ex-

---

61. Oakley, *Empty Bottles*, 1–10.
62. Kraynak, *Christian Faith and Modern Democracy*.
63. Aquinas, *Aquinas: Political Writings, Cambridge Texts in the History of Political Thought*, ed. and trans. R. W. Dyson (Cambridge: Cambridge University Press, 2002), xvii.

perience suggest that Aquinas remained to an extent a prisoner of the conventions of his time. The third argument seeks to explain in part why: Aquinas read Aristotle too simplistically.

Much research on *De Regno* has centered around Aquinas's familiarity with the *Politics*. Eschmann, for instance, argues for the composition date of *De Regno* on the basis of what we know about Aquinas's reception of the *Politics*.[64] But even if Aquinas had had access to the *Politics* when he wrote *De Regno*, that hardly necessitates that he knew it well. Perhaps at the time of writing *De Regno* Aquinas was not critically engaged with the Aristotelian political science of regime form, but rather used Aristotle's language to conceptualize preexisting medieval thought. We have already raised this possibility with the *provincia* and the *civitas*. On this account, Aquinas utilizes Aristotle's language to explicate medieval understandings of monarchy as the best regime but without being challenged by the nuances and subtleties of Aristotle's arguments, subtleties that would raise questions about the limitations of monarchy as a regime.

But perhaps Aquinas has more control over his presentation of monarchy in *De Regno* than these first three arguments assume. Let us consider, for instance, Aquinas's audience. Aquinas is writing a *speculum*, and so this text is addressed to a king. We might wonder, then, if this audience and this *genre* will impact Aquinas's presentation of his regime typology. Perhaps he only presents his typology selectively, aware that he is writing to a monarch, who, after all, is not interested in a theoretical disquisition into regime types, and particularly not those of regime forms other than his own. On that account, Aquinas could be fully aware of the caveats and qualifications that he is leaving out but sees no difficulty with those omissions given his audience. Indeed, Aquinas might

---

64. Eschmann, *On Kingship*, introduction, xxvi–xxx.

wish to avoid belaboring this typology so as to proceed more expeditiously to a topic of greater concern. Perhaps, too, Aquinas has a rhetorical strategy behind his typology, and employs it for its hortatory effect on his royal reader rather than for its theoretical value. That would explain why Aquinas hints at the excellence of monarchy in I.1 before he explicitly addresses the question of the best regime: Aquinas means for the whole typology to be a moral exercise for the king, to let him feel like David, the *servus meus* of God.

One would then wonder what Aquinas means to do with this rhetorical strategy. Perhaps he simply means to flatter the king. This *speculum*, after all, was probably written to curry favor with the Cypriot royal house.[65] A more charitable reading, however, is that to which we have already adverted: Aquinas wants to predispose the king to take the duties of his royal office seriously. By framing monarchy as unreservedly the best regime, Aquinas can at once secure the trust of his royal reader and also spur him to acts of greater justice. Rather than browbeating the king for his inevitable injustices, Aquinas elevates the task of the monarch by exalting the kingly office, an exaltation founded, of course, on the king's deep obligations to justice. Aquinas can then emphasize the implications of satisfying those obligations within the context of that exaltation of the king.

This consideration about audience might lead us to reject the premise that Aquinas in *De Regno* is uncritical in his advancement of monarchy as the best regime. For on this account, his elevation of monarchy is a rhetorical strategy, not a philosophical blindspot. Another possibility, one that is not mutually exclusive, is that he is being advised in his use of the term "monarchy." As we noted earlier, "monarchy" in the medieval context need not preclude some

---

65. Eschmann, *On Kingship*, introduction, xxx–xxxi.

constitutional element.[66] If this is true, then we need to see how Aquinas "tempers" or moderates monarchy. Indeed, given Aquinas's emphasis on monarchy's superlative justice, we hope that he will spell out under what conditions monarchy can be just. That *De Regno* might yet contain arguments that temper Aquinas's endorsement of monarchy as the best regime is not a strong claim, but it is a wise one given how early we are in the text.

Conclusion: *De Regno* I.1–2

The early chapters of *De Regno* offer a powerful teaching on fundamental questions of politics. Against expectations that Aquinas's teaching in *De Regno* would be theological or removed from politics, he has provided a sophisticated philosophical analysis of the naturalness of politics, of the multiplicity of regime forms, and of monarchy as the best regime. We also see signs that Aquinas will utilize conventions of the *speculum* with facility. He is not writing a treatise, and so we ought not to read *De Regno* as one.

Aquinas has also, however, left us with a number of questions. Perhaps the greatest one is whether Aquinas will moderate his defense of monarchy as the best regime. Why are his arguments for monarchy at I.1–2 so unqualified? As we have seen, those reasons could be philosophical, but they might also be rhetorical, revealing more about the structure and purpose of this *speculum* for Aquinas. As a related issue, will Aquinas make more room for nonmonarchical regimes? An answer to this question might be Aquinas's articulation of the conditions under which monarchy cannot flourish. Such a specification would then set the terms by which communities might choose to institute other regime forms.

Also unresolved at the end of I.1–2 is Aquinas's interpretation of political naturalism. Is Aquinas finally gesturing toward a

---

66. Blythe, *Ideal Government*, 39–59; Black, *Political Thought*, 136.

more Aristotelian *telos* for the city, or is it a more Augustinian or even Ciceronian notion? Aquinas's grasp of Aristotle has at times seemed tenuous, and his emphasis on survival and necessity in the origins of the *civitas* does indeed resemble the Ciceronian tradition. And while Aquinas has argued for the end of the community as treating its citizens like *liberi* rather than *servi*, he has not specified the end of the *liber*.

We have to wonder, then, if Aquinas uses Cicero to balance Augustine and Aristotle, as Nederman has it of other medieval thinkers, or if Aquinas ultimately juxtaposes Augustine with Aristotle. After all, Aquinas has had remarkably little to say about the Fall and sin, doctrines that would indicate the influence of Augustine and would seem to require Cicero. For that matter, Aquinas has said nothing of the church or the law. And his invocations of revelation have largely served to prop up monarchy. Looking ahead, then, we will wonder if and when Aquinas will invoke the great questions of "church and state," also looking for clues as to why he chooses to delay such conversation.

While in *De Regno* I.1–2 we have seen little trace of the tyranny that has concerned so many scholars, tyranny does indeed become a focus in the subsequent section. As we move on to *De Regno* I.3–6, we will have to ask why Aquinas's focus shifts from the excellence of kingship to tyranny and how it bears upon the perplexities raised by I.1–2.

CHAPTER 2

The Augustinian Earthly City

De Regno I.3–6

I.3–6 informs one of the most common interpretations of *De Regno*: it is obsessed with tyranny. As Keys puts it, in *De Regno*, Aquinas seems "more centrally occupied with avoiding or mitigating tyranny than with elaborating the simply best civic way of life."[1] It is I.3–6 that gives the text this reputation for tyranny, which, as we have noted, is a serious obstacle to the study of *De Regno*. For it is not obvious why one would read a medieval text with so little to say about the best regime, a work so far removed from the Aristotelian character of Aquinas's other works, or for that matter a text that promises but purportedly fails to supply remedies for tyranny, as Dondaine worries.[2]

Yet this long treatment of tyranny comes only after Aquinas's fulsome encomium to monarchy in I.1–2. And while the overall tenor of I.3–6 certainly raises a question as to the practical possibility of the regime laid out in I.1–2, it never directly contradicts the teaching of I.1–3. In other words, Aquinas offers a substantive teaching about both monarchy and tyranny in the first chapters

---

1. Keys, *Aquinas, Aristotle, and the Promise of the Common Good*, 64.
2. Dondaine, *De regno ad Regem Cypri*, préface, 423.

of *De Regno*, uncertain as the relationship between those two teachings may be. Thus, the fundamental question to be put to *De Regno* is not why Aquinas dwells on tyranny in it but rather why he juxtaposes two radically different accounts: a promising vision of rational politics grounded in political naturalism and the goodness of monarchy, and a bleak picture of seemingly inevitable tyranny, in which politics is the domain of sin and injustice. Why does he juxtapose the two teachings, and how does he resolve their apparent contradiction?

Further, Aquinas makes clear that he must treat on tyranny not despite the advantages of monarchy but because of them. Monarchy, he argues, bears an ambiguity, issuing in the just and unjust rule of one. This ambiguity, in turn, bears upon the Aristotelian question of the naturalness of politics and the Augustinian denial of such naturalness. For at stake is whether the close association between tyranny and monarchy negates for practical purposes the theoretical excellence of monarchy, and perhaps even the naturalness of politics. We will see that Aquinas preserves the excellence of monarchy and the naturalness of politics while fully cognizant that humans can turn away from justice.

And to repeat from the introduction to this study: our reading of *De Regno* does not require that we exaggerate the differences between Aristotle or Augustine or the subsequent traditions that ambiguously represent them, but we should contemplate sensitively the action whereby Aquinas invokes and reconciles their arguments for the benefit of his royal student.

The Caprice of the Tyrant: I.3

Now that Aquinas has presented the six regimes in I.1, and the best regime, kingship, in I.2, he turns in I.3 to the worst regime: tyranny. He begins the chapter by noting that what is contrary to the best is the worst. And what is best, he has proven, is monarchy. Tyranny as the opposite of monarchy is therefore the worst regime (I.3.22).[3] "[A] united force [*virtus unita*]," Aquinas argues, "is more efficacious in producing its effect than a force which is scattered or divided" (I.3.23). This was a reason to prefer kingship over other regimes. Yet a united force can do good or do evil. The king as a united force does great good. The tyrant is also a united force, but a force directed toward injustice. Thus, among unjust governments, the more united the ruling element, the more harmful the rule will be. Tyranny, therefore, bests oligarchy and democracy in the harm it can do.

Tyranny is also the worst regime with respect to Aquinas's distinction between the common and the private: "Moreover, a government becomes unjust by the fact that the ruler, paying no heed to the common good, seeks his own private good [bonum privatum]. Wherefore the further he departs from the common good the more unjust will his government be" (I.324). Aquinas then explains that oligarchy seeks the good of the few (*bonum paucorum*) and so is more unjust than democracy's pursuit of the *bonum multorum*. Tyranny seeks the good of just one (*bonum tantum unius*), however, which is the greatest departure from the common good of all: "For a large number is closer to the totality than a small number, and a small number than only one" (I.3.24).

Aquinas then returns to the metaphysics of I.2 on the superiority of kingship as another proof of tyranny's injustice. Good things ensue from one perfect cause; evil "results from any one partial defect.... Thus ugliness results in different ways from many causes; beauty in one way from one perfect cause." Aquinas here vouches for the providence of this arrangement: "It is thus with all good and evil things, as if God so provided that good, arising

---

3. Cf. *Ethics* VIII (Dondaine, *De regno ad Regem Cypri*, préface, 452).

from one cause, be stronger, and evil, arising from many causes, be weaker." What is good is stronger than what is evil, because evil depends on many causes. Evil can arise from any defect in a cause, and the more defects, the more evil. Yet the more evil something is, the more causes it depends on for its character. Evil is thus an ever-shifting attribute, for its specific defectiveness changes whenever one of its many causes is removed or altered. The political consequences of this teaching are straightforward:

> It is expedient therefore that a just regime[4] be that of one only in order that it may be stronger; however, if the regime should turn away from justice, it is more expedient that it be of many, so that it may be weaker and the many may mutually hinder one another. Among unjust regimes, therefore, democracy is the most tolerable, but the worst is tyranny (I.3.25).

Tyranny in its goal or final cause, injustice, could be not further from kingship. Yet in its formal unity, as the rule of one, it is the unjust regime most parasitic on kingship. Democracy in its multiplicity of unjust rulers is the most removed from kingship: it cannot share in the formality of kingship's unity. Because the rulers are many, however, it is a weak regime. What makes democracy so defective, then, is also what limits its efficacy: "the many may mutually hinder one another."

Aquinas gives over the second half of I.3 to the evils of tyranny (I.3.26–29), emphasizing the experience of subjects under the tyrant. It is an account structured around that most Augustinian notion, *libido*. He argues in I.3.26 that tyranny is also shown to be the worst regime by "the evils which come from tyrants." The tyrant seeks his *bonum privatum*, not the *bonum commune*. Different tyrants are motivated by different passions, and the same

---

4. Eschmann often translates *regimen* as "government," which is not always helpful when Aquinas has in mind the regime forms.

tyrant can be driven by multiple passions. Thus, the tyrant not only commits injustice by seeking his *bonum privatum*: in so doing, he propagates pervasive and persistent instability throughout his regime. "Nobody," Aquinas elaborates, "will be able firmly to state: This thing is such and such, when it depends on the will of another, not to say upon his caprice [*libido*]" (I.3.26). "Keep far from the man who has the power to kill," Aquinas quotes Sirach 9:13, because "he kills not for justice's sake but by his power, for the lust of his will [*pro libidine voluntatis*]."

Libido is a charged word for Aquinas, recalling Augustine's theological history of Rome in *The City of God,* V.12–21. On Augustine's account, the desire of the Romans to control other peoples was absolute, an insatiable appetite. And while the Roman project began with vice that imitated virtue, it eventually gave over entirely to a vice that sought the eradication of all virtue. Thus, it is no surprise that Aquinas's model tyrant herein seeks total control of his subjects, body and soul. The tyrant does not seek "merely" to control his subjects "in corporal things" but also "hinders their spiritual good." As Aquinas has it, they do not seek to control their subject in spiritual matters only for their need to control them. They also fear "all excellence in their subjects to be prejudicial to their own evil domination. For tyrants hold the good in greater suspicion than the wicked, and to them the valour of others is always fraught with danger."

As Aquinas goes on to describe in I.3.27, the tyrant fears in all their forms the virtues of and friendship between others. The tyrant will "sow discords among their subjects [*subditos*]," nurture preexisting ones, and "forbid anything which furthers society and cooperation among men," including marriage.[5] Aristotle's *Politics*, the likely source of this section, contains no reference to

---

5. Eschmann renders *subditi* variously as "the people" and "subjects."

tyrants suppressing marriage.[6] One possibility for marriage's inclusion here is that Aquinas has in mind marriage primarily between powerful families, alliances that would pose a threat to the tyrant.[7] But as a Christian, Aquinas's concern with marriage will naturally exceed that of Aristotle, not only as the natural basis of society but also as the sacramental basis of society, as well.

If we take a step back from this passage, moreover, we can see that Aquinas has introduced two new considerations: the spiritual good of the citizens, and the general virtue of subjects under a tyrant. With his statement that the tyrant "hinders" the citizens' "spiritual good," Aquinas refers for the first time to the relationship between spiritual goods and politics. It is a thin teaching. Aquinas is not arguing that kings promote the spiritual good of their subjects, although he could well be implying that. Here Aquinas only commits himself to the claim that it would be an injustice for a ruler to hinder that good.[8] If Aquinas were saying nothing more than that, he would be speaking in the tradition of Augustine's *The City of God*, which emphasizes the negative power of government in matters spiritual more than the positive power. Nowhere in I.1–3 does Aquinas speak of the king's task being directly related to the spiritual good of his subjects but rather to the temporal good of peace (I.2.17, 20). And yet here Aquinas speaks of the spiritual ills that the tyrant can cause.

More generally, this section offers Aquinas's first substantive references to the virtues of the citizens. In some detail, Aquinas describes just how hateful such virtue is to the tyrant. The tyrant views virtue as a threat to his rule, insofar as virtuous men can

---

6. Eschmann, *On Kingship*, introduction, 17, n. 11; cf. *ST* III.65.2 ad 1.

7. See Blythe, *On the Government of Rulers*, introduction, 69, n. 39.

8. Douglas Kries, "The Virtue of Religion in the Political Thought of Thomas Aquinas," *Proceedings of the PMR Conference* 15 (1990): 103–15.

work together to overthrow him, but the threat comes to dominate his thinking and further divides his soul. Indeed, Aquinas ends the paragraph on a biblical note to this effect: "The sound of dread is always in his ears and when there is peace, that is, when there is no one to harm him, he always suspects treason" (Job 15:21). It is no surprise, then, that few virtuous men are to be found in the tyrannical regime, as Aquinas illustrates in a florilegium of quotations from Aristotle, Cicero, and St. Paul:

> For, according to Aristotle's sentence [*NE* 1116a 20], brave men are found where brave men are honoured. And as Tullius says [*Tuscul. Disp.* I, 2, 4]: "Those who are despised by everybody are disheartened and flourish but little." It is also natural that men, brought up in fear, should become mean of spirit and discouraged in the face of any strenuous and manly task. This is shown by experience in provinces that have long been under tyrants. Hence the Apostle says to the Colossians [Col 3:21]: "Fathers, provoke not your children to indignation, lest they be discouraged."[9]

In I.1–2, Aquinas emphasizes the relation between the reason that rules man and the man that rules men. But what the tyrant loves is what flourishes in the regime; what he hates, dies. The "loves" of the city, as Augustine would say, factor also in this series of quotations. Aristotle and Cicero attest to the formative influence a regime's paideia has on its citizens.

The quotation from St. Paul speaks at a different level: the family. Aquinas has already mentioned the family once before, as we saw at I.3.27. Here Aquinas seeks to emphasize that the head of a family exercises an influence over his children analogous to that of the leaders of a regime over their subjects.[10] Perhaps Aquinas means to echo Augustine's claim that the family can become a sort of refuge from society, a place to cultivate excellence in a limited

---

9. cf. Dondaine, *De regno ad Regem Cypri*, préface, 453.
10. Aquinas makes a similar claim at *ST* I-II.90.3 ad 1, primarily to emphasize that the command of the father falls short of law.

way and endure until circumstances are more auspicious for championing virtue. Thus, Aquinas might seek through this quotation to point out the importance of the family not only as analogous to the city but also to remind his readers, as many Christian thinkers before him did, that the family can have a kind of autonomy from the regime that allows it to function as both a source of renewal for that regime.[11]

De Regno is littered with quotations of Solomon, and the paragraph that concludes I.3 is no exception. While these Solomon quotations seem to support without extending Aquinas's conclusions, at times they allude to more than Aquinas explicitly states. Consider the second quotation: "When the wicked rise up men shall hide themselves?" (Prv 28:28). Aquinas explains: "It is no wonder, for a man governing without reason, according to the lust of his soul [*secundum animae suae libidinem*], in no way differs from the beast." This is not simply an interpretation of the text but rather an allusion to Aristotle's claim that those who live outside of the polis must be either beast or God. The tyrant who thinks himself a god is actually the beast who destroys the polis in trying to secure his possession of it.

As we noted above, I.3 inaugurates the section of *De Regno* that tinges the whole work with an association of tyranny. Indeed, I.3 has been engrossing in part because Aquinas is therein far more direct about the nature of tyranny than he has hitherto been about the nature of kingship. Aquinas presents an impressive metaphysics of tyranny, one predicated on the multiplicity and weakness of its contradictory causes and elaborated with history and scripture. Aquinas has made a more thorough and concrete case for the inferiority of tyranny (I.3, or nine chapters) than for

---

11. Compare Augustine's famous discussion at *The City of God* XIX.17 on the need in bad regimes for families to be such a refuge.

the superiority of monarchy (I.2, at five chapters). This has allowed him to say more about the nature of injustice and the slavish regime than about that of the best regime.

Not only is length at issue, but also quality: while Aquinas's defense of monarchy as the best regime was an abstract argument from unity and the imitation of nature, his vilification of tyranny descends immediately into practical details, granting us a knowledge of the concrete politics of tyranny. While we have a vague impression that the king fosters virtue and friendship, seeking order and concord, Aquinas's presentation does not teach us a great deal about how the king should do so. Aquinas's political naturalism at times has hewed closer to that of Cicero than of Aristotle. We also do not know how the king's rule relates to that of the church, but Aquinas spells out in great detail how the tyrant destroys virtue and friendship among the citizens and encourages faction and vicious hate. Indeed, even Aquinas's first reference to the spiritual in relation to the temporal comes in his description of the tyrant.

Does this picture of tyrannical politics undermine that of monarchy presented in I.1–2? Strictly speaking, it should not: Aquinas has said nothing to reject his arguments for the naturalness of politics or the goodness of monarchy. Indeed, he means for his catalogue of the horrors of tyranny to be an argument for monarchy.

Yet Aquinas's presentation of tyranny at I.3 raises doubts. How can monarchy be prevented from lapsing into tyranny? And if the perversion of the best is the worst, should human communities as a practical matter simply avoid the best in the first place? Just how likely is monarchy to be perverted into tyranny? As for political naturalism, if human nature is so inclined toward living in community, what in human nature also lends itself to such unjust behavior? And what aid can be offered to human nature to prevent such injustice?

We may also wonder if Aquinas has a rhetorical purpose in juxtaposing his hopeful image of monarchical politics with his grim portrait of tyranny. Perhaps Aquinas means for this *speculum principum* to set before his royal reader two fundamental options, the selection of one being determinative for all future discernment. Aquinas might well wish to impress upon the king the gravity of his royal office, underlining the dangers of tyranny even more than the positive aspects of monarchy.

Here we cannot avoid the presence of Augustine. I.3 presents a gloomy, bleak picture of politics that accords well with many popular depictions of Augustine's politics. Aquinas's description of tyranny fits with the "Augustinian" notion that politics is coercive and a punishment for the Fall. The structure of *De Regno*, moreover, is surprisingly Augustinian. For whatever beautiful words we can adduce about justice (I.1–2), the lot of man described at I.3–6 is far worse. But if Aquinas were adopting an "Augustinian" posture here, then he would seemingly reject the claims of I.1–2, according to which man is political and living in community promotes his excellence. Or, at the very least, he would be offering two very different teachings to our king, lessons which stand in need of reconciliation.

Deciding how far Aquinas's teaching here is "Augustinian," however, is no easy matter. There is a venerable Augustinian tradition associating the great saint's political teaching with sin and coercive government. More broadly, Augustine has long been associated with two strands of Christian thought: the "Two Cities" doctrine, whereby Christians place little faith in earthly rulers to do more than maintain a bare peace, and a "political Augustinian" tradition, which advocates the subordination of political authority for the instrumental utility of the church.[12]

---

12. Oakley, *Empty Bottles*, 123, 127, 137–42; Black, *Political Thought*, 7, 49, 93; and

Both strands are radical flattenings of Augustine's own thought, however, particularly in their reduction of the spiritual dynamics of grace and sin to earthly institutions. They also profoundly contradict each other in many of their theoretical assumptions and practical effects. Yet these strands are admittedly parasitic on Augustine's own ambivalence toward politics. For while in *The City of God* Augustine tends to emphasize the limited ability of man to reach happiness due to the effects of sin, and thus the limited ability of human political authority to work for man's happiness, in his later writings Augustine often urged the use of state power against the Donatist, seemingly believing that political authority could go some way in promoting the faith. And even within any one work of Augustine, he rarely seems to state and expand on any of his political theses systematically.[13]

This ambivalence can probably not be resolved at the level of politics. As Augustine's best interpreters have understood, he was never so much concerned with politics narrowly as with the grand drama of souls within salvation history: how humans were wounded in turning away from God, and how Christ heals them and reunites them with God the Father.[14] If Augustine had a "systematic" coherence, then, it is at the level of theology, not politics. While it might be logically possible to extract "political" theories out of Augustine, that enterprise is fraught, and not made easier by treating his political theory as somehow independent from his theology.[15] Thus, scholars and others who take his theology seri-

---

Michael J. S. Bruno, *Political Augustinianism: Modern Interpretations of Augustine's Political Thought* (Minneapolis, Minn.: Fortress Press, 2014), 1.

13. Bruno, *Political Augustinianism*, 6.

14. Robert Dodaro, *Christ and the Just Society in the Thought of Augustine* (Cambridge:
    Cambridge University Press, 2008), 27–71; Bruno, *Political Augustinianism,* n. 4 at 10; 106 et seq on Fortin.

15. Oakley, *Empty Bottles,* 127.

ously are more likely to identify the salient teachings that shape what we might take up as Augustine's "political" teachings.[16]

Such ambivalence must be borne in mind when asking how thoroughly I.3 is "Augustinian." Aquinas, of course, was a masterful exegete of Augustine, as he had to be to meet the scholarly standards of the day. He was also well aware that many of his contemporary interlocutors were members of the Augustinian tradition and thus would have been well-placed to navigate Augustine's teachings.

We can first note that, thus far, Aquinas's *De Regno* does not fit the pattern of "political Augustinianism." Aquinas has not prescribed a "theocracy," whereby state power is subjugated to religious authority. As we noted, this strand of Augustine's legacy tends to emphasize the power of the state, and the power of the church over the state, by universalizing Augustine's arguments that Roman power could legitimately be brought to bear upon the Donatists. He has not suggested, however, that the coercive power of politics ought to be used primarily to restrain or punish sinners. For that matter, Aquinas has had little to say about the power of monarchy in terms of inculcating virtue, let alone the faith. All he has said that is that the tyrant tramples spiritual goods.

But our analysis of *De Regno* does not obviously bring Aquinas in line with the "Two Cities" interpretation of Augustine's earlier career. Aquinas has had much to say about the human person's political nature, a nature that in principle allows man to grow in virtue and toward happiness in the earthly *civitas*. Thus, any "Two Cities" interpretation of *De Regno* would have to contend with the fact that Aquinas seems to maintain *pace* Augustine some form of political naturalism. Moreover, if Aquinas has revealed the dan-

---

16. See, for example, Dodaro, *Christ and the Just Society* and Bruno, *Political Augustinianism*.

gers of tyranny in I.3–6, he has urged no flight from the earthly city. Indeed, Aquinas has had nothing to say thus far in *De Regno* about the church, much less the *civitas Dei*.

As goes political naturalism, we can see how I.3 deepens our understanding of what is at stake in Nederman's line of questions. Given the complexity of both Augustine's thought and the traditions he inspired, however, it is worth extending Nederman's thesis beyond Augustine to encompass the Augustinian tradition.[17] Perhaps Cicero is used by medieval thinkers as a mediator between Aristotle and the Augustinian tradition, rather than between Aristotle and Augustine himself. But given Augustine's complexity, which is far richer than the flattened interpretation of him offered by the Augustinian tradition, is it really necessary to invoke Cicero to bridge the gap between Aristotle and Augustine? Or might Augustine's vision of a Christ-centered society itself be reconcilable with Aristotle? While we cannot answer these questions now, Nederman's Cicero thesis comes to be a rich source of reflection on the political naturalism of *De Regno*.

I.3 without doubt reflects a certain Augustinian mood. Yet Aquinas's most "Augustinian" section makes no direct reference to the Fall or sin, although he does reference "spiritual good." Aquinas has also presented the lesson of I.3 not as the whole truth about politics but as a reality that somehow has to be integrated into a larger picture of politics, or perhaps into something still larger than politics. If Augustine envisioned politics within the grand sweep of the human soul's relationship with God, after all, we might wonder if Aquinas has anything like that in mind for his *speculum* as well.

---

17. See Oakley, *The Mortgage of the Past*, 80.

Between Tyranny and Monarchy: I.4

Aquinas has argued that tyranny is the worst government because it is "the contrary of the best" (I.3.22). To restate the obvious, then, tyranny and kingship are very different in one respect but very similar in another: while one is directed toward justice and one toward injustice, they are both the rule of one. This presents a practical problem: "Because therefore the best and the worst regime are latent in [*existit in*] monarchy, i.e. in the rule of one, the royal dignity is rendered hateful to many on account of the wickedness of tyrants," (I.4.30).[18] The rule of one issues in both royal and tyrannical governance. This fact presents a considerable difficulty for kings, because in the popular mind kings are hateful through their association with tyranny. This is not just a theoretical confusion, but a practical one, as Aquinas goes on to explain: "Some, indeed, whilst they desire the rule of a king, fall under the cruelty of tyrants, and exceedingly many rulers exercise tyranny under the pretence of the dignity of a king" (I.4.30). Communities seeking to install a king often end up with a tyrant. Then, too, many tyrants take advantage of this confusion, ruling behind a façade of royal justice. This chapter is primarily historical, with Aquinas offering two examples of monarchy becoming hateful because of its confusion with tyranny: the case of Rome (I.4.31–33) and the Hebrew people (I.4.34).

Rome's early kings made the word *rex* detestable, although they were not kings but tyrants, Aquinas argues (I.4.31).[19] The aristocratic regime that subsequently developed had much to recommend it. "For it frequently happens," Aquinas reasons, invoking

18. Dondaine notes that some manuscripts omit *regimen*/"regime" (Dondaine, *De regno ad Regem Cypri*, préface, 453).

19. See Andreas Kalyvas, "The Tyranny of Dictatorship: When the Greek Tyrant Met the Roman Dictator," *Political Theory* 35, no. 4 (2007): 412–43.

Sallust, "that men living under a king strive more sluggishly for the common good.... But when they see that the common good is not under the power of one man, they do not attend to it as if it belonged to another, but each one attends to it as if it were his own." This is a startling admission on Aquinas's part. He has had nothing ill to say of monarchy, and little at all about rule by the few. I.3, which considered the best regime, notably omitted that option. Now he not only suggests that kingship can lead men to a tepid defense of the common good but that aristocracy can be a greater boon to that good. A city under rotating leaders, Aquinas continues, can sometimes achieve more than those under kings: "small services extracted by kings weigh more heavily than great burdens imposed by the community of citizens" (I.4.32). Indeed, he argues, the Roman republic incorporated the plebeians quite successfully, through the army, and the wealthy stinted nothing toward the defense of the common good in time of need.[20]

Yet this regime, too, came to an end. "Continual dissensions" led to civil wars, and those wars spelled the demise of their liberty. Then arose the empire, whose emperors, while avoiding the title *rex*, were monarchs nonetheless, and often tyrannical ones. While some were just rulers, Aquinas admits, "most of them became tyrants towards their subjects while indolent and vacillating before their enemies, and brought the Roman commonwealth to naught" (I.4.33). Aquinas argued at the beginning of the chapter that men seek kings but end up with tyrants, and tyrants masquerade under the name of king. In the Roman example, however, tyrants explicitly did not do this: they eschewed the name king just because of the associations with tyranny it raises. The emperors claimed instead to rule for Rome as new consuls.

    20. Stoner, James R. "Was Thomas Aquinas a Republican?" 12–13, paper presented for the annual conference of the Southern Political Science Association, New Orleans, January 5, 2007.

This last claim, however, is a disturbing one, as Aquinas appears to agree with Sallust that the citizens of the Roman republic loved the common good in a way that they did not under the old kings. Why, then, did this republican virtue not prevent tyranny? How were the emperors able to abuse the common good? One clue is these "continual dissensions" that Aquinas mentions without explanation. However these dissensions started, they eventually built up to civil war. We can connect this discussion to Aquinas's discussions in I.1–2 about the need for unity in rule. Perhaps in Rome's early period, it benefited from the diversity of citizens; later, however, this diversity turned into faction. It then became internally divided and vulnerable, at first to Roman strongmen, later to foreign invaders. If such is the case, we might wonder how strong the virtue of the citizens was.

More speculatively, we might connect this dynamic to the war that so quietly pervades this section. Rome, after all, built itself on the military spirit of its citizens: this is how it incorporated them into a predominantly aristocratic mixed regime. So long as Caesar had Gauls to subdue, Rome had new treasures for its leaders and new lands for its plebeians. But when this military spirit turned inward, the wars became internal, and the "continual dissensions" we puzzled over were simply the fruits of her partial virtues brought home. The collapse of the republic culminated in tyranny. In other words, Rome in abandoning monarchy opened itself to tyranny. It would indeed seem that in attempting to become a *provincia*, Rome became less than a *polis*.

The example of the Hebrews is similarly complex. The Hebrew people, Aquinas begins, were ruled by judges but persuaded God to grant them kings (1 Sam 3:18), but these kings were wicked and led them into idolatry and then into "captivity." The rule of judges was no good thing, Aquinas argues, for owing to the Hebrews' weakness "they were ravished on all sides [*undique diripiebantur*] by their enemies." Yet they fared no better under kings. Strikingly, according to Aquinas, the initial difference between their condition under judges and under kings was not temporal but spiritual: "they departed from the worship of the one God and were finally led into captivity" (I.4.34). They abandoned judgeship because of temporal failures, but kingship gave way to spiritual and temporal failure. Thus, as Aquinas stated in the beginning of this chapter, they desired a king but fell under tyranny. Aquinas here, moreover, echoes his claim in I.4 that tyranny leads to the spiritual detriment of subjects. Again, however, piety is only negatively connected with justice: Aquinas links tyrannical injustice to impiety, without explicitly linking piety to justice.

The Hebrew example might help us to make more sense of Aquinas's account of Rome. The decline of Rome seems caused in part by the lack of unity in the ruling element, a point that Aquinas has repeatedly stressed. But note something more. If the Roman tyrants did not call themselves kings, it is because the Roman people themselves did not want kings. Yet the Romans did seek a just regime, aristocracy, and after becoming a republic finally ended in an unjust regime, tyranny. What is more, it was precisely the emperors' avoidance of the title *rex* that made the Romans blind for so long to their usurpations. One might wonder if, as with the Hebrews, Rome's decline relates to its orientation to the common good. Perhaps any regime pursued for the wrong reasons, whether monarchy or otherwise, leads to tyranny. Note, for instance, that after they overthrew their kings, the Roman citizens each began to work toward the common good "as if it were his own" (I.4.31). This sounds initially like an endorsement of the Roman polyarchy. At some point, however, the Romans came to care for their own private goods more than the common good, and they were ruled by men who were animated by that same greed. It seems that, like the Hebrews, the Romans sought regime change not because of the inferiority of their regime but because they wanted to grasp power for themselves. Perhaps Sallust did not have it quite right: although he wrote that they worked toward the common good, it would seem, in fact, that they worked toward it not as common but as something to be grasped for themselves. Then Aquinas would seem to be warning that changing regime forms often happens as a result of a community's illegitimate deliberation on the ends of political society.

What are we to conclude from this chapter? Not only are monarchy and tyranny closely linked theoretically: their close identification has considerable practical implications. Thus, Aquinas can conclude: "Danger thus lurks on either side: whether while the tyrant is feared the best rule of the king is missed, or, that while desired the royal power turns into [*convertatur*] tyrannical wickedness" (I.4.35).

This chapter could be of no comfort to our king, for if the chapter seemed to begin with a need to explain why the people can confuse monarchy for tyranny, then the chapter concludes with a strong argument that these regimes are not confused but fused. And so Aquinas has led us to see that the greatest danger of monarchy is not that kingship easily lapses into tyranny but rather the perception that kingship easily lapses into tyranny. We thus could consider I.4 part of the Augustinian mood that pervades I.3.

Further, we might consider this chapter as, again, part of a *speculum principum*. If the confusion between tyranny and monarchy is such that many subjects are deceived between the two, it is possible that some rulers are also deceived by this distinction. Then it would not simply be the case that some tyrants pretend to be kings, but rather that some kings "fall under the cruelty" of their own tyrannical rule. Such a teaching would not only be a highly edifying one for our Cypriot but also reinforce the lesson of chapter 4, according to which tyrannical rule is a slavery first and foremost of the tyrant himself. For perhaps this slavery begins with a kind of ignorance of the nature of justice.

Perhaps this chapter is even an argument against monarchy. While Aquinas does not argue anything in I.4, as in I.3, to expressly contradict I.1–2, he has exposed in I.4 a teaching that must be reckoned with: for all the strengths of monarchy, it has a terrible weakness, that is, its tendency to lapse into tyranny. We thus must wonder if Aquinas will find a way to prop up monarchy against its seemingly inevitable decline into tyranny.

Preserving Tyranny: I.5

I.4 obscures the distinction between kingship and tyranny gradually developed over the first four chapters.[21] We might have formed the impression from I.4 that kingship must be avoided to circumvent tyranny. We might have even decided that kingship is not the best regime, at least for practical purposes, because it deviates so readily into tyranny. If this is a possible conclusion from I.4, Aquinas means to disabuse us of it in I.5. *Pace* scholars who find in *De Regno* a theory of politics abandoned to tyranny and sin, Aquinas advocates for just monarchical rule even in the face of pervasive injustice. He thus opens I.5: "Now from monarchy, if converted into tyranny, less evil follows than from an aristocracy [*regimen plurium optimatum*] when corrupted" (I.5.36). Tyranny produces less evil than oligarchy, Aquinas argues. It is not clear

---

21. While not significant to the meaning of their teaching, the parts of *De Regno* on tyranny contain an impressive amount of variants across manuscripts in words for tyrant and tyranny, mostly differences in case. See, in particular, Dondaine, *De regno ad Regem Cypri*, préface, 452 and 454.

how this is possible, given that in I.3 we learned that the contrary of the best is the worst, and that tyranny is the contrary of the best regime.

Aquinas explains. Dissension most often arises from polyarchy (*regimen plurium*), and such dissension pervading a multitude "runs counter to the good of peace." A tyrant does not destroy this good, however, but only "obstructs some goods of particular men" (I.5.37). Dissension in a polyarchy, we are left to infer, thus does more damage to the good of peace than does tyrannical dissension.

This is a puzzling claim, for the chaotic picture of tyranny that Aquinas presents in I.3–4 is not one of injury to "some goods of particular men" but of violence to society at every level. The sentence, however, continues with a weighty caveat: "unless there be an excess of tyranny [*excessus tyrannidis*] and he rages [*desaeviat*] against the entire community." Aquinas seems to be arguing that in most cases, the corruption of monarchy does not lead to an "excess of tyranny" but only some milder form of it. In that case, the dark Augustinian picture of I.3 arises not out of mild tyranny but only the "excess of tyranny" that "rages against the entire community" and to the mortal detriment of the common good.

Aquinas offers two more arguments for why oligarchy is more dangerous than tyranny. The first is this: that which produces dangers with greater frequency is to be avoided, and polyarchy (*regimen multorum*) turns to oligarchy more often than monarchy turns to tyranny. This proceeds from Aquinas's arguments in I.3–4, according to which evil arises from multiple causes. When many rule, there is a greater chance that any one of them will abandon the common good. And when any one of them does this, the entire group of rulers is threatened by internal strife. This strife, in turn, leads to dissension among the people. But the monarch is only one man, so there is no chance of him being drawn into conflict with other rulers. And when he does fall away from the common good, "it does not immediately follow that he proceeds to the total oppression of his subjects, which is the excess of tyranny [excessus tyrannidis] and the worst wickedness in government, as was shown previously" (I.5.38).

While I.5 might seem to contradict I.3, that contradiction is apparent, according to Eschmann, only because I.3 "proceeds on the supposition of an absolute and total tyranny, which is here expressly set aside."[22] This is true so far as it goes. Aquinas uses the phrase *excessus tyrannidis* here, the same one he employed in the previous paragraph (I.5.37) to distinguish the serious tyranny that apparently rarely happens from the more mild or moderate tyranny that he compares with oligarchy in this chapter. As with the previous argument, Aquinas argues here that a king can fall away from justice without lapsing into unrestricted tyranny, and again seems to imply that this moderate tyranny is the more likely outcome.

But Aquinas has come close to equivocation. He defines tyranny in the most awful terms at I.3 in contrasting it with kingship, but in I.5 he minimizes its negative aspects so as to contrast it favorably with oligarchy. Aquinas would seem to execute this sleight of hand, in turn, because of what comes in between: tyranny at its worst, he argues in I.4, is a serious argument against monarchy altogether. Taking into full account the argument of I.5, however, the confusion between kingship and tyranny we saw in I.4, although still a grave matter, would then seem to arise from a relatively rare manifestation of tyranny. Thus, Aquinas can claim that the effects of the corruption of aristocracy are typically worse than those of the corruption of kingship, eliminating a doubt as to

---

22. Eschmann, *On Kingship*, introduction, 22, n. 1.

whether we should really prefer monarchy. This would be particularly welcome news to our royal reader, who might have formed the impression that monarchy frequently descends into total tyranny. But Aquinas now tells him that such occurrences are not common, and that only a mild form of tyranny normally ensues.

As a pedagogical device, Aquinas's procedure here has much merit: he makes clear to the king at I.3 that unjust forms of monarchy are truly deplorable and to be avoided, while also reassuring the royal reader at I.5 that monarchy itself is not therefore to be avoided. We might wonder, however, if Aquinas genuinely believes that tyranny tends to be mild rather than excessive and is thus overstating the case for the practical excellence of monarchy. If Aquinas does believe mild tyranny to be common, and that monarchy and tyranny are frequently confused, then the source of confusion rests in the fact that what appear to be just monarchies are, in fact, often mild tyrannies. That conclusion would again indicate that Aquinas has overstated the case for the practical excellence of monarchy.

Aquinas's last argument that the perversion of polyarchy is worse than that of monarchy is yet another surprise: not only does polyarchy devolve into oligarchy more often than kingship does into tyranny, but "a polyarchy deviates into tyranny not less but perhaps more frequently than a monarchy" (I.5.39). In the case of dissension among multiple rulers, "it often happens that the power of one preponderates [*unum super alios superare*] and he then usurps the government of the multitude for himself." This fits with Aquinas's concern in the previous paragraph that it requires only one unjust ruler to pervert polyarchy, and that very ruler, in turn, can spawn tyranny by deposing the other rulers. Aquinas can thus sum up the historical record he has investigated in I.3–5: "There has hardly ever been a polyarchy that did not end in tyranny." Aquinas again presents the Roman republic as his example. The lengthy rule of magistrates gave way to "the most cruel tyrants," disintegrating under the pressure of civil wars and dissension, fomented by a parade of ambitious and selfish supposed republicans. This is the same history Aquinas presented at I.4.33, although in that chapter Aquinas notes that kings preceded the magistrates. Now Aquinas's point is clearer: tyranny cannot be avoided by rejecting kingship. In fact, the degeneration of polyarchy itself reveals a monarchical principle, and a tyrannical one at that.

Aquinas therefore ends this chapter with a restatement of the problem that lurked beneath the surface of I.4 and was brought to the fore in this one:

> The strongest objection why monarchy, although it is the best form of government, is not agreeable to the people is that, in fact, it may deviate into tyranny. Yet tyranny is wont to occur not less but more frequently on the basis of a polyarchy than on the basis of a monarchy. It follows that it is, in any case, more expedient to live under one king than under the rule of several men (I.5.40).

I.5 has thus been an impressive recovery of the excellence of monarchy after the fears about it stoked throughout I.3–4. In comparing monarchy favorably with the worst of tyranny, and comparing oligarchy unfavorably with mild tyranny, Aquinas paints tyranny as such in the worst light, while being more forgiving toward those instances of mild tyranny that are perhaps no more than minor detours from kingship.

Aristotle also spoke of two kinds of tyranny.[23] Concerning

---

23. Blythe's helpful appendix of Aristotelian citations records no reference to this passage of the *Politics* (Blythe, *On the Government of Rulers*, 293–94; cf. Keys, *Aquinas, Aristotle, and the Promise of the Common Good*, 15–21). Aquinas did not complete a great many of his works, of course, and a disproportionate number of his incomplete works are Aristotelian commentaries (Torrell 2005). Given how few of Aquinas's works directly

how to preserve tyrannies, Aristotle writes that tyrants have two choices: first, the "traditional way," by which the tyrant attempts to control his citizens and territory to the greatest possible extent, or second, an apparently novel way, by playing the part of a king, winning the people over to him.[24] "One can get an understanding of" this second way, Aristotle says, "from the way kingship is destroyed." As one destroys kingship by making it more tyrannical, Aristotle explains, so one can "save" tyranny by making it more kingly. While the emphasis is on the tyrant "appearing" to be good, according to Aristotle, he must conduct himself in a decent way most of the time for this ploy to succeed. This tyrant could easily be mistaken for an imperfect king trying to become better, but perhaps this is Aristotle's intent: in so acting, the tyrant's reign will "be more noble and more enviable," and he will render himself "nobly disposed for virtue," and "not wicked but half wicked."[25]

Admittedly, we cannot know for certain whether Aquinas read this portion of the *Politics:* Aquinas's *Politics* commentary ends abruptly early in book III. The first "method," however, matches Aquinas's *excessus tyrannidis*: the tyrant who pants after power and possessions, who incurs universal hatred and must take extraordinary steps to preserve himself. The second, the tyrant who appears royal, seems to correspond to Aquinas's moderate tyrant, the king who departs only minimally from justice.

But granting a similarity between these teachings, what is Aristotle trying to accomplish through this teaching, and could the same be said for Aquinas? Simpson offers a helpful commentary

---

impinge on politics, it would be fascinating to know whether his failure to complete his *Politics* commentary indicates less a dissatisfaction with Aristotle's teaching on politics than a greater interest in other subjects, most obviously the systematic theology that absorbed his later years.

24. Aristotle, *Politics* 1314a29–1315b10.
25. Aristotle, *Politics* 1315a40-b10.

on this portion of the *Politics*.[26] If it seems strange that Aristotle should offer advice on preserving tyranny, we might consider that a citizen or sage may very well be asked to advise an unjust monarch on such matters. While a citizen might have to say something about the "traditional" method of preserving tyranny, both because it is an obvious solution and because it is one any tyrant would know, Aristotle advises that such a citizen point out a better way to the tyrant. Holding to the pretense of advising a tyrant, such a citizen could suggest another way to preserve tyranny, one that happens to be in the self-interest of the tyrant and of his people precisely because it directs him and his people toward justice. Thus, this section of the *Politics* could function as a kind of education for the less-than-perfect monarch whose rule must be directed toward kingship and justice.

But this is the point of *De Regno* as well. For if a tyrant is not necessarily a raging slave to erotic lusts, but perhaps often a misguided or inexperienced ruler who is only somewhat unjust, then Aquinas could well believe that such rulers can be steered back toward justice. And so in a sense, Aquinas plays the role of the citizen or sage who advises the tyrant. Aquinas first warns of the dangers of full-blown tyranny (I.4), a teaching that might very well persuade the king against the wisdom of Aristotle's "traditional" method of preserving tyranny. In I.5, Aquinas then reminds the king that his own departures from justice are in any event not likely to be great, but only mild forms of tyranny. Thus, the king can feel confident that he is neither a tyrant nor liable to be replaced by polyarchy. The next trick, of course, would be to actually habituate the virtue of justice in the king, but Aquinas has laid the groundwork for disposing the king toward such virtue.

26. Peter Simpson, *A Philosophical Commentary on the Politics of Aristotle* (Chapel Hill: University of North Carolina Press, 1998), 411–15.

A reading of I.5 easily resolves the doubts engendered by I.4 and reinforces the claim that *De Regno* needs to be read with a regard for its rhetorical form as a *speculum principum*. Aquinas has offered robust arguments that monarchy is good theoretically and practically: excessive tyranny is not inevitable. Yet politics must guard against the mild tyranny of fallen monarchy.

Surprisingly, I.5 has more of an Aristotelian than Augustinian tone. Even should Aquinas not have read Aristotle on "preserving" tyranny, Aquinas's refusal to equate mild tyranny with a rejection of the possibility of just politics is a far cry from the Augustinian traditions of his day. Instead, Aquinas's distinction between mild and excessive tyranny allows him to reassert the possibility of just government through monarchy, a move that should remind us of his distinction between rule over the *liber* as *causa sui* and over the *servus*. In this staunch defense of justice, his emphasis rings thoroughly Aristotelian, but he has only complicated our understanding of this work's political naturalism: if human nature is so inclined toward living in community, what in human nature also lends itself to such unjust behavior? And what can politics do about it?

Aquinas's "Appeal to Heaven": I.6

Aquinas argues in I.5 that kingship is the best defense against tyranny yet: the disposition to foster a just monarchy and not the acceptance of a second-best regime secures politics against injustice. In other words, we should give monarchy, despite its potential for tyranny, a second look. Aquinas opens I.6 with a reiteration of this point. He then proposes to show how tyranny can be prevented among monarchs and states three conditions for avoiding tyranny: selecting the right man, carefully arranging his government, and tempering his power. Aquinas cites 1 Samuel 13:14 in explanation of the first condition:

"Wherefore Samuel, commending the providence of God with respect to the institution of the king says: 'The Lord sought a man according to his own heart, and the Lord appointed him to be prince over his people'" (I.6.42). This quotation is a bit faulty, missing that Samuel is, in fact, warning Saul that Saul's kingdom will be destroyed and that he will be removed from the throne.[27] It is curious that Aquinas does not quote the verse quite accurately or fully, as the overall effect is negative: Saul has been a failure as a king, not a success. As Aquinas often quotes scripture from memory, perhaps he mistakenly misquotes the scripture. And although he would have been mindful not to add or subtract a word from scripture, perhaps Aquinas's paraphrase was subtly shaped by his desire to emphasize the first part, according to which "The Lord has sought out a man after his own heart." In any event, this passage makes clear that, ultimately, God places men on thrones, whether just or tyrannical. While one could certainly infer this signal fact from Aquinas's discussion of monarchy, we here find Aquinas's most direct claim about monarchy being divinely instituted. Rhetorically, it would also be quite meaningful to the royal reader given his fears in I.3–4 concerning the practical value of monarchy. The quotation only adds to the argument of I.5 that monarchy remains the best regime.

The stated purpose of I.6, preventing tyranny, occupies only these first two paragraphs of the chapter. As Dondaine and Eschmann note, this is a disconcerting lacuna in the text, not least because Aquinas has thus far devoted more attention to the evil

---

[27]. The scholarly attribution of this quotation reflects Aquinas's own seeming confusion. While the verse Aquinas has in mind seems to be 1 Samuel 13:14, with Samuel speaking, Busa thinks it to be from the first book of Kings, Kenny gets the book right but thinks Daniel is speaking, and Eschmann, in the introduction to *On Kingship*, attributes it to 1 Kings and Daniel.

qualities of the tyrant than to the character of the just king.[28] Moreover, Aquinas has staked much on securing the excellence of kingship against the peril of tyranny. The reader hopes Aquinas will explain how to arrange royal government so as to avoid tyranny, including how his power might be tempered. The remainder of this long chapter, however, is given over to provision for the king lapsing into tyranny. And even then, it will turn out to bear chiefly on the populace rather than on the tyrant.

If Aquinas had written on tempering royal power, what might he have argued? Some scholars argue that a fuller treatment of this third consideration would have shown Aquinas to be advocating a constitutional or limited monarchy.[29] That could well be true, and it would accord with the argument of Aquinas in the so-called "Treatise on Law" in the *Summa Theologica*.[30] Yet *De Regno* is not a treatise but a *speculum principum*. We must ask, in other words, if Aquinas's apparent failure to address tempering royal power is a genuine lacuna or a deliberate decision not to discuss this topic here. We might think that Aquinas does not discuss the selection of a king because it is a moot point for our king: he has already been selected. This king, moreover, already has a government in place, which might explain Aquinas's silence on the arrangement of the king's government. If this is the case, Aquinas might not simply be avoiding wasted space: he might also want to avoid causing affront to an imperfect king and an imperfect government. He has, after all, gone to great lengths to compare kingship favorably with other regimes (I.2–4). There may also be some deeper strategy at work. Perhaps Aquinas once again focuses on tyranny

---

28. Eschmann, *On Kingship*, introduction, xviii; Dondaine, *De regno ad Regem Cypri*, préface, 423.

29. Eschmann, *On Kingship*, introduction, 24, n. 3 (citing *ST* I-II.105.1) and A. J. Carlyle and R.W. Carlyle, *A History of Mediaeval Political Theory in the West*, vol. 5 (Edinburgh: W. Blackwood & Sons, 1936), 94.

30. Oakley, *The Mortgage of the Past*, 114–5.

to give our king a negative teaching, an indirect discourse on kingship through a treatment of its unjust opposite.

Having scanted the questions with which he begins I.6, Aquinas proposes to move on: "Finally, provision must be made for facing the situation should the king stray into tyranny" (I.6.43). He does not take long to make his point.

Aquinas rejects tyrannicide. Such attempts rarely succeed, and when they do, they often lead to the rule of men as bad as or worse than the original tyrant. If there be no excess of tyranny (*excessus tyrannidis*), to recall Aquinas's favorite phrase, then the people should tolerate their tyrant, and private individuals should never take it on themselves to act in the name of the people, as this Aquinas thinks inevitably leads to faction (I.6.46–8). Aquinas vigorously opposes tyrannicide with scripture, arguing that it "is not in accord with apostolic teaching," citing 1 Peter 2:18–19: "For if one who suffers unjustly bears his trouble for conscience' sake, this grace." Aquinas adduces the early Christian martyrs of imperial Rome as witnesses to this teaching.

Thus far, Aquinas's teaching is quite traditional: even unjust political authority should be respected and not resisted for what later generations would call "light and transient causes." Alongside this conservatism, however, Aquinas also advances his more novel claims about excessive tyranny. If, as Aquinas suggests here, tyranny falling short of *excessus tyrannidis* generally ought to be tolerated, then that only complements his claim that mild tyranny is not an unconscionable threat to justice: it is no worse than perverted polyarchy and does not merit resistance. And the more this is the case, the more it is also true that the lapse of monarchy into tyranny is not a strong argument against monarchy.[31]

31. See Michael D. Breidenbach and William McCormick, SJ, "Aquinas on Tyranny, Resistance, and the End of Politics," *Perspectives on Political Science* 44, no. 1 (2014): 10–17.

Yet a tyrant's reign may become unbearable, Aquinas admits, a necessary concession given his description of excessive tyranny at I.3–4. In such case, the manner of proceeding varies. A people can depose a tyrant if they by right placed him in office. If some higher authority set up the king, such as an emperor, appeal should be made to that authority, who can depose the king. Yet if no human effort or help against the tyrant can be had, one option remains: prayer. To be more precise: "recourse must be had to God, the King of all, who is a 'helper in due time in tribulation,'" quoting Psalm 19:16 (I.6.51). For only God can turn (*convertat*) the heart of the tyrant to the common good by softening his heart or remove the tyrant whom He deems "unworthy of conversion." Aquinas lists a few examples of this, including, somewhat humorously, the drowning of the Egyptian pharaoh in the Red Sea at the climax of the Hebrew exodus (I.6.51).

While this recourse to prayer will strike many modern readers as strange, two things are worth noting here. First, Aquinas does not mention appeal to the pope. The centuries preceding *De Regno* saw innumerable controversies over the temporal power of the pope and his ability to depose rulers, especially with regard to the ancestral homeland of the Norman king of Cyprus, France, not to mention Aquinas's own native Italy. That power, moreover, was often conceived vis-a-vis the Holy Roman Emperor, who Aquinas does mention. He does not, however, raise the papacy here.[32] Is this because Aquinas does not wish to distract his reader with contemporary issues likely to inflame his passions? Or is Aquinas maintaining his silence on the church, which thus far has gone unmentioned? It is particularly curious that Aquinas does not invoke

---

32. Léopold Genicot, "Le *De Regno*: Spéculation ou réalisme?" in *Aquinas and Problems of His Time*, ed. G. Verbeke and D. Verheist (Leuven: Leuven University Press, 1976), 3–7.

papal power in this sphere given Aquinas's frequent references in I.3–4 to the spiritual harm that tyrants do their subjects.

Second, Aquinas does not invoke God's power over earthly things as a formulaic expression of piety. Rather, the conversion of the people is a concrete strategy against sin. Prayer to the divine, Aquinas says, will be efficacious only if the people themselves turn away from sin: "for it is by divine permission that wicked men received power to rule as a punishment for sin" (I.6.52). God gives the people a tyrant in his anger at their sin. Thus, Aquinas cites Job that God "makes a man that is a hypocrite to reign for the sins of the people" (Job 34:30). As the reign of a hypocrite, tyranny is confirmed as at the worst regime, and the tyrant himself is the worst sort of man. Yet it this regime and this ruler, Aquinas urges, that nations can sometimes come to deserve. Aquinas thus makes clear that tyranny is not always just an isolated political problem of the bad man with political power. Rather, the tyrant reflects and arises from the sin of a whole society. We again hear echoes of Augustine's *City of God*, for this sounds much like the earthly city (*civitas terrena*) or city of man. In fact, Aquinas ends I.6 with one of this book's most Augustinian lines: *Tollenda est igitur culpa, ut cesset a tyrannorum plaga*, or "Therefore sin must be obliterated, that the plague of tyrants may cease."

The contrast between Aquinas's call for recourse to God against tyranny and John Locke's "appeal to Heaven" is instructive.[33] Aquinas's argument here is not a prescription for institutional change but for spiritual conversion. Whereas Locke urges his reader to recall the foundational if prudential role that a people must play in instituting and dissolving government, Aquinas means with this teaching to remind the king that God alone is

---

33. John Locke, *Two Treatises of Government*, Cambridge Texts in the History of Political Thought, ed. Peter Laslett (Cambridge: Cambridge University Press, 1988), II.XIV.168.

finally sovereign over human affairs. Ultimately, then, humans attain true justice not by selecting the right leaders but by conforming themselves to God's sovereignty. Thus, this appeal to God might not be as "pious" or metaphorical as we think. Aquinas is a theist and believes that God provides for all creation. While his call for man's conversion might indicate a certain lack of hope in man, it by no means indicates the same of God.

This interpretation of I.6 accords well with Aquinas's criticism of ancient Rome in I.4. Aquinas hinted at I.4.31–2 that Rome's decline into empire involved the citizens' resolve for the common good under the late republic, but he largely accented the dissension between rulers. The account of I.6, however, would seem to attribute to the citizens a larger role in Rome's slouch toward tyranny, for if the rulers devolved into tyrannical vice, perhaps the citizens did as well. In that case, unjust citizens would in a sense deserve that tyranny, and would indeed have produced the individual tyrants. We might even think that the rulers and the ruled are bound by a culture of moral failure. As we noted at I.3, there are echoes here of Augustine's famous treatment of Rome in *The City of God*, V.12–21. "What unites the people in common is not a virtuous end, but a vicious one."

Does Aquinas here open the door to tyrannicide? As Wyllie notes, in a letter addressed to a king, we can hardly expect Aquinas to have been so direct,[34] but we can note this: many Aquinas scholars argue with Gilby that Aquinas developed in his views on tyrannicide, moving from approving it in the *Commentary on the Sentences* to rejecting it in the *Summa Theologica*.[35] If Finnis is right, however, to reject such a change in the thinking of Aquinas,

---

34. Robert Wyllie, "Reconsidering Tyranny and Tyrannicide in Aquinas's *De Regno*," *Perspectives on Political Science* 47, no. 3 (2018): 155.

35. Thomas Gilby, *The Political Thought of Thomas Aquinas* (Chicago: The University of Chicago Press, 1958), 289; noted by Finnis, *Aquinas*, 288.

and we date *De Regno* between these two works, then one might think that implicit in Aquinas's advice to the king is a legitimation of tyrannicide not obvious from the text of *De Regno*.

That said, in *De Regno,* Aquinas seems to assume that the tyrant has acquired his power legitimately. He divides the question, we noted, between tyrants placed in office by the people and by a higher authority. This matters, because, as Finnis notes, in Aquinas's early works, he counsels patience and forbearance in the case of legitimate rulers. Such tyrants should be removed through proper authorities, while usurpers may be resisted however necessary.[36] It is entirely possible, then, that in *De Regno,* Aquinas has in mind only the sort of ruler that his reader presumably is, and that in following the theory of the *Commentary,* he has no reason to broach or endorse tyrannicide.

I.6 has done little to settle our picture of monarchy. While we might remain persuaded that monarchy remains the best regime, Aquinas has offered few clues as to how one prevents tyranny from imperiling justice. Instead, he emphasizes how to respond to tyranny post hoc: with a return to God. What precisely is the main thrust of I.6 if mild tyranny is to be tolerated, and salvation from full tyranny requires divine intervention? We would have a better grasp of this question if we knew just how pervasive Aquinas takes mild tyranny to be, and why he skimps on his description of selecting a just king in I.6. For if mild tyranny is pervasive, and selecting a would-be just king is not something Aquinas takes to be worth bothering about, then a rather incomplete image of politics emerges from *De Regno*. It is not as hopeless as interpreters have suggested, but it nevertheless offers few clues for how the picture of rational politics in I.1–2 can be instantiated.

36. Finnis, *Aquinas*, 288.

Conclusion: *De Regno* I.3–6

As I argued at the beginning of this chapter, the question to put to the early chapters of *De Regno* is not why Aquinas dwells on tyranny but rather why he juxtaposes two radically different accounts of politics: a promising vision of rational politics grounded in political naturalism and the goodness of monarchy (I.1–2), and a dark picture of tyrannical politics as the domain of sin and injustice (I.3–6). We have identified at least three reasons for this juxtaposition.

First, we can at least partly reject the common claim of a stark contrast between the two sections, for in I.3–6, Aquinas holds out more hope for politics than prima facie seems to be the case. Aquinas argues that harsh tyranny is more the exception than the rule: mild tyranny is more common than an excess of tyranny and, moreover, is apparently tolerable. Aquinas also suggests that there are ways to arrange and temper royal government such as to prevent tyranny, although he does not elaborate on this point. Most importantly, Aquinas reminds his Cypriot reader that the tyrant and his subjects are in the hands of God. This is a classic application of Aquinas's theology, and it is also rhetorically significant: the king knows that grave dangers abound in politics, and his recourse should ultimately be not to himself but to God.

This reference to rhetoric leads to the second reason for the juxtaposition. As we have noted, Aquinas is not writing a theological textbook: he intends this work to be useful to a king. The presentation of the teaching dictated by the principles of practical philosophy might not be the presentation best suited to teaching a politically active ruler. As for what that pedagogy might consist of, we have seen that Aquinas wishes to build up the king's sense of the dignity of monarchy but also to place the horrors of tyrannical rule before him. The images of tyranny and slavery that

Aquinas presents to the king are terrifying, and surely they would lead most rulers to seek justice, a justice that the king has already been brought to believe he loves from the flattering depiction of himself in I.1–2. This would again be taking a page out of Aristotle's lessons for educating tyrants.

There are at least two clear examples of this indirect teaching. The first example bears on the question of political naturalism. Whereas in I.1–2 we hunted for clues as to Aquinas's understanding of man's political nature, in I.3–6 we find strong hints that Aquinas subscribes to Aristotle's political naturalism, except that the teaching is negative and primarily in the spiritual rather than the temporal realm: the tyrant can obstruct the spiritual good of his subjects. Thus far, Aquinas's strongest statements of political naturalism have not been the putatively "Ciceronian" claims of I.1–2 that man needs political community for his necessities, but rather the "Augustinian" claims of I.3–6 that tyranny deprives citizens of spiritual goods. Indeed, rhetorically, I.6 echoes the *prooemium*, in which Aquinas reminds the king that God is king of all kings, and that the king must rule with an eye toward God's justice. Now, when Aquinas has his opportunity to argue how tyranny can be avoided and mitigated, he invokes that relationship between God and ruler. It is a tantalizing invocation, however, as he does not spell out its practical applications. Nevertheless, commentators who have seen in I.6 a desolating picture of politics should see that the chapter's closing references to God apply not only to the tyrant's injustice but also to the king's justice.

The second example concerns the limitations of monarchy. In I.1–2, Aquinas begins to lay down a political philosophy organized around the nature of community and the excellence of kingship. But where one might have expected him to explain to his reader the duty of the good king and the nature of the common good he serves, Aquinas instead ventures into an extended discussion of tyranny, particularly the practical problems associated with tyranny as closely related to, and thus popularly identified with, kingship. This prompts Aquinas to reassert his defense of monarchy as the best regime, no doubt to the relief of the Cypriot. That defense, however, requires Aquinas to distinguish moderate from extreme tyranny. Aquinas thus masterfully champions the excellence of monarchy in *De Regno* but at the cost of admitting the prevalence of mild tyranny. Aquinas has thus admitted that monarchy in practice is not the flawless, perfect exemplar of justice that the king might have taken away from I.1–2.

To belabor the second point: the juxtaposition between monarchy and tyranny forms a part of Aquinas's pedagogy in *De Regno*, one that relies on an indirect teaching of the limitations of monarchy through an illustration of the horrors of tyranny.

An indirect or negative teaching is a valuable thing. In the uncertain and chaotic activities of daily politics, concrete instructions of any kind are valuable. Negative teachings, moreover, set boundaries within which prudence and ambition can be exercised. The Ten Commandments are stated in largely negative terms, for instance. In short, it is no small matter that Aquinas has supplied the king with a negative teaching in the early chapters of *De Regno*.

A negative or indirect teaching, however, does not always clearly correlate with a positive or direct teaching. If *De Regno* has set our royal reader on a course of politics to avoid the easily identifiable dangers of tyranny, we could worry that he still lacks a firm knowledge of that toward which his governance should advance. Aquinas leaves unanswered how the just monarch can facilitate the acquisition of spiritual goods for his citizens that the tyrant deprives his citizen, and in what relation that activity stands to the acquisition of the temporal common good.

The Augustinian Earthly City

This brings us to our third reason for the juxtaposition between monarchy and tyranny in I.1–6: the need for a theological foundation to politics. As we have already seen, Aquinas has set out the spiritual evils of tyranny, albeit without much theological elaboration. Thus, the juxtaposition between tyranny and monarchy bears a certain asymmetry, namely that we know the spiritual ills of tyranny but not the spiritual goods of monarchy. The juxtaposition and its asymmetric character, then, points to the need for a careful account of the spiritual goods of monarchy. The elaboration of those goods, in turn, would supply a resolution to the tension between the two regime forms.

Indeed, the paucity of theologically weighty teachings in I.1–6 should lead us to suspect that Aquinas has intentionally withheld such data. While Aquinas promises in the *prooemium* a gift worthy of a king and fitting the office of a theologian, Aquinas puts scripture and theology to light use in these first chapters of *De Regno*.[37] In a book written by a theologian for a king, Aquinas has said little about the virtue or piety that would even necessitate a turn to the Bible, nor has he spoken explicitly of any end or happiness of man the knowledge of which would require such wisdom. Scripture has been used to illustrate or deepen some arguments, but Aquinas has not used revelation to ground any positive teaching.[38] His discussion of the God-king analogy takes its principles from natural theology. While invocations of scripture like David being *servus meus* are suggestive, we do not know if this is meant to be a seal on Aquinas's philosophical teaching or if a king's service to God should lead him to act beyond or against reason. There is certainly no "political theology" thus far.[39]

---

37. Jordan, "*De Regno* and the Place of Political Thinking in Thomas Aquinas," 157–60.
38. *ST* I-II.98–108; see Kries, "The Virtue of Religion."
39. See Eric Nelson, *The Hebrew Republic* (Cambridge: Cambridge University Press, 2010), 142, n. 3; Jacques Maritain, *An Essay on Christian Philosophy*, 100.

Admittedly, if I.1–6 of *De Regno* seem philosophical insofar as systematic theology is conspicuously absent from it, it is a thin political philosophy. Aquinas has not shown that reason can secure justice in man's community against the perils of tyranny. Moreover, we may have found a teaching more Ciceronian than Aristotelian, if man's needs and utility are indeed the key to his political nature.[40] Aquinas has acknowledged that the point of living in society is living, but certainly not that it is living well. *Pace* Manent and Dawson, then, Aquinas's great political work thus far cannot be accused of exaggerating in a "neo-Aristotelian" fashion the autonomy of the temporal from supernatural concerns.[41]

As we continue through *De Regno*, then, we will look for Aquinas to invoke well-known features of his political theology, particularly the natural law and the church-state question.[42] Those teachings, whatever their form, will undoubtedly bear upon our questions about monarchy, tyranny, and political naturalism.

---

40. Eschmann, *On Kingship*, introduction, 4, n. 2, 3; cf. Pinckaers, *The Sources of Christian Ethics*, 432.

41. Pierre Manent, *An Intellectual History of Liberalism*, trans. Rebecca Balinski (Princeton, N.J.: Princeton University Press, 1996), 11–12; Christopher Dawson, *The Formation of Christendom* (San Francisco: Ignatius Press, 2008), 253, 261, 280, and 286.

42. Guerra, "Beyond Natural Law Talk," 14, n. 2.

CHAPTER 3

The Reward of the King

De Regno I.7–12

Thus far in *De Regno,* Aquinas has urged our king to fulfill the promises of his royal office, bolstering his belief that political authority is natural and that kingship is the best regime. Yet kings are in constant peril of becoming tyrants, and their citizens will often be suspicious of them. This is for good reason: tyranny is the worst regime and a nightmare for all who live under it, and it is too often confused with just monarchy. Thus, we are led to continue reading *De Regno* not only because of a speculative interest in how Aquinas will complete his teaching and reconcile these seemingly disparate sections of *De Regno* but also because, like Aquinas's royal reader, we have seen both the urgent need for an effective teaching against tyranny and the apparent limitations of monarchy in preventing tyranny. We can hope this teaching will include a further specification of how the king is to execute his office.

I.7–12, or *De Praemio Regis* ("The Reward of the King"), has been the focus of controversy concerning the proper ordering of the text of *De Regno*.[1] As Dondaine notes in the Leonine preface

---

1. The compiler of the later textual tradition *De Regimine Principum* combines the last two. chapters of book I, what is I.11 and I.12 in this study (Eschmann, *On Kingship,* introduction, xiv; Dondaine, *De regno ad Regem Cypri*, préface, 443).

to *De Regno*, those debates have centered on why Aquinas chooses to discuss the reward of the king after his disquisition on the travails of tyranny and before any substantive discussion of the task of the king, and whether with this section Aquinas introduces a practical consideration into the putatively theoretical first book of *De Regno*.² Yet such controversies have been carried out in the absence of close textual analysis of the work. Therefore, the two-fold purpose of this chapter will be to grasp the teaching of I.7–12 and clarify its teaching vis-à-vis that of I.1–7 about the proper order of these sections. This second task should illuminate answers to our questions from chapters 1 and 2, including about political naturalism and the as-yet unmentioned subjects of the law, the church, and revelation in general.

The Magnanimous King: I.7

I.7 begins promisingly:

> Since, according to what has been said thus far, it is of the king to seek the good of the multitude, the task of a king may seem too burdensome [*onerosum*] unless some proper good [*proprium bonum*] should come to him from it. It is fitting therefore to consider in what is a fitting reward [*conveniens praemium*] for a good king (I.7.53).³

This paragraph is an abrupt shift in focus: 1.3–6 concern tyranny, and now Aquinas proposes to treat not the long-awaited duties of the king but their reward. While Aquinas has previously asserted that "it is the king's duty to seek the common good," he has said little as to what that common good is or of what that duty consists. This idea has been articulated in I.1 as a purely theoretical matter, not as a practical one: the practical dimension of *De*

---

2. Dondaine, *De regno ad Regem Cypri*, préface, 432; Eschmann, *On Kingship*, introduction, xiv–xxi.

3. Eschmann renders *praemium* variously as "reward" and "advantage."

Regno has dwelt only on tyranny.⁴ Thus, it is the more striking that Aquinas asserts that the king's duty may seem "burdensome," perhaps "too burdensome," save it should be accompanied by some "good" to the king. Yet Aquinas has taken pains to show that the tyrant bears tremendous burdens because the tyrant rules for himself, not for the common good. Why, then, would Aquinas emphasize the burdens attached to the opposite of tyranny, kingship? Moreover, given that the king works for the common good, not his own, private one, why would Aquinas associate the attainment of justice with a reward for the king and not with the advantage of the common good? Does the king really work for the sake of the common good?

Seemingly oblivious to such considerations, Aquinas goes on to consider whether honor and glory could be the king's reward. Aquinas cites the reports of Aristotle and Cicero that some men say that honor and glory are the rewards proper to a prince (I.7.54).⁵ "For it is in the heart of all men to seek their proper good," the reasoning seems to go, and "if the prince is not content with glory and honor, he will seek pleasures and riches and so will resort [*convertitur*] to plundering and injuring his subjects." Aquinas thus recalls the arguments of I.3, also invoking Aristotle and Cicero, that tyrants hate virtue and so suppress it in their subjects. Perhaps, then, honor and glory are loved by the king.

But Aquinas finds five problems with this conventional opinion (I.7.55–59). First, Aquinas argues that "nothing seems [*videtur*] more fragile among human things than the glory and honor of men's favor," for they rest on the "fickle" opinion of men (I.7.55).⁶

---

4. Eschmann, *On Kingship*, introduction, xvi.

5. Dondaine directs us to Augustine, *The City of God* V.13 (Dondaine, *De regno ad Regem Cypri*, préface, 457).

6. Eschmann renders *fragilius* as "perishable." Dondaine notes that some manuscripts read *esse* for *videtur* (Dondaine, *De regno ad Regem Cypri*, préface, 457).

Second, Aquinas cites Cicero's *De officiis* to argue that the need for glory and honor "takes away greatness of soul," turning men into slaves. If, as previously stated, honor and glory depend on the good opinion of others, then "he who seeks the favor of men must serve their will in all he says and does" (I.7.56). Aquinas argues in support of this conclusion that "the inordinate desire for glory is to be guarded against; it takes away freedom of soul, for the sake of which great-souled men [*magnanimis viris*] should put forth all their efforts." If being great-souled is to be valued among princes, Aquinas argues, and the king aims to be a *causa sui* and *liber*, then seeking glory and honor through the good graces of other men is not the way to that greatness of soul.

These first two reasons concern the prince. The third relates to his people and the common good, for Aquinas next argues that "it is injurious [*nocivum*] the multitude if such a reward be set up for princes" (I.7.57). This should animate us: as we noted above, Aquinas has not yet spoken concretely of the king's duties to the multitude. The virtuous man, Aquinas argues, has no concern for glory, yet if glory is the reward for princes, then good men will not become princes on account of that glory. Kingship will rather attract the wrong sort of man.

Aquinas's fourth reason argues that "dangerous evils [to the multitude] come from the desire for glory" (I.7.58). A prince's desire for glory often leads to the ruin of his country, first because such a prince risks destroying himself and his army through warfare, and second, when they finally do lose, through the country's eventual subjection to those foreign combatants. This adds flesh to our concern at I.1 that the *provincia* would turn out to be a defective regime if its orientation toward military affairs—however it originated—led not only to a diminished concern for virtue but even to the extinction of the community itself.

Moreover, Aquinas fifth and finally notes, another effect of glory-seeking is to be feared: hypocrisy. In yet another reference to Augustine's *City of God* V.12, Aquinas argues that virtue is difficult: simulation of virtue, easy.[7] "Ambition drives many mortals to become false," Aquinas quotes of Sallust. "They keep one thing shut up in their heart [*pectore*], another ready on the tongue, and they have more countenance than character [*ingenium*]." But Christ, Aquinas argues, would call these men hypocrites, people who "do good work that they may be seen by men." Even the man who does apparently good deeds can be vicious, in other words. Aquinas has not mentioned material goods as a reward other than in what he reports of Cicero and Aristotle. But the analogy is obvious: just as the honor-seeking prince will defraud his subjects by imitating the appearance of a man who deserves glory, so the pleasure-loving man will place those goods that give him pleasure above the common good. This teaching recalls Aquinas's discussion at I.3 of the tyrant who masquerades as a king. But can such a fraud hide that he is "a plunderer and abusive," or that he is "presumptuous and a hypocrite?" Perhaps, as in the case of the Romans, such attributes become known to the people only after they become powerless to depose him. We might also think that, as in the case of the Romans, the kind of people who set up and maintain such a monarch are also the kind of people who will themselves become increasingly hypocritical as they participate in the same game for riches and honor. This would explain why Aquinas urged the reform of the people as a resolution to the problem of tyranny (I.6).

Aristotle and Cicero seem to endorse honor and glory, Aquinas argues, "because it is more tolerable for him to seek glory than to desire money or pursue pleasure" (I.7.60). The desire for glory

---

7. Dondaine, *De regno ad Regem Cypri*, préface, 457.

depends on the opinion of other men. To the extent that these other men are good, then, the man seeking their favorable opinion will play at being good from his outsider's perspective. He will not know why what he does is good, and he will lack genuine prudence, but he at least follows the lead of those who do. Thus, the hypocrisy that Aquinas earlier castigated has a silver lining. Considering that "few men reach true virtue," such hypocrisy might even be necessary in many regimes. Perhaps the hypocrite will be taught toward justice in this way. But how long will the hypocrite be restrained to good works by the accidental presence of good men in his regime? This is, of course, Augustine's question at *The City of God* V.12–21. As Aquinas goes on to argue, if "the one who desires to domineer lacks the desire for glory," then nothing will restrain him in his pursuit of power and "he will surpass the beasts in the vices of cruelty and lust" (I.7.60). Aquinas puts forth Nero as an example of such a man, reminding us again of the degeneration of the Roman love for glory and honor. Aquinas then summarizes the conclusions of this chapter:

> Indeed all this is quite clearly contained in what Aristotle says in his *Ethics* [1124a 16] regarding the magnanimous man: Not that he seeks honor and glory as something great which could be a sufficient reward [*praemium*] of virtue, but that beyond this he demands nothing more of men. For among all earthly goods the chief good, it seems, is that men bear testimony to the virtue of a man (I.7.60).[8]

Aquinas mentioned this magnanimous or great-souled man in passing earlier. From this passage, we know him as someone who deserves and seeks honor, yet not as "a sufficient reward" for his virtue. When we turn to Aristotle's treatment of magnanimity ($\mu\varepsilon\gamma\alpha\lambda o\psi\nu\chi\iota\alpha$) in the *Nicomachean Ethics*, we see that it is no ordi-

---

8. Eschmann's translation changes the emphasis of this line: "True, he does seek honour and glory, but not as something great which could be a sufficient reward of virtue."

nary virtue but an embellishment or crown on the others.[9] What is interesting for our purposes is the magnanimous man's relative independence from other humans. He has little truck for the opinion of vicious or petty men: he and not they know what virtue is. The magnanimous man instead seeks the good opinion of those he knows to have worthy opinions. Yet because the magnanimous man knows what virtue is independently of such men, then he is in no sense their slave, as though seeking merely to please them regardless of what true virtue is. He knows he deserves honor from them, but as something due to him by his nature rather than as a gift in their favor to be withheld arbitrarily.[10]

This magnanimous man seems to be something like the *liber* at I.7.56. He is free from the opinions of other men, and free from an inordinate striving after glory or goods below it. In I.1, we learned that the free man is *sui causa*: he acts toward his own end, not as an instrument of another (I.1.10). Here Aquinas gives flesh to that terse abstraction: the *liber* is not under the power of the opinion of other men, but rather is guided by virtue. Guided by virtue, he might see glory and honor as the highest things to be had on earth, but they will not satisfy him. In some sense, liberty is the fruit of magnanimity: the cultivation and ordering of the virtues such that one sees in full why one ought to be virtuous in the first place.[11]

---

9. Aristotle, *Nicomachean Ethics*, 1123a34–1125a35.

10. See Robert Faulkner, *The Case for Greatness: Honorable Ambition and Its Critics* (New Haven, Conn.: Yale University Press, 2008), 44.

11. Debate has arisen as to whether Aristotle's notion of magnanimity stands in tension with or even contradicts other aspects of Aquinas's own thought, for example, Larry Arnhart, "Statesmanship as Magnanimity: Classical, Christian & Modern," *Polity* 16, no. 2 (1983): 263–83; Carson Holloway, "Christianity, Magnanimity, and Statesmanship," *The Review of Politics* 61, no. 4 (1999): 581–604; and Mary M. Keys, "Humility and Greatness of Soul," *Perspectives on Political Science* 37, no. 4 (1996): 17–22. Let us note for now that Aquinas seems in *De Regno* to invoke magnanimity for a narrow purpose: to suggest what

It is also curious that throughout this chapter the life of pleasure is discussed only briefly and then only as inferior to the life of honor. Perhaps Aquinas means to present the magnanimous man as an attractive alternative to our princely audience's possibly pleasure-seeking ways. Aquinas appeals to the king's desire for honor and glory, which desire can often lead men to repress their desires of pleasure. Aquinas then presents the magnanimous man who is above even honor and glory, which could, as we suggested above, flatter the king's sense of autarky.[12] Thus, the magnanimous man looks most attractive to the king, and since the magnanimous man is surely above sensible pleasures, then so will be our king.

Whatever its final significance, the emphasis on magnanimity in I.7 seems to flatter the king's sense of self-sufficiency and power. His is a splendid task, the chapter assures him in its opening, and earthly things of the kind petty men seek after are beneath him. Beneath this rhetoric, however, is the suggestion that the king can and should attain to great virtue to become this magnanimous man. This would not only be reassuring to the king, who would fear after reading I.3–6 that kings never avoid tyranny, but also because we can hope that Aquinas will show the king, and us, just how the king is to become magnanimous. For surely, then, we would have a firmer grasp of the duties of kingship and the nature of the common good it serves.

Thus, I.7 seems to have more answers than earlier chapters have had. The magnanimous man has given us something of a picture of the *liber*: in pursuing his own end, he is not drawn to

---

a virtuous person will not seek after. And perhaps Aristotle himself had reservations about the great-souled man as the pinnacle of virtue. On that question, see Susan D. Collins, "Moral Virtue and the Limits of the Political Community in Aristotle's *Nicomachean Ethics*," *American Journal of Political Science* 48, no. 1 (2004): 47–61, and Jacob Howland, "Aristotle's Great-Souled Man," *Review of Politics* 64, no. 1 (2002): 27–56.

12. Howland, "Aristotle's Great-Souled Man," 46–49, 53, n. 44.

earthly things, including the caprice of others, but rather to the reward of virtue. After the dire description of politics in I.3–6, our king has received some encouragement of reward and in being a magnanimous man above earthly things.

But why does Aquinas introduce the problem of the reward of the king in the first place? For one thing, it seems to answer a possible objection to I.3–6: whatever the injustice of tyranny, the tyrant often meets with considerable rewards in this life. In fact, Aquinas argues herein, even if the tyrant gained all of the earthly goods that he pants after, he would still be unhappy, and, thus, all the more would the magnanimous prince be unhappy with such rewards. This at the end of I.7 should be clear also to our princely audience.

The reward of the king also seems to bear on what we remained in ignorance about through I.6. Citizens wish to avoid a tyrant and so abandon monarchy, but with what, then, is it that they should replace the tyrant? For if any regime can eventually slide into tyranny, then every regime must guard itself against it. In considering the just reward of the king, Aquinas considers what royal reward would be good for the people, what kind of reward would attract the kind of ruler whose governance would benefit the common good (I.7.57–9).

Aquinas has not yet identified, however, the reward of the king. In this way, it is most telling that Aquinas has invoked Aristotle's magnanimous man, for it is not clear even on Aristotle's terms why the magnanimous man would want to participate in the fullness of political life for the benefit of others. While he must engage in public life if he is to do great and noble things for others, what this man "to whom nothing is great" should gain from those actions is less obvious.[13]

13. Keys points to the strange inhumanity of this virtuous man (Keys, *Aquinas, Aristotle, and the Promise of the Common Good*, 144–47), noting that Aristotle describes the

On another note, the sorts of arguments that Aquinas makes in I.8 about the end of man can be found in a variety of philosophical sources dating back to ancient times.[14] As a Christian theologian, however, Aquinas perhaps elaborates this category of "earthly" goods to oppose it to some "spiritual" or "supernatural" category. Yet we await any notion so explicitly theological in *De Regno*. Thus, we may wonder if and when Aquinas will invoke such concepts, and what their effect will be on his political teaching.

God's Royal Minister: I.8

With "worldly honor and the glory of men not sufficing as reward for royal cares [*sollicitudini*]," what reward is sufficient to the king (I.8.61)? The next paragraph states it up front:

> It is proper that a king look to God for his reward [*praemium*], for a servant looks to his master for the reward of his service. The king is indeed the minister of God [*minister Dei*] in governing the people, as the Apostle says: "All power is from the Lord God" [Rom 13:1] and God's minister is "an avenger to execute wrath upon him who does evil" [Rom 13:4]. And in the Book of Wisdom [6:5], kings are described as being ministers of God. Kings therefore ought to look to God [*expectare a Deo*] for the reward of their rule [*regimine*] (I.8.62).

This is a breathtaking statement. After numerous chapters detailing the evils and uncertainty of political life, a key dynamic of which was the futile endeavor to save kingship from tyranny, we were told in I.7 that the king as a selfless ruler deserves a great re-

---

magnanimous man as "he to whom nothing is great" three times in the *Nicomachean Ethics* (1123b32–3, 1125a3–4, and 15–16).

14. See, especially, the *Phaedo* (including the four arguments for the immortality of the soul, 61c-107a) and *Symposium*; *NE* I and X, especially the claim at 1177B that what is best and most divine about man is more than human; Cicero's *De finibus malorum et bonorum*, which takes the question for its very title; and C. S. Lewis's cornucopia of such sentiments as an appendix to his *The Abolition of Man*.

ward. We are now told that the king is not just any public-spirited person, but a minister of God. Thus, the *servus meus* that Aquinas invoked at I.1 was no metaphor. And the king's reward will thus come from God himself, but Aquinas has not identified that reward.

Aquinas continues by arguing that temporal goods are ambivalent goods, for God rewards kings good and bad with temporal goods. Wicked kings are God's slave: God grants tyrants the temporal goods to defeat God's enemies. This is a new gloss on the distinction between *servus* and *liber* first raised in chapter 1. The tyrant is the slave not only of his passions and intemperate desires (I.3.26) but also of God. This recalls Aquinas's earlier suggestion that the magnanimous man is free from inordinate attachments to goods beneath him. The king, then, is presumably free in embracing God's will. But then in the *liber* would coincide the *causa sui* and the *minister Dei*.

This discussion draws out an ambiguity at the beginning of I.8.62. Citing St. Paul's famous chapter from his Letter to the Romans, Aquinas argues that all power is from God (Rom 13:1). Therefore, the king is a minister to God and should be obeyed, not resisted (13:2). Indeed, kings enforce God's justice as an "avenger" for God's "wrath"(Rom 13:4). Paul's teaching would seem to present no problem for subjects of just kings, but what of subjects of tyrants, those monarchs who in not serving their subjects seem also not to serve God? Must their subjects serve them? And, if they do, how do they avoid becoming slaves? Is the subject of a *servus* thereby not also a *servus*? Perhaps the answer to such questions must begin with I.5. If the citizen is not drawn immediately to violence against the tyrant but contemplates the end of his community and what would serve it, then his eventual course of action would not be one of animal-like reaction against the tyrant but rather the fruit of his own intellect. Thus, he would in that sense not be a *servus* to the tyrant.

Yet God does not always reward the tyrant, as Aquinas's two quotations concerning Nebuchadnezzar indirectly make clear. In the first, God tells Ezekiel that he has given Nebuchadnezzar no reward for unknowingly doing God's bidding in besieging Tyre (Ezek 29:18). It is, in fact, this citation that Aquinas offers as evidence that God rewards the tyrant.[15] But when Nebuchadnezzar is finally rewarded, it is emphatically to fortify him in God's mission (Ezek 29:19). So if God often enough does "reward" tyrants for their service to him, then how does God reward those kings of pious intention? Aquinas answers this question in closing this long paragraph:

He promises them not an earthly reward [*mercedem*] indeed but an everlasting one and in none other than in Himself [*nec in alio quam in se ipso*]. As Peter says to the shepherds of the people of God (1 Pet 5:2,4): "Feed the flock of God that is among you and when the prince of pastors [*princeps pastorum*] shall appear, i.e. the King of kings, Christ, you shall receive a never-fading crown of glory," concerning which Isaiah says (28:5): "The Lord shall be a crown of glory and a diadem of joy to His people" (I.8.62).[16]

This quotation answers many questions. The reward of the just king is not more or better temporal goods than those given to the tyrant, or it is not just that. Further, the king does not just look to God for a reward, as though that reward could be something other than God. Rather, the just king's reward is in God. Note that Peter refers to Christ as *princeps pastorum*. Aquinas embellishes this with *id est rex regum, Christus*, emphasizing that Christ is King of

---

15. This verse immediately follows "Now God sometimes rewards kings for their service by temporal goods, but such rewards are common to both the good and the wicked" (I.9.62), quoted above.

16. *erit dominus sertum exultationis et diadema gloriae populo suo.*

kings, including of the Cypriot, in the same way that Peter calls Christ the Shepherd of shepherds, that is, over the church leaders to whom Peter speaks. Aquinas here echoes his description of God in the *prooemium* as "King of Kings."

If the king is a *liber*, then his role is yet one of service or ministry to God. The phrase *minister Dei* can be traced to Romans 13 and Wisdom 6, with many indirect allusions in the Psalms and the Old Testament to the Davidic kingship. Aquinas uses the phrase over a hundred times in his works, and again particularly with reference to scripture and the priesthood, for example, *ST* II-II.87.1.[17] But he also makes use of the phrase in the *Summa Theologica* with specific reference to political rulers. Two are worth mentioning. At *ST* II-II.60.2 ad 2, Aquinas argues that judges and magistrates can lawfully judge as an act of justice insofar as they are ministers of God: "A judge is appointed as God's servant; wherefore it is written (Dt 1:16): "Judge that which is just," and further on (Dt 1:17), "because it is the judgment of God." At *ST* II-II.19.3 ad 1, Aquinas argues that political authorities "inflict punishment" as "God's minister," and thus to fear that authority's punishment is not blameworthy "worldly fear" but praiseworthy "servile or initial fear."[18] These *Summa* passages might be taken to emphasize a "sacral kingship," whereby the king's authority is unlimited and uncontestable because divine. But they emphasize the essentially ministerial function of political power: the king serves God, not by the king doing his own will, as in Baroque notions of divine kingship, but by executing God's justice. To the extent that the king fails in that task, then, his ministry is not divine.

If the *Summa* passage affords ambivalent support for divine kingship, the usage of *minister Dei* in *De Regno* contrasts even

---

17. A search of Brepols' "Latin A" database shows 106 usages of the term in his opera.
18. This famous distinction traces back at least in part to the Rule of St. Benedict.

more strongly with prevailing notions in Aquinas's time of "sacral kingship." While sacral kingship was particularly imputed to the Holy Roman Emperor, the ideology was far from absent from the Cypriot king's native France. It would have also been particularly potent in the Crusader states, as we have already noted, as a justification for Christian incursions into Muslim territories.[19]

But Aquinas makes clear in I.1–2 that the origins of politics are natural, not divine. Political community and authority arise out of human nature and human ends. Further, as we noted in I.3, the work of politics is not a glorious deification of the king, but hard and painful work, trials in which the king often finds himself listing dangerously close to mild tyranny. What is sacred about kingship in the presentation of *De Regno*, however, is its reward. Curiously, however, the *minister Dei* is not presented as a *minister Ecclesiae*, which is to say a servant of a church or theocracy. So far, Aquinas has not said that the king's rule is subject to church, but to God. And even were the king is somehow subject to the church, Aquinas in I.7–9 yet argues that his reward is for doing his own political activity, not for obeying the church.

In a word, then, Aquinas's invocation of *minister Dei* synthesizes what has been latent in *De Regno* from the *prooemium*: the king serves God's justice, but not as a mini-god himself. If he is not an exalted divinity, however, his political activity also has a certain integrity that sets him apart from hierocratic arrangements. Thus, the greatest example of revelation in *De Regno* thus far serves to affirm man's natural activity, activity that Aquinas also justifies with reason as being by nature.

I.8 thus far has completed the philosophical argument of I.7 with revelation: that which completes man is had from God. In what follows, Aquinas returns to moral philosophy to sketch

---

19. Oakley, *The Mortgage of the Past*, 162–68.

out three arguments about how the God of revelation fulfills the promises of the happiness posited or sought out by ethics. The first argument sets up the other two. "The reward of virtue is happiness," Aquinas argues, and "this is placed in the minds of all who use reason" (I.8.63). And what is virtue?[20]

The virtue of anything whatsoever is explained to be that which makes its possessor good and renders his deed good. Moreover, everyone strives by working well to attain that which is most deeply implanted in desire, namely, to be happy [*felicem*]. This, no one is able not to wish. It is therefore fitting to expect as a reward for virtue that which makes man happy [*beatum*]. Now, if to work well is a virtuous deed, and the king's work is to rule his people well, then that which makes him happy will be the king's reward [*praemium*] (I.9.63).[21]

Here, we are again entering unfamiliar territory for *De Regno*. After his harrowing account of the vice and sin endemic to politics in I.3–6, Aquinas now defines virtue and happiness as the means and end of all human activity. In defining happiness as the end of virtue, Aquinas also seems to be going beyond his discussion of the magnanimous man, whose ends in action are ambiguous. We noted in I.7 that Aquinas seemed to present the magnanimous man as attractive because of his freedom from earthly goods, without saying exactly what kind of goods the magnanimous man was thereby free to embrace.

But this all raises a larger question: what is happiness? Aquinas goes on to define it: "Happiness, we say, is the ultimate end of desires [*ultimum desideriorum finem*]." Here, ultimate means final and universal, final in the sense that it is desired for its own sake,

---

20. Aristotle, *Nicomachean Ethics*, 1106a15.
21. While Aquinas argues in other places that *beatitudo perfecta* can only be had in the afterlife, he never distinguishes the terms *felicitas* and *beatitudo* in *De Regno*. See Anthony J. Celano, "The Concept of Worldly Beatitude in the Writings of Thomas Aquinas," *Journal of the History of Philosophy* 25, no. 2 (1987): 215–26.

not for some further good, or that for which it is desired for would be real happiness.²² It is universal in the sense that only what is universal satisfies the intellect (I.8.63). Thus, happiness is "the perfect good" in the strongest sense of the word "perfect": per-facere, or completely or fully made or done. We might recall from I.8 that no earthly good could be such a thing. And Aquinas says here: "Thus, nothing earthly can make man happy, so that it may be a fitting reward for a king" (I.8.63).

Aquinas's second argument from reason runs as follows: what perfects something is higher than it, just as gold added to silver perfects the silver. Happiness, Aquinas argues, is just this sort of thing: it perfects man because it is his ultimate or final good. Turning to the human mind, however, we see that all things on earth are beneath it. This we learned in I.6, although Aquinas spoke there only of "man." As for man's mind, Aquinas singles out what is highest in man: his rational soul.²³ It is, after all, matter that we see around us on earth. It is man's soul that stands above it. So man's fullest happiness will be that which completes his soul. This cannot be had among earthly things. Thus, Aquinas cites Augustine's discussion of happy Christian princes: they are happy in hope, not in fact. We can call them happy insofar as they act with justice and in the hope of eternal happiness.²⁴ "But neither is there any other created thing," Aquinas argues, "which would make a man happy and which could be set up as the reward for a king" (I.8.64). Happiness consists in finding one's perfection, which can be thought of as one's "end," but also in a sense as one's cause or source, that which determines what one ought to become. And

---

22. Compare Aristotle, *Nicomachean Ethics*, 1097b20–1098a-19.

23. Aristotle, *Nicomachean Ethics*, 1177b25–1178a8.

24. Augustine, *City of God* V.24. Dondaine notes variants of *felices dicimus* and *beaficamus* in Aquinas's Augustine citation (Dondaine, *De regno ad Regem Cypri*, préface, 459).

the source (*principium*) of created things is found not in other created things but whatever stands before creation, the creator.

Aquinas's third argument from reason is brief. "[T]he human mind knows the universal good through the intellect," he writes, "and desires it through the will: but the universal good is not found except in God." Aquinas affirms here what we might have noticed before: the integral connection between the intellect's faculty of knowing and the will's faculty of desiring in the moral act of deliberation. The tyrant follows *libido*, Aquinas suggested at I.3. The king must conform his will to reason. As if to confirm this, he cites King David from Psalms: "What have I in heaven? And besides Thee what do I desire upon earth? It is good for me to adhere to my God and to put my hope in the Lord God" (Ps 73:25, 28). David invokes both his knowledge of and desire for the good.

Aquinas then closes the chapter. Just as those who do not seek earthly glory and honor are those that receive it, so those who rather seek heavenly glory and honor receive both. He again invokes the example of Solomon, who sought to be godly and was honored by other good men on earth for it. Solomon sought to be a "citizen with the saints and a kinsman of God," which language would well strike a chord with the king, who would be reminded of a lower kind of citizen to which he must attend, one who is actually controlled by the king, and kinsmen of the worst kind: fierce competitors in dynastic struggle.

We can draw many points from these three arguments from reason, but I will focus on four. First, Aquinas has herein articulated the beginnings of a potent ethics. We saw him in I.8.63 lay out a definition of happiness and virtue that depends on the greatest good of man's highest faculties. It is an ethics, moreover, that Aquinas has expanded beyond the king to discuss man as such. We have been waiting for this. Since I.1, we have wondered about the relation between the good of the individual and the common good. This is a difficult project rhetorically: Aquinas has moved slowly but deliberately from the *prooemium*, in which the king was a great and noble addressee, to the end of I.8, in which the king can hope to be not a king at all but a citizen of a kingdom far above his. That kingdom, of course, is God's, the *Rex regum* pointed out in the *prooemium* itself.

Second, this moral philosophy centers on happiness. Perhaps this need not be controversial. Yet when one considers the range of Western ethics, whether philosophical or theological, one would rarely get the sense that happiness is central to ethics, with the focus typically on obligation.[25] Of course, Aquinas has yet to say a great deal about how this happiness will transform our understanding of political life as adumbrated at I.3–6. Most notably, how does this image of the king as a *minister Dei* complete the king-God analogy in I.1? What end does the king seek, for himself and for his people, as God's minister?

Third, while Aquinas has laid out philosophical arguments for the kind of end that man must seek, that end can only be identified by revelation. Thus, in I.8.64, Aquinas stipulates that man's good is neither material nor created, the latter a point that arguably would not be clear without revelation. In I.8.65, Aquinas similarly invokes Psalms to remind us that the good sought by the will and intellect is none other than the Christian God. Such examples seem to suggest that for Aquinas, a purely philosophical ethics would be impossible: it would not know the great fact of man's end.[26]

---

25. Pinckaers, *The Sources of Christian Ethics*, 8–13, 26–31.
26. As Maritain puts it: "For this [natural ethics] lacks two things: the knowledge of the true ultimate end to which man is actually ordained, and the knowledge of the integral conditions of man's actual existence" (*An Essay on Christian Philosophy*, 63).

And even should man be able to identify his end by reason, I.3–6 is a reminder of the morass of daily life: the false starts, confused intentions, and failed attempts that often mock the very idea of a moral life, and this not least in politics. Yet the Bible tells man just this thing, that man has an end and that it is God. Thus, revelation proposes a teaching that both lays out a teaching that could be had from philosophy, on man's end, and gives it a concrete completion: that end is God. Yet revelation would then have a second-order teaching, one according to which things that can and should be known by all men through reason may, in fact, be most obscure to them. This is, of course, a point Aquinas makes at *ST* I.1.1.

The fourth and final point I will make here is obvious but fundamental: Aquinas has entered into this treatise on ends by a sleight of hand. He moved from a search for the reward of the king (*praemium regis*) to a search for the end of man (*finis hominis*). To be more precise, Aquinas moved from the reward of the king to the reward of the magnanimous man in I.7, and then to man as such in I.8. This is a momentous shift, with ramifications of at least six kinds. First, to state the obvious, this shift is a shift from the political to the anthropological: Aquinas does not merely inquire into the reward of a particular class of political elites but of the person as such. Second, it is a shift from the individual good to the common good: beatitude is not simply something for the individual king but the common destiny for all persons. Third, by corollary, this reward is not a private good of a person to be had against other people, but it is a good proper to the person. Fourth, Aquinas also shifts beyond the human: from the end of humans to the end of humans that is God. Fifth, as is implied but not stated, he also shifts from human exertion to God's grace. Sixth, all of these dimensions imply a complicated shift from the reward as accidental to an end as necessary. Somehow, the reward of the king is not just an arbitrarily selected prize for kingship but deeply embedded in the human condition.

The sum effect of these shifts is to embed the king in the life of his people and in God's providence. The king in seeking his own reward must seek the common good of his citizens and turn his sights toward God. Indeed, Aquinas has brought together Aristotelian teleology and Augustinian theology. Aquinas uses the Aristotelian language of ends to link man's heavenly end to terrestrial activity that is social, political, and rational.[27]

Politics is not simply a means to an end beyond it but somehow an important human activity. It is, after all, a ministry to God. And while Aquinas never suggests that beatitude is the reward that the king merits through the king's own human exertions, Aquinas nevertheless links the *visio Dei* with the *ministerium Dei*.

Given this emphasis on beatitude, it is tempting to say that I.8 shows a greater influence of Augustine on Aquinas than previous sections. Augustine's influence in this chapter is perhaps most clear in Aquinas's citation of "Such Christian emperors we say are happy, now in hope, afterwards in very fact when that which we await shall come to pass." Aquinas's argument in I.8 would seem to agree with the overall tenor of *The City of God* V.24–25.

This citation, however, should be assessed with the following caveats. First, Aquinas has cited *The City of God* after arguing for the integrity and nobility of politics at I.1–2, teachings that Augustine does not always clearly embrace. Second, Aquinas has never argued for theocracy, a concept often associated with the later, anti-Donatist Augustine. Third, while Aquinas has made it clear in I.3–6 that politics is no easy undertaking, he has never claimed that justice is impossible (XIX.21; 24), or that the state is nothing

---

27. Black, *Political Thought*, 23.

more than a band of robbers (IV.4), as Augustine argues elsewhere in *The City of God*. Finally, to ward off a particular interpretation of V.24–25, it should be clear that Aquinas has never argued in *De Regno* for anything like Augustine in *The City of God* V.17: "As far as this mortal life is concerned, which is finished in a few days, what difference does it make under what rule a man lives who is soon to die, provided only that those who rule him do not compel him to do what is impious and wicked?"

If these caveats lead us back to the impression that Aquinas is fundamentally still Aristotelian in *De Regno*, however, we should recall Aquinas's tepid endorsement of political naturalism in I.1–2. And while Aquinas has been willing to speaking of man's proximate ends like peace and the unity of peace, he has now identified a final end for man, one that goes well beyond the moral philosophy of Aristotle.[28] We can expect that end to be highly consequential to the undertaking of *De Regno*.

These considerations, by the way, suggest strongly that Eschmann's judgment that *De Regno* does not accord with Aquinas's mature teaching on the origins of political community is wrong, although it would require further work to trace out the understanding of Avicenna developed across the works of Aquinas. We can at least say this: *De Regno* I.1 lays out the necessity of political community, but I.8 lays out its end in excellence.

The Storm-Tossed Ship of State: I.9

In I.9, Aquinas sets out to prove that "they who discharge the kingly office worthily and laudably will obtain an elevated and outstanding degree of heavenly happiness": *eminentem obtinebunt caelestis beatitudinis gradum*. So he must answer two questions.

---

28. Mary Nichols, Response to Robert Bartlett, *American Political Science Review* 89, no. 1 (1995): 152–55.

What is an "outstanding degree of heavenly happiness"?[29] And why is kingly office worthy of it?

Aquinas begins from the formulation: "For if happiness is the reward of virtue, it follows that a higher degree of happiness is due to greater virtue" (I.9.68). Why does a king deserve it? For Aquinas, this has something to do with the king ruling, not only himself, but others.

Aquinas argues that those who rule others manifest more virtue than those over whom they rule, comparing the ruler and subject to a teacher and student (I.9.69). In framing good laws and exhorting them to virtue, the king is teaching his subjects to become good themselves. Yet the virtue of a king stands above that of any teacher, for he leads an entire multitude. Aquinas quotes Aristotle: "But the good of the multitude is greater and more divine [*divinius*] than the good of one man."[30] While this line raises many questions, Aquinas at least wants to impress upon the king that the good of the multitude is of a different order from that of the individual. As a private person "is praised by men" for a public spirit through which he helps others and strengthens his community, so the king is praised all the more for devoting his life to such acts of justice. He does not simply perform such deeds but through his good rule makes those very acts possible (I.9.71).

Aquinas also argues that "The greatness of kingly virtue also appears in this, that he bears a special likeness to God [*praecipue Dei similitudinem gerit*], since he does in his kingdom what God does in the world." The more similar that something is to God, Aquinas writes, "the more acceptable it is to Him." If kings are most like God in this respect, then kings are the most acceptable

---

29. *ST* I-II.95.2.
30. Aristotle, *Nicomachean Ethics*, 1094b7.

or "the most pleasing to God and are to be most highly rewarded by Him" (I.9.72).

Aquinas gives two examples of kings being acclaimed god-like by their regime: the Hebrew judges in Exodus and the Roman emperors. The Hebrews were originally ruled by judges, because God alone was to be their king (1 Sam 8). As for the Roman example, it perhaps simply reflects man's natural apprehension of the quasi-divine nature of kings. Yet the Romans did not call their emperors *divus* in mere metaphor: many emperors were treated exactly as gods, both in the respect they were accorded and in the scope of things they were allowed to do. Aquinas's quotation from Ephesians helps us to make sense of this difficulty: "Be you therefore imitators of God as most dear children" (Eph 5:1). Imitation has this ambiguity, namely that one aspires to be like another while still being other than that person. This particularly holds when one seeks to imitate the ground of being itself, like God.

This argument recalls at least two others in *De Regno*. There is first the argument for the excellence of monarchy from unity: art should imitate nature, and nature is always rule by one, including God's rule of the cosmos (I.1.19). It is only in I.8 that the king's relation to God comes to be seen in a positive light, that as *minister Dei*, or minister or servant of God (I.8.62). As heirs of the seventeenth century, we immediately worry that such god-king comparisons can only be put to cynical use.[31] It would seem, however, that Aquinas shares our concerns. The king must be encouraged to think of himself not only as the winner of great rewards but also as a servant of God who bears great virtue and performs great deeds for his people to deserve those rewards.

As if to reinforce that this kingly duty will not be easy and will

---

31. Nelson, *The Hebrew Republic*.

not come with sure material gains, Aquinas moves on to a startling argument. Kings are like sailors on ships battered by "stormy waves": in such conditions, even experienced sailors can be "bewildered."³² Kings are always at the center of tumults that test their virtue. Compounding these difficulties, Aquinas argues, are the constant temptations posed by earthly riches and the flattery of men. The vagaries of politics can lead to the misfortune of anyone.

The very difficulty, then, of acting well, which besets kings, makes them more worthy of greater reward [*eos facit maiori praemio dignos*]; and if through weakness [*infirmitatem*] they sometimes do amiss [*peccaverint*], they are rendered more excusable before men and more easily obtain forgiveness from God provided, as Augustine says, they do not neglect to offer up to their true God the sacrifice of humility, mercy and prayer for their sins [*peccatis*] (I.9.73).³³

The king who struggles for virtue will be forgiven for those times when he falls short of perfect virtue, and even rewarded for his efforts. Thus, he should not fear the struggles against tyranny that he has been promised. He should not fear, in other words, that in undertaking this task he should subject his soul to great dangers. And our Cypriot audience should not fear that, already a king, he cannot face this task that Aquinas presents him. Rather, he should see God's grace as giving him the strength to face the law.

The image of the king as a sailor in a ship on a storm-tossed sea might remind us of the image of tyranny at I.3–6. Tyranny arises from multiple and contradictory causes and ruins friendship, marriage, and even the most basic economic relations through random and arbitrary violence. Moreover, Aquinas warns us that "mild

---

32. Gregory the Great. *The Book of Pastoral Rule*, trans. George E. Demacopoulos, Popular Patristics Series (Crestwood, N.Y.: St. Vladimir's Seminary Press, 2007), I.9.

33. *Peccaverint* might be better translated by "sin," especially given its close proximity to *peccatis* in the Augustine quotation. "Do amiss" is Eschmann's translation.

tyranny" occurs regularly, seemingly beyond the control of the king. It is telling, then, that Aquinas refers to kings as "sailors," not as "pilots." The term "governor" in its Latin root, *gubernator*, comes from the Greek κυβερνήτης for pilot, and metaphors about the ship of state and the prince as pilot are as old as politics. Aquinas could mean to undercut the navigational competence of the king as pilot and thus metaphorically to remind the king that his control of his community is weak. If the king comes to ruin from these waves, however, at least he maintained order in his own soul as those of his familiars as best he could. In a way, the king-pilot is a sailor just like anyone else on the boat, perhaps comparable to the citizens at I.6 tossed about by the stormy chaos of tyranny.

Aquinas ends the chapter by again comparing our king to King David, to whom was promised by the prophet Zachariah a perfect share of beatitude in the afterlife. David won his reward, the quotation reminds us, by carrying out the work of God among David's people. Again, Aquinas seems to be balancing exhortations to the king to be a virtuous leader with encouragement not to lose heart.

Aquinas then writes: "This was also in some measure realized [*somniatum*] among the Gentiles, for they thought to transform into gods the rulers and preservers of their cities." This final quotation is a gloss on Aquinas's earlier comments (I.9.72) about the Roman habit of divinizing their emperors. Unlike David, those emperors did not know the true God. Unlike David, then, they could not serve the people for that true God. Or at least they could not do so knowingly or willingly, to recall the case of the tyrants who unwittingly fulfill God's ends (I.2). In a sense, then, Aquinas is calling on the Cypriot to be an even greater prince than the emperors of Rome.

I.9 has a relatively limited scope. If the king is to seek his end in God and not in material things, we might wonder why he should be a king at all. Is not beatitude the gift of every Christian? But Aquinas assures the king that his reward will be that of a great saint. Like David, he will be well seated at the heavenly banquet. Yet even though the reward be great, there is a great risk involved in seeking it. The perils of tyranny laid out at I.3–6 are so pervasive in part because of the attractiveness of earthly goods, which lead them away from the execution of their office and so from their divine reward. Moreover, the desire to rule for one's own good, and to the exclusion of others, can lead to a kind of *libido dominandi*. Perhaps with this risk in mind, Aquinas explains with great patience in I.9 the tremendous reward of the king who serves God as he can, even if maladroitly. In so articulating that reward, Aquinas thereby reinforces the lessons of I.7–8 while subtly reminding the king that he must avoid tyranny.

Fools, Infidels and Friendless Tyrants: I.10

I.10 opens with a recapitulation of I.7–9:

> Since such a grand reward [*praemium*] in heavenly happiness [*caelesti beatitudine*] is set before kings if they have acted well in ruling, they ought to keep careful watch over themselves in order not to turn to tyranny. For nothing ought to be more acceptable to them than to be transferred from the royal honour, to which they are raised on earth, into the glory of the heavenly kingdom. Tyrants, on the contrary, who desert justice for a few earthly advantages [*terrena commoda*], are deprived of such a great reward that they could have obtained by ruling justly (I.10.75).

The reward of the king is incredibly desirable, for kings receive both the heavenly glory they seek and the earthly glory they have voluntarily rejected as an end in itself. The tyrant, however, loses everything: both the earthly goods he seeks and the great reward he could have had by ruling well. While we have heard much of the temporal woes of the tyrant in I.3–6, and the great supernatural reward of the king at I.8–9, this is the first time that Aquinas has connected these lessons to warn the tyrant: the tyrant loses beatitude. The lesson is clear, Aquinas urges: "How foolish it is to sacrifice the greatest and eternal goods for trifling, temporal goods no one could not know but a fool or an infidel" (I.10.75).[34]

This line might seem flattering to our king, for he will of course not think himself a fool or infidel. The fool (*stultus*) is one who lacks knowledge; the infidel (*infidelis*) lacks faith. Perhaps the fool is someone who sees the advantages of earthly goods but does not know either the supremacy of heavenly ones or the obstacles that the pursuit of earthly goods can place between one and heavenly goods.[35] The infidel, on the other hand, has no faith in a supernatural happiness: he would see earthly goods as the highest end for which man can strive, or at least not see something beyond them, even if he admitted to their inadequacy. After the reward promised at I.7–9, the king might concur in Aquinas's judgment here.

But we might reject tyranny and yet find ourselves unsure at I.10 what the proper alternative ought to be. While Aquinas has presented a compelling contrast between the reward of the king and the tyrant, we can doubt he has laid out how choosing the heavenly over the earthly reward can lead to moderate and rational politics. Moreover, even were it possible, how can Aquinas persuade us that the average king—not the ideal king—will rise to this challenge? In any event, in speaking of this "fool" and "infidel," it would seem that we have crossed a sort of divide, after which Aquinas's audience is no longer the would-be tyrant but

---

34. This line echoes Mark 8:36: "For what shall it profit a man, if he gain the whole world and suffer the loss of his soul?"

35. See Hobbes' fool in *Leviathan*, ed. Edwin Curley (Indianapolis, Ind.: Hackett, 1994), xv.

the man who, being neither an infidel nor a fool, is safe from the temptation of tyranny. We, like the king, are in a more purified state of ignorance than we were at the *prooemium*.

We should further be glad to have considered these questions, moreover, as Aquinas is poised with the next line to take them up: "It is to be added further that these temporal advantages for which tyrants abandon justice work to the greater profit of kings when they serve justice" (I.10.76). Aquinas seems to speak to the fool who thought that the tyrant could benefit from temporal goods, or that infidel who thought that in serving God one might lose the ability to serve men, that is, no longer be secure in earthly possessions. But how will Aquinas support this claim?

Aquinas begins by arguing that "among all worldly things [*mundana omnia*] there is nothing that seems worthy to be preferred to friendship" (I.10.77). Most critically, "Friendship unites [*in unum conciliat*] virtuous men and preserves and promotes virtue." It also promotes pleasure, such that "There is no tyrant so cruel that friendship does not bring him pleasure." Aquinas relates a story of Dionysius of Syracuse, who was so touched by the friendship of two men, one of whom he had decided to kill, that he not only pardoned the man but also asked to be included in their friendship.[36] There is something pitiable about tyrants, for tyrants deny themselves friendship: "For when they do not seek the common good, but their own good," he argues, "there is little or no communion between them and their subjects." Aquinas makes the simple point that friendship requires something in common between would-be friends, however low. But tyrants and their subjects have nothing in common. The definition of the tyrant, after all, is he who rules for his private benefit, not for the

---

36. Dondaine credits this tale to Valerius Maximus (Dondaine, *De regno ad Regem Cypri*, préface, 461).

common good (I.1.10). We recall that the tyrant treats his subjects like slaves, seeing nothing good in them save what he can take for himself (I.3). The tyrant oppresses his subjects through injustice, and the subjects feel "not loved but despised [*contemni*]": "Nor have tyrants any reason to complain of their subjects if they are not loved [*diliguntur*] by them, since they do not act towards them in such a way that they ought to be loved [*diligi*] by them (I.10.78)." Aquinas has thus far made no connection between tyranny and love, making this a surprising argument. The first Latin verb for love he uses here, *amare*, has a range of connotations, from the innocent and romantic to the lascivious.[37] *Dilectere*, the other word, is the preferred word for "to love" in the Vulgate, including the Great Commandment (Matt 22:35–40), and has a more elevated ring to it. Aquinas thus manages in this short section to appeal to a wide range of human relations. Just as importantly, he denies them all to the tyrant. This is the point of the portrait of Dionysius from above. The only thing stronger in Dionysius's heart than his desire to oppress is his longing to share in friendship. How could a tyrant want to resign himself to such a life? Yet he does.

Note that Aquinas opened this argument with the statement, "the very temporal advantages for which tyrants abandon justice work to the greater profit of kings when they observe justice." Thus far, however, Aquinas has only emphasized the temporal advantages lost to tyrants. Aquinas next considers kings. Kings "are loved by many when they show that they love [*se amare demonstrant*] their subjects" (I.10.78). Kings act not only in justice by serving their subjects, but also in love. That is, there is established between them a kind of friendship.

Aquinas speaks here to the fool: the one who doubts that just politics are possible. It is not hard to see that a tyrant will win

---

37. Lewis & Short, "*amo, amare*."

little affection from his subjects, because his whole rule aims at their destruction, or at least at their slavery. But this point also speaks to the king, for the king's service to the common good is a kind of love that is the ground for friendship between him and his subjects. Indeed, as Aquinas goes on to write, "the consequence of this love is that the government of good kings is stable, because their subjects do not refuse to expose themselves to any danger whatsoever on behalf of such kings" (I.9.79). For love of their king, subjects will do anything. This is a power political tool, and Aquinas claims it constituted a significant part of the power of Julius Caesar over his soldiers and Augustus over his subjects. "Therefore," Aquinas concludes, "it is no easy task to shake the government of a prince whom the people so unanimously love."

This teaching is a solution to Aquinas's astonishing suggestion that the Romans were wise to abandon their kings for a republic (I.4.31). In light of the discussion at I.10, the trouble with monarchical Rome would seem to be that the kings were no longer thought to serve the common weal through their rule, only themselves. If kings truly manifest a kind of friendliness toward their subjects, however, and serve them as friends would serve friends, then this difficulty vanishes. Indeed, all can love one king more easily than multiple rulers or a faceless council. And then they do not begrudge the king great sacrifices. So it would seem that a king in establishing a friendship between himself and his citizens could avoid this problem and restore the practical advantages of kingship.

While Aquinas's discussion of the just king makes it clear that political life itself depends on a kind of friendship, in the case of tyranny, he has thus far emphasized how deeply tyrants regret the loss of friends. Now he spells out the political consequences of this lack of friendship between tyrants and their subjects: "The gov-

The Reward of the King

ernment of tyrants, on the other hand, cannot last long because it is hateful to the multitude, and what is against the wishes of the multitude cannot be long preserved" (I.10.79). Aquinas presents two arguments explaining the instability of tyrannical regimes: an argument from chance (I.10.80) and a critique of fear (I.10.81).

The first directly proceeds from the above claim: the tyrant is odious to the people. The tyrant, of course, will seek to control their power to resist him: he oppresses them at every turn. Yet can this regime always keep him safe?

For a man can hardly pass through this present life without suffering some adversities.[38] In the time of adversity, occasion cannot be lacking to rise [*insurgendi*] against the tyrant; and where there is an opportunity there will not be lacking at least one of the multitude to use the occasion (I.10.80).[39]

Tyrannical regimes are predicated on a kind of false order, false because tyrants have no popular support, but also because they depend on a stability that no regime can maintain. For no one can escape chance. Even the best rule of law, Aristotle warns, cannot provide for every situation, least of all a crisis.[40] The rule of a tyrant, of course, is decidedly less stable than that of the best laws. What weakens the tyrant is that his power depends on his personal and pervasive use of power, what Aristotle calls the first method of preserving tyranny.[41] Should the tyrant survive to die in office, his legacy will be completely undone by his death, yet Aquinas emphasizes here that such longevity is unlikely, for the lack of love between the tyrant and his subjects means that the subjects con-

---

38. The manuscript traditions offer *adversitates* and *diversitates* here (Dondaine, *De regno ad Regem Cypri*, préface, 462).
39. Eschmann adds "his." "In his time of adversity."
40. Aristotle, *Politics*, 1286a7–23.
41. Aristotle, *Politics*, 1314a29–1315b10.

stantly prepare for and await the moment of the tyrant's weakness. Where they find pleasant and noble the task of serving the king whom they love, they find pleasant and noble the task of deposing the tyrant whom they hate.

The second method through which the tyrant maintains his power is fear, but fear, Aquinas argues, "is a weak support," for it engenders hate and desperation (I.10.81). Prolonged fear leads to conditions that Aquinas compares to building pressure: the moment the pressure can expand, it does so, releasing untold violence against the tyrant. Fear, in other words, is only as good a tool of social control as the power behind it. What is more, Aquinas argues, this "very fear itself is not without danger, because many become desperate from excessive fear" (I.10.81).[42] Desperation, of course, makes man unpredictable because he becomes irrational. He may even "despair of safety," which "impels a man boldly to dare anything." This is a curious parallel with Hobbes, who worries that the fear of violent death will not hold down the vainglorious,[43] but Aquinas does not seem to have only the vainglorious in mind. Anyone who values the justice that the tyrant tramples, Aquinas is suggesting, could be led to desperate and unpredictable acts. They return fear with fear. Thus, tyranny not only depends on a level of order that no regime can maintain, but its very attempt to maintain order fosters disorder.

At I.6, Aquinas strenuously urged against tyrannicide and against resistance to unjust rulers in virtually all circumstances. Yet here, Aquinas warns that the tyrant will likely be deposed. Those tyrannical regimes spared from this fate, he says, are those

---

42. The Latin of an extraordinary section: *Sed nec ipse timor caret periculo, cum ex nimio timore plerique in desperationem inciderint. Salutis autem desperatio audacter ad quaelibet attendenda praecipitat. Non potest igitur tyranni dominium esse diuturnum.*

43. Hobbes, *Leviathan*, vi.39, xi.11–12.

regimes that "were not very tyrannical but in many things imitated the moderation of kings [*regalem modestiam*]" (I.10.82). He again references Aristotle's discussion in the *Politics* of the second method of preserving tyrannies (1315b11–39). The allusion comes at a good time for our king. If he worries through Aquinas's description of the fragility of tyranny that his own kingdom is beyond help, Aquinas immediately reassures him: do your best to imitate the moderate king, and you will endure. "Moderation" is well chosen: it represents less the crown of virtue than a certain disposition to be ordered toward virtue, particularly not to be intemperately controlled by love of inferior goods like pleasure or honor.[44] This would be the direction in which our royal reader would need to move, after all.

Aquinas opens the next paragraph with a quotation from Job 24:30: "He makes a man who is a hypocrite to reign for the sins of the people" (I.10.83). Aquinas explains that no one "can be more truly called a hypocrite than the man who assumes the office of king and acts like a tyrant, for a hypocrite is one who mimics the person of another, as is done on the stage." Aquinas has raised the problem of hypocrisy before. The difficulty of extrinsic goods like honor is that they can be gained through subterfuge, in this case the simulation of virtue. So the tyrant might take office under the

---

44. Aristotle, *Nicomachean Ethics*, 1117b23–18a26. Cf. *ST* II-II.161.4 *sed contra*: "Origen says (Hom. viii super Luc.): 'If thou wilt hear the name of this virtue [humility], and what it was called by the philosophers, know that humility which God regards is the same as what they called *metriotes*, i.e. measure or moderation.'" Keys notes that Aquinas makes no such connection in his *Commentary on the* "Nicomachean Ethics" (Keys, 2005, 164). *De Regno,* of course, predates both works, and so perhaps foreshadows his approach in the *Summa,* but note Pinckaers' argument that the Aristotelian organization of the *Secunda pars* obscures the significance of humility for Christianity. See Servais Pinckaers, OP, "The Sources of the Ethics of St. Thomas Aquinas," in *The Ethics of Aquinas*, ed. Stephen J. Pope (Washington, D.C.: Georgetown University Press, 2002), 21–23.

pretense of assuming kingship, when, in fact, he strives for tyranny. Thus, another layer of irony: in the tyrant's quest for order, he must upturn the very order by which he gains power.

After explaining the hypocrisy of tyrants, Aquinas writes: "All this becomes still more evident if we consider the divine judgment.... Hence God permits tyrants to get into power to punish the sins of the subjects." The word "permits" (*permittit*) is crucial: God's involvement in this play takes advantage of the tyrant's willingness to oppress and the subjects' sin. Where God does seem to be more active is the length of the tyrant's reign: just as God gives the people a tyrant in his wrath, he deprives that tyrant of his rule swiftly in his mercy. Aquinas then again quotes Hosea, as at the crucial conclusion of I.5: "I will give thee a king in my wrath" (Hosea 13:11).

The last argument of this chapter concerns the temporal goods that the just king enjoys. Now that Aquinas has said something toward the ways in which the tyrant is deprived of temporal goods, he can return to his claim at the beginning of the chapter, according to which kings and not tyrants benefit from the temporal goods for which tyrants abandon everything. The argument is simple: tyrants expend all of their resources on securing their regime. They must employ "a great many satellites" to protect themselves against subjects, and they must pay these satellites "more than they [the satellites] can rob from their subjects" (I.10.84). In other words, they must pay their mercenaries an amount sufficient to dissuade them from bribery, theft, and corruption. Kings, on the other hand, need not pay such mercenary arms to hold down their subjects, but, in fact, can even ask for service from their subjects. This, we remember, is because kings can become a kind of friend to their subjects when they serve the common good. Thus, the tyrant loses through taking from his subjects, while the king gains from giving to them. Moreover, citizens gain from kingship because the king at the very least does not seek to plunder them as a tyrant would.

Aquinas ends the chapter on a seemingly minor point about fame. "It seems superfluous to speak about fame," he writes, but then he does just that (I.10.85). This apparently trifling matter would be of tremendous importance to our royal reader. Perhaps he has been persuaded of the dangers of seeking honor and glory for their own sake. Yet it would delight him to know, as Aquinas goes on to tell him, that good kings are praised by men, and, in fact, that those praises echo long after the death of the good kings. It would confirm the king's sense of the dangers of tyranny to read that "the name of the wicked kings straightaway vanishes or, if they have been excessive in their wickedness, they are remembered with execration." Thus, Aquinas can seal the lessons of I.7–10 by assuring the king that he will receive everything he desires in ordering his rule to higher goods.

We might recall, however, that at I.10.73 Aquinas states that the difficulties of kingship will test the best of kings. We can doubt, then, that Aquinas is preaching a "Health and Wealth Gospel" to the king. The temporal realm is profoundly ambiguous: the king is as subject as the tyrant to chance (I.10), unjust resistance (I.6), and the sloth of his own subjects (I.4) as any tyrant: he is a sailor on a boat that he does not pilot or captain (I.9). Yet Aquinas has presented persuasive arguments that the king stands in a better position than the tyrant to rule justly, especially if he can educate his subjects to be as good as he is. And if we follow Solon's dictum to judge a man's happiness only after his death, then we know that the tyrant will only know the most fleeting happiness in life, and none in death.[45]

---

45. See Aristotle, *Nicomachean Ethics*, I.9–11.

I.10 evinces a potent blend of classical political naturalism and Christian concern with both the Fall and beatitude. Aquinas concurs with Aristotle on the centrality of friendship for political life, and sees it as the key to the king's temporal success. Indeed, I.10 offers the strongest affirmation yet of Aristotelian political naturalism, notably only after the disclosure of divine beatitude as man's final end at I.2.19. On a more Augustinian note, Aquinas locates the tyrant's weakness precisely in his inability to engage in civic friendship with his subjects. Taking the sweep of I.7–10, the tyrant often loses temporal advantages because of his lack of friendship, and the king often loses temporal advantages because of the tempestuous nature of politics. But it is the king who has a chance at attaining the common good for his subjects, because it is the king who has a chance at attaining beatitude for himself. He would thus be a fool or infidel not to heed Aquinas's counsel.

The Damnation of Tyrants: I.11

I.11 begins on a surprising note.[46] Arguing that material goods redound to the service of kings, not tyrants, Aquinas goes on to write: "The tyrant, moreover, loses the surpassing beatitude [*excellentissima beatitudine*], which is due as a reward [*praemio*] to kings and, what is still more serious, brings upon himself great suffering as a punishment" (I.12.87). We might not have realized that the punishments of the tyrant laid out in I.10 were only losses in the temporal order. It is only after thoroughly explicating them that Aquinas moves on to consider the tyrant's supernatural punishment. We might have expected Aquinas to write on the supernatural first, given that this is the more horrifying and final one.

---

46. Other editions, including that of the *Corpus Thomisticum*, differ from Eschmann in combining I.11 and I.12 into one chapter. Because those editions also divide I.1 into I.1,2, their combined I.11–12 is numbered as I.12 rather than I.11.

The Reward of the King

Indeed, in I.7–10, he first speaks of the king's celestial reward at great length, only later mentioning, as a sort of concluding aside in I.10, the temporal reward of the king. Perhaps the allure of temporal gains is strong for the less-than-perfectly virtuous prince, such that Aquinas sees an urgent need to emphasize that tyrants gain material goods, in addition to the opportunity afforded by his recent depiction of tyranny. For the king, however, Aquinas begins with his heavenly reward because this will fortify the king to accept the great sacrifices necessary to rule justly, but then in I.8, he initiates a criticism of earthly goods as the king's reward. In some sense, then, Aquinas adopts a deflationary tactic toward earthly rewards for both tyrant and king.

Aquinas emphasizes in this early part of I.11 that the supernatural fate of the tyrant is as surpassingly horrible as that of the king is sublime: "death in the judgment of men, and in the judgment of God eternal damnation" (I.11.87). This is because of the gravity of trespassing against the common good (I.11.87); their proud lack of repentance (I.11.88); the long-term effects they have on their kingdom (I.11.89); and the dignity of the office they hypocritically occupy (I.11.90). Three points emerge from this discussion.

First, Aquinas's treatment of repentance and pride. The tyrant does not repent for his crimes against man and God; rather, he embraces them, "puffed up by the wind of pride, deservedly abandoned by God for their sins, and besmirched [*delibuti*] by the flattery of men" as they are (I.11.88). This is a searing critique of pride, and while a Christian theologian's criticism of pride might not surprise us, it might lead us to rethink the scattered references to the magnanimous man in *De Regno*. For it is a kind of pride or sense of self-worth that constitutes his sense of superiority to the earthly goods that Aquinas wishes our king to be above. The pride of the tyrant also looks suspiciously like that of the magnanimous man, at least in this way: neither recognizes anything greater than him in the city. The tyrant takes everything for himself; the final good is simply his good. The magnanimous man has some sense of the common good at least insofar as he seeks to serve it for honor and glory, and in this sense, he depends on other people who will benefit from his deeds and will give him honor. Yet he does not seem satisfied by this reward, as though he were not really acting for that common good. We might wonder yet again what good "he to whom nothing is great" finally seeks, and how he avoids succumbing to the temptations of tyranny if he never finds a good noble enough to match his self-estimation. And were this pride of the magnanimous man to lead him to value himself to other men, he might also extend that contempt to God.[47]

This brings us to our second point about I.11: the long-term effects of tyranny. At I.11.89, Aquinas explains that the "malice of their impenitence" extends beyond the lives of tyrants, for "taking their accustomed habit [*sua consuetudine*] for authority, they hand on their boldness in sinning to posterity." The *auctoritas* of the tyrant might simply be that by which he justifies his own actions, yet in oppressing his people by those actions, he inspires fear and desperation in his subjects (I.11.81) such that they too might be drawn into sin. Perhaps through their struggles, they might even come to see violence and resistance against authority as inherently good. Aquinas might have wished to guard against this dynamic by his strong words against resistance (I.6.52), yet the tyrant's in-

---

47. Aristotle, *Nicomachean Ethics* X. And yet: "Aristotle did not look upon God as Creator nor as exercising conscious government and providence, but regarded him as the final Cause alone.... The virtuous man of Aristotle is, in a sense, the most independent man, whereas the virtuous man of St. Thomas is, in a sense, the most dependent man, that is, the man who realizes truly and freely expresses his relation of dependence on God." See Frederick Copleston, SJ, *A History of Medieval Philosophy* (New York: Harper & Row, 1993), 410–11.

fluence might yet be subtler. Perhaps if the people choose to bear their suffering under the tyrant—perhaps they are not so good themselves—the tyrant might establish a *paideia* in which his *consuetudo* comes to be seen by many as an authoritative judgment as to the best way to live. One could envision a "slippery slope" effect across generations by which what seems forbidden becomes merely dubious, then acceptable and even desirable. No one, strictly speaking, intends such a dynamic: the tyrant simply seeks his own goods, and the people, apparently of weak virtue, imperceptibly slouch into it, whether under the reign of one tyrant or a number of them. Thus, the glory-seeking tyrant will at best be remembered by execration, and at worst will be forgotten (I.11.85).

We will third note the language of Aquinas's final argument. In I.11.90, he argues that the dignity of the office trespassed by the tyrant especially recommends the harsh punishment of the tyrant. The language evokes strongly the teaching of I.8, that of the king's office as *minister Dei* (I.8.62). The dignity of the royal office is that of "executors and ministers of His [God's] government," and so the punishment for violating that trust is greater than that for other offices, just as an earthly king punishes his own ministers more harshly than he does his subjects for crimes. Aquinas cites the Book of Wisdom's warning to "ministers of His kingdom" about protecting (*custodere*) "the law of justice" and "walk[ing] according to the will of God." Aquinas fittingly concludes this section with Isaiah's promise of punishment to Nebuchadnezzar, the tyrant whose punishment by God was offered as proof at I.8.62 that all kings serve God. By this point in *De Regno*, our king has become accustomed to thinking of himself as a minister of God, and Aquinas can articulate the full implications of the notion. What is striking about this passage, after all, is that it goes beyond the king's failure to protect the common good, to repent for their crimes or to provide for posterity. Rather, Aquinas singles out the dignity of the office as *minister Dei*, a teaching that only reinforces the nobility of the common good that the king is to defend.

At the outset of this chapter, we noted that I.10 concerns the temporal disadvantages of tyranny, and that only at I.11 does Aquinas take up the supernatural punishment of tyranny. Yet I.11 justifies that supernatural punishment in terms of the horrific earthly consequences of tyranny: the tyrant tramples on the common good, the tyrant sets up his *consuetudo* as a perverse *paideia* that inures his people to injustice, and so on. Even the last argument, according to which the tyrant fails in his duty as *minister Dei*, is coupled to the health of the polity. Serving as a *minister Dei*, in fact, is Aquinas's explanation of the God-king analogy that has struck us as so curious throughout *De Regno*. It is, to be sure, a specifically Christian and theological reading of the philosophical neo-Platonic God-king analogy. Yet Aquinas has made the best of philosophy and theology in these two chapters, showing that to be a good *minister Dei* is to fulfill the promises of the excellence of monarchy. It is evident from reason that temporal rewards are more likely to go to the king, not to the tyrant (I.10), yet for the king who might grasp such arguments less clearly, revelation powerfully supports the conclusions of reason (I.11). Thus, even if in the uncertainties of politics injustice seems to pay, Aquinas reminds our king that what he gains in life as a tyrant will be infinitely outweighed by what he loses in death. The king, moreover, comes into that reward by serving as a good king, by promoting the common good.

Conclusion: *De Regno* I.7–12

I.12 closes book I, and summarizes our progress:[48]

If therefore temporal goods abound and come to kings, and an eminent degree of beatitude [*excellens beatitudinis gradus*] is prepared for them by God, and tyrants are for the most part frustrated in seeking the temporal goods that they covet, subjected to many dangers, and, what is more, are deprived of eternal goods [*bonis aeternis*] and singled out for the gravest punishments, those who take up the duty of ruling must zealously strive to serve their subjects as kings, not as tyrants (I.12.91).[49]

This sentence reorganizes *De Regno* as it synthesizes its teaching: any king, seeing the king's reward (I.7–9) and the frustrations and punishment of the tyrant (I.3–6; I.10), will exercise the duties of kingship (I.1–2) with ardor and hope. Most notably, what has thus far come last in *De Regno*, "The Reward of the King," now comes first. In this, it bears a certain parallel to the beginning of I.10, which prefaced the punishment of the tyrant, save that there, Aquinas had not completed outlining the frustrations of the tyrant's rule (I.4–6) with his punishments (I.10–11). Recall that before I.7, in fact, the instability and perils of tyranny, not the tyrant's punishment, were the dominant theme of the work. But they are clearly related. Thus, Aquinas's introduction of the theme of the reward of the king initiates the lesson in how to avoid the ills of tyranny. In some sense, this is his refining of the best regime (I.1–?), for Aquinas herein has shown what the ruler of the best regime must be, namely a *minister Dei*.

---

48. This chapter is combined with the preceding one in some editions (Eschmann, *On Kingship*, introduction, xiv).

49. Eschmann renders *regendi officium* as "the office of kingship." Dondaine notes variants of *susceperunt* and *suscipiunt* for "take up" (Dondaine, *De regno ad Regem Cypri*, préface, 463).

In this restatement, we see Aquinas's skillful synthesis of Aristotelian teleology and Augustinian theology, a synthesis that only appeared as an awkward juxtaposition in I.1–6: God's grace alone affords man an end that is itself in God, yet that end is nevertheless set as the end of human life. This is a crucial point, for in I.3–6, we learned that mild tyranny is nearly unavoidable. I.19, however, assures our king that the seemingly inevitable minor injustices of politics need not deprive our king of beatitude, provided he indeed steers clear of radical tyranny.

The revelation of man's end through grace is also significant insofar as I.1–6 were theologically thin. Now we know that the ruler serves as *minister Dei* and for beatitude. Specifically, we saw Aquinas move in I.7–8 from the question, "What would induce a king to rule?" to "What would make a human being happy?" This involves two shifts: a changing notion of "reward" to "end," and a concurrent shift from the king to the human person. The reward of the king will be greater than that accorded to the citizen, but all virtuous persons enter into beatitude. Thus, we might think that the good person, the *liber,* and the good king, the *minister Dei*, have at least that in common. But what is the *liber* or *sui causa*? At I.6, we thought he might be the magnanimous man, the one free from attachment to earthly goods beneath him. But then, why does he act? The thrust of I.7–8 seems to be that only in acting in view of a worthy end can one be rational. This end, of course, is finally God. Thus, the *sui causa* directs his actions toward the attainment of happiness, which Christian revelation shows to be the God of Abraham, Isaac, and Jacob.

Yet these theological considerations have not led to a theocratic turn in *De Regno*. Aquinas also emphasizes that true kingship is not sacral or theocratic: while it is divine in its reward, there is no suggestion that it is anything but natural in its origin and activity, and there is no talk of being a handmaid to the church. Politics remains possessed of its integrity, another nod to the Aristotelian tradition.

In this shift from a "reward" to an "end," we have seen a synthesis of Aristotle and Augustine that has elevated but also grounded politics: the reward of the king for persevering in noble but difficult politics becomes the end of the king whose fulfillment of man's naturally political nature is affirmed by a God-given end. Indeed, Aquinas has surprisingly introduced divine revelation to set moderate if noble expectations for politics. Aquinas has made clear throughout book I that even the best regime will have unjust aspects in practice, and its reward in beatitude does not demand that every imperfection be eliminated. Further, that reward has not led Aquinas to argue that the king must serve stringent requirements of theocracy.

Restatement: *De Regno*, Book I

Yet this epilogue also highlights two perplexities in the textual ordering of book I. First, why does Aquinas proceed from the perils of tyranny (I.3–6) to the reward of the king (I.7–12)? Second, to return to our earlier question, does I.7–12 resolve the tension between I.1–2 and I.3–6? Or, as Dondaine and Eschmann ask more plainly: does I.7–12 belong at the end of book I?

The first question arose as soon as we turned to I.7, as the shift from tyranny to the reward of the king is not a little surprising. This first question, moreover, acquires particular importance when we consider that I.7–12 is essentially a treatise on ends, thanks to Aquinas's sleight of hand at I.7, whereby he shifts from speaking of the "reward of the king" to the end of the human person. What might strike us at this point is where this discussion of the human end appears in other works of Aquinas, or indeed of many other moral thinkers through the ages."[50] Such inquiries often begin practical works, as a given end allows us to make sense of a human action, and so that ultimate end "renders intelligible all those choices and activities that human life comprises."[51] As Aquinas himself writes: "Although the end be last in the order of execution, yet it is first in the order of the agent's intention. And it is this way that it is cause."[52] The end is the final achievement of action, so the end occurs or comes into being last temporally. Yet it is the cause of all action because it is that in view of which the action is undertaken.

Such an end-centered conception of ethics inevitably turns on the question of the final end, or happiness. As Pinckaers writes: "To anyone with an open mind, one huge fact stands out in the history of morality: for the ancients, Christians and pagans alike, the question of happiness was primary."[53]

But if the question of final ends is central for Aquinas, why does it not begin *De Regno*? Why, in other words, does Aquinas place this section at the end of book I and after his treatment of tyranny? The great Thomistic scholar Eschmann's reservations about this epilogue help to address these difficulties, for he reminds us that *De Regno* is not a treatise but a *speculum*, and thus its components are arranged pedagogically. That pedagogy, I argue, depends on the interplay of the theoretical and practical, and the dynamic between the Aristotelian and Augustinian traditions. This latter dynamic will open up an answer to our second question.

---

50. Illustrative citations for Aquinas's numerous reiterations of this teaching, including at the beginning of the "Questions on Law": *ST* I-II.1.3; I-II.1.5; I-II.18.6; I-II.90.2; I-II.94.2; and II-II.43.3 can be found in Gregory Froelich, "The Equivocal Status of *Bonum Commune*," *The New Scholasticism* 63, no. 1 (1989): 38–57.

51. Froelich, "The Equivocal Status of *Bonum Commune*."

52. *ST* I-II.1.1 ad 1.

53. Pinckaers, *The Sources of Christian Ethics*, 18.

Eschmann argues that Aquinas fails to execute the plan that he sets forth in the *prooemium* and recapitulates in the epilogue.[54] Most glaringly, in the *prooemium,* Aquinas promises to discuss two subjects: the "origin of kingship" and "the things which pertain to the office of a king." Yet the last chapters of book I concern not the origin of kingship, but rather its reward and the punishment for tyranny. The reward of the king is a practical rather than a theoretical consideration, Eschmann concludes, and thus belongs in book II, with "the things that pertain to the office of the king."[55]

What can we make of this claim? Prima facie, Eschmann could have a case, although we might simply lack a text between I.6 and I.7 that justifies this organization.[56] But we might also question Eschmann's assumptions, particularly the practical nature of "The Reward of the King" and how to read *De Regno.*

As to the practical nature of I.7–12, we noted that I.7–12 is not simply a statement of the reward of the king but a treatise on ends or happiness. In other words, Aquinas asks in this section not only the practical question of what reward would motivate a king to perform his task but also the theoretical question of end or telos of man as a creature. To be sure, the answer to that question has profound practical implications. Indeed, the centrality of ends for ethics and politics has profound implications for the relationship between practical and theoretical reason in politics, as Eschmann would have known. A practical activity like politics must be conducted in view of its end, and this particularly applies to politics,

---

54. Eschmann, *On Kingship,* introduction, xiv–xxi.
55. Eschmann, *On Kingship,* introduction, xvi. Dondaine's concern is characteristically more muted: he only notes that it is difficult to see how I.7–12 relates to the investigation of the *regni originem* promised in the *prooemium* (Dondaine, *De regno ad Regem Cypri,* préface, 423).
56. Jordan, "*De Regno* and the Place of Political Thinking in Thomas Aquinas," 161–62.

where the question of the end looms large. Yet there can be no doubt that the identification of man's end has a theoretical dimension to it. Thus, I.7–12 is more theoretical than Eschmann argues, and the attempt to isolate one part of *De Regno* as theoretical and another as practical, then, will miss Aquinas's education of the king.

What of how Eschmann reads *De Regno*? Eschmann sees the *prooemium* as a kind of plan for the work and expects Aquinas to march through it in a deductive fashion. In fact, however, *De Regno* is a *speculum principum*, and its content and style will be dictated at least in part by pedagogical concerns.[57] For instance, Aquinas's initial discussion of the best regime at I.1–2 is uncritically laudatory of monarchy, yet we have subsequently seen Aquinas indicate in several places the limitations of monarchy. This organization does not reflect a scattered, fragmentary attempt at a treatise, however, because Aquinas is not writing a treatise. He is not writing a treatise, in turn, because he is not writing for a scholar but for a politically active prince. Instead, this organization reflects Aquinas's method of guiding his reader from uncritical and self-interested ideology of monarchy to a more nuanced understanding of his royal role as mediated by the travails of politics and the glory of rewards beyond riches and fame.

Given that Aquinas structures *De Regno* with an eye toward the education of the king, it should come as no surprise that Aquinas reserves the issue of final ends to I.7–12 for pedagogical reasons. It is a pedagogy, I argue, that plays on the relationship between the theoretical and the practical, but also the Aristotelian and Augustinian traditions.

In terms of theory and practice, Aquinas reserves the discussion of the king's reward for the end so as to emphasize the

---

57. Roguet, *Du Gouvernement Royal*, vii.

The Reward of the King 145

difficulty and nobility of politics. Aquinas roughly correlates his argument for the nobility of politics with his theory of monarchy, and his argument for the difficulty of politics with his practical digression on tyranny. The reward of the king resolves these tensions because it is both practical and theoretical.

As we have already noted, Aquinas emphasizes the nobility of politics throughout I.1–2. He does so by presenting politics theoretically: with a metaphysical justification of monarchy as the most just regime form; in his seeming denial that other regimes can be adopted as practical alternatives to monarchy's theoretically pure justice; and perhaps most especially in his strong if vague claims that the king serves the common good of his people.

While I.1–2 highlights the nobility of monarchy theoretically, I.3–6 turns toward a more practical description of the horrors of tyranny and the difficulty of avoiding it. This section to be sure contains much of theoretical interest, but compared to I.1–2, Aquinas here is pleased to descend into considerable detail about the quotidian exigencies of tyranny, even down to the tyrant's lack of friends. In short, then, the king arrives at I.7–12 with a palpable sense of politics' arduous nobility. Politics is laudable and worthy in principle, but in practice, it often fails to achieve those laudable ends, instead risking the king's very soul.

Aquinas introduces the reward of the king as a resolution to that tension: the king deserves beatitude for the nobility of his activity, and he can earn it even should he fail at his task. In other words, as a theoretical matter, it is an end that along can satisfy the human person, and as a practical matter, it is a good that God gladly gives humans. In his characterization of the monarch as a *minister Dei*, Aquinas presents the king not as someone who can flawlessly execute the theoretical promise of monarchy but as a servant seeking to cooperate with God as best as the king can.

These considerations about why Aquinas would end book I with the reward of the king have implications for our second question: why does Aquinas juxtaposes I.1–2 with I.3–6? For if one way to understand I.7–12 is as a theoretical-practical resolution to the tension between the theory of I.1–2 and the practice of I.3–6, another way to characterize I.7–12 is as a resolution to the "Augustinian" and "Aristotelian" elements of *De Regno* that are juxtaposed in book I. I.7–12 is the resolution to those two moments, and so comes later in the text so that Aquinas can lay out that tension for the inspection of the king before it is resolved. Thus, what is "Augustinian" and "Aristotelian" in these two moments concerns not only the historian of political thought but the office and activity of the king.

The tension that Aquinas lays out in juxtaposing I.1–2 and I.3–7 is not mysterious: it is the great divide between two hallmark theses of Christian political thought: that man is naturally political, and that in his fallen state he is profoundly antisocial. At stake in this tension is the integrity and end of man's terrestrial and political activity. Nederman suggests that Aquinas need not settle this division because Aquinas is an Aristotelian.[58] On that account, Aquinas sides with the tradition of Christian thought that emphasizes man's political nature against the Augustinian tradition that emphasizes man's fallen nature.

Yet there are at least two difficulties with Nederman's suggestion. First, as a matter of fact Aquinas does enter into the debate between the Aristotelian and Augustinian traditions. We have seen that *De Regno* offers a striking contrast of political visions that could be termed "Aristotelian" and "Augustinian": I.1–2, in which man is presented as naturally political and the great goal of *unitas pacis* seems possible, and I.3–6, in which politics is "the

58. Nederman, "Nature, Sin and the Origins of Society," 5.

devil's playground," in Maritain's amusing words.[59] Indeed, for some scholars, *De Regno*, far from being typical of Aquinas's "Aristotelian" tendencies, betrays a remarkably Augustinian note, but this would be to ignore the Aristotelian aspects of *De Regno*.[60] Again, Aquinas's emphasis on I.3–6 on tyranny is striking not only *in se* but also because it follows the putatively Aristotelian I.1–2.

A second problem with Nederman's claim is more fundamental: even should Aquinas as a theologian have followed the teaching of Aristotle on political naturalism, as a Christian he could not have ignored the importance of the Fall for his political thought, not least in an intellectual climate in which Augustine was tremendously important. In other words, even if Aquinas takes Aristotle's thought as controlling for his politics, which is not clearly the case for *De Regno*, Aquinas will still need to clarify how that teaching dovetails with traditional Christian teaching on the Fall. Thus, Nederman's challenge applies to Aquinas more than Nederman realizes, even should Aquinas not finally invoke Cicero to resolve the tension between man's natural political nature and his fallen nature.

The question remains as to how Aquinas resolves his philosophical adherence to Aristotle's political naturalism and his Christian adherence to the doctrine of the Fall. He does so, I argue, through I.7–12. Again at the risk of reductivism, we can see I.7–12 as synthesizing the naturalism of I.1–2 and the Augustinianism of I.3–6. Man's political activity does indeed have an integrity arising from his rational nature, despite the fear that sin and vice impede that activity. Indeed, his political activity is even hallowed by a divine end. Political activity does not secure man's final

---

59. Jacques Maritain, *Integral Humanism* (New York: Scribners' and Sons, 1968), 103.
60. Keys, *Aquinas, Aristotle, and the Promise of the Common Good*, 64.

end, however, nor are the temporal ends achieved through that activity man's final end. Beatitude is man's final end, and it comes to him despite the Fall. It comes to him, moreover, from God, not from his own exertions. It is not simply the reward of nature.

To recapitulate: Aquinas seeks to affirm through *De Regno* two critical theses so often associated with the warring "Aristotelian" and "Augustinian" traditions: that man is naturally political, and that in his fallen state he is antisocial. By presenting the force of each of these theses for politics before resolving them, he can not only unequivocally affirm their importance but also the need to resolve them.

While such a method of arranging *De Regno* has engaging theoretical implications, we might also inquire into its pedagogical implications. The Cypriot king, after all, is no political theologian or political scientist: his purpose in reading this would be to learn something that can be of practical value for his rule.

The pedagogical value of this arrangement of *De Regno* is parallel to its theoretical value: Aquinas desires to bring to the attention of the king both two distinct moments of political life and their resolution in God. Aquinas wants the king to see the seriousness of each fact about man: that political activity fulfills something deeply natural in humans, but that this political activity does not complete or fully realize humanity. Human political activity really does have a relative end, but it is difficult to acquire, and it is not man's final end. Aquinas wants to exalt the king's understanding of politics and justice, but wants the king to see himself as an unprofitable servant.

The king, then, will learn thoroughly not only that the excellence of his rule is profoundly rooted in human nature but that the difficulty of political activity is also profoundly rooted in human nature, or at least in fallen human nature. The reward of the king will emerge as a reinforcement that he will indeed be rewarded for his political activity, despite the vicissitudes of politics. That reward, however, is not something he can grasp from himself: it comes from God, and the king learns that his reward is not something that ordinary political activity could ever inspire.

If this basic argument is right, then we have something of an answer to the question of why Aquinas appears "Ciceronian" at times in *De Regno*, which is to say ambiguous about politics' ability to secure man's final end. To be sure, Aquinas does not use Cicero to juxtapose Aristotle with Augustine or the Fall or church. Rather, Aquinas presents politics as ends-directed in I.1–2 without elaborating fully on the temporal ends of politics. Thus, I.1–2 appear Ciceronian not because Aquinas does not wish to relate politics to man's final end but because he wishes to draw that connection later in the text.

If some matters are clearer at the end of I.12 than they were in I.1–6, we have as yet remaining questions. First, what are the practical consequence of the king's status as a *minister Dei*? While Aquinas argues in I.1 that the king governs in his kingdom as God governs the world, he has had little to say of practical significance concerning this. Aquinas has now, however, added to this designation the title *minister Dei*. What concrete significance does this have for political activity? How ought the king to rule? And will that practical guidance add to Aquinas's thin teaching on how to avoid tyranny?

Second, what is the relationship between the temporal end of politics and beatitude? As we noted, Aquinas's argument about the proper reward for the king moves from goods that are often taken to be conventional ends of politics, including glory and honor, to goods which seem surpassingly better, indeed fully satisfying to man's highest faculties, especially beatitude. But can politics lead or help lead man qua citizen to that happiness? And if some other institution must play a role in leading a man to this happiness, for example, the church, then Aquinas must explain the relation between the king and that other institution.

Third, will Aquinas have anything to say to modern politics that is pluralistic or skeptical about ends, whether temporal or supernatural? At the risk of anachronism, what room in this polity Aquinas will leave for the person who sees that the human person has ends and that they seem to go beyond the earthly, but who does not see that God is that final end? If we connect this concern with the two questions I just asked, then we might ask: what would a government look like that somehow fulfills not only a community's end of beatitude but also fosters each man's inquiry into just what his happiness really is? To answer such questions would be to respond to the "infidel" of I.19.

CHAPTER 4

The Politics of Revelation

De Regno II.1–8

Our investigation of book I has shown *De Regno* to convey a teaching of considerable theoretical and practical significance, despite the claims of scholars like Finnis.[1] Most obviously, Aquinas has presented a fulsome teaching on political naturalism, monarchy as the best regime, the king as *minister Dei*, and beatitude as the reward of the king and the common good of all persons.

Yet what does Aquinas ultimately hope for us to take away from *De Regno*? Book II provides answers to such questions. Indeed, although less has been written on book II than any other part of *De Regno*, it promises from the outset answers to puzzles that bedevil the interpreter of book I. In particular, as we noted at the end of chapter 3: what are the practical consequence of the king's status as a *minister Dei*, and what is the relationship between the temporal end of politics and beatitude?

More broadly, book II provides a model or picture of politics, something lacking hitherto in *De Regno*. By synthesizing the seemingly disparate parts of *De Regno*, Aquinas illuminates for his royal reader the role of political activity within God's creation and

---

1. Finnis, *Aquinas*, 228–31, 287–88.

governance of the world, a role that Aquinas presents in prosaic but noble terms in II.5–8. Tellingly, Aquinas's account of that role challenges as much as justifies the king's ministry as *minister Dei*.

A reading of book II must also confront the concern of Eschmann that II.3–4 is a rupture in the text, as he thinks it digresses from the plan of II.1.[2] Dondaine is reserved in his evaluation of this passage: he notes that Eschmann "perceives" a rupture and then adds that Aquinas's thought on the two powers is not "of a perfect clarity."[3] I argue, however, that II.3–4 present an important teaching on the king's role as *minister Dei* that completes the promise of II.1 and the prologue of *De Regno*.

The Government of Nature: II.1

II.1 opens with a welcome promise. It will treat on "what the duty [*officium*] of the king is and "what a king ought to be" (II.1.93).[4] This duty will be uncovered, Aquinas writes, by considering "the pattern of the regime of nature [*regimen naturalis*]." For art is an imitation of nature, he argues, "from which we accept the rules to act according to reason." Thus, II.1 is the practical continuation of I.2, which defined kingship as the most excellent regime. It also continues I.2 in another way: after the notably theological treatment of beatitude and the *minister Dei* in I.7–12, Aquinas here signals a return to a more philosophical enterprise, namely the consonance of the duties of the king with reason and nature itself.

If we are to learn of the royal office from nature, Aquinas argues, then we should consider the government of nature. He explains that the government of nature is two-fold: universal and particular (II.1.94). As for the universal, "all things are held to-

---

2. Eschmann, *On Kingship*, introduction, xix.
3. Dondaine, *De regno ad Regem Cypri*, préface, 423–24.
4. Cf. Dondaine, *De regno ad Regem Cypri*, préface, 441.

gether [*continentur*] under the rule of God [*Dei regimen*], who by His providence governs all." The particular is analogous to the universal and is found in man. Aquinas then explains the parallel between the two governments: reason governs the powers of the soul and the body as God governs the spiritual and corporeal bodies of the universe: "And thus in a certain manner reason obtains in man as God obtains in the world." But this way of speaking only equates a single man with God, and we have repeatedly noted that man is "naturally a social animal living in a multitude." Thus, we should note that this analogy holds not only for the reason in one man but also for the reason of the man that governs a multitude of humans. Indeed, Aquinas argues that this analogy of reason's role "principally pertains to the office of the king."

We noted at I.1.3 that Aquinas argues that reason rules the soul of each person, and that one person rules over other people. But Aquinas only now explicitly argues that the reason of that person rules over other persons. The government of man over men will have to be more than the instinct of animals, but it must also be something more than the willful caprice of the tyrant, which in some sense is worse than rule by beasts (I.2). The first consequence of this teaching is practical:

Therefore let the king recognize [*cognoscat*] that this is the office that he has taken up, that he is to be in the kingdom what the soul is in the body, and what God is in the world. If he reflects[5] seriously upon this, a zeal for justice will be enkindled in him when he contemplates that he has been appointed to this position in place of God, to exercise judgment in his kingdom; further, he will acquire the gentleness of clemency and mildness when he considers as his own members those individuals who are subject to his rule (II.1.95).

---

5. *Recogitet, consideret, respiceret* and *attingeret* in various manuscripts (Dondaine, *De regno ad Regem Cypri*, préface, 464).

This passage bears a resemblance to I.2, but the teaching is crucially different. Aquinas emphasizes the difference between metaphysics and politics: the king cannot simply spontaneously assume his place in the hierarchy of governments that justifies monarchy as best: he must "recognize" and "reflect" on it through reason. In so doing, he will predispose himself to a "zeal for justice" that will aid his service *in loco Dei*. Justice, we saw at I.1, requires knowing how to lead fittingly a multitude of free persons who act for their own sake, to their end. He will thus come to understand the place of judgment and clemency in serving his people.

Aquinas names another way in which the king cannot simply assume his place in the metaphysical hierarchy of governance as though parachuted from Heaven: the king must grow in virtue to execute his particular government under God. In this passage, Aquinas names four virtues requisite to rule: justice, judgment (*iudicium*), clemency, and mildness (*mansuetudo*). He also names them in complementary pairs, connecting justice with judgment, and clemency with mildness. Aquinas has previously mentioned justice, but now he pairs it with judgment, a word closely connected to prudence. Aquinas in many of his works uses *iudicium* in its Scholastic sense as an exercise in prudence, the judgment of choice that finally issues in act (*ST* I.79.8, I-II.13). Prudence requires experience with the contingent and the changing.[6] Yet *prudentia* is more than just than the application of this knowledge. One can only practically reason well when one can discern the proper ends of action and pursue the means to achieve them. To be prudent, one must be a virtuous person who knows and seeks the good in his activity.

Thus, the word arises at a pivotal moment in *De Regno*. The

6. Aristotle, *Nicomachean Ethics* VI; see Aquinas, *Commentary on "Nicomachean Ethics,"* bk. VI, lects. IV and VII.

end that prudence pursues is precisely what was promised at I.1, namely that of the *liber* living in a multitude, but revealed only at I.7. We saw that the tyrant's misery results from his failure to act in view of the person's proper end, and we have received many urgings not to deliberate on ends. Thus, while Aquinas has never directly raised the notion of prudence until now, *De Regno* has been a kind of education in prudence throughout.

Mildness and clemency, meanwhile, are virtues Aquinas desires that the king direct to his subjects. Aquinas links these two virtues as parts of temperance in the *Summa Theologica*, where he explains that mildness moderates the passion of anger, whereas clemency moderates external activities, particularly punishments (*ST* II-II.157.1 *respondeo*). Aquinas means to encourage the king to cultivate his virtues such that he can perform his tasks justly and prudently, yet also temperately. Aquinas does not here invoke the fourth cardinal virtue, courage, which, in fact, goes unmentioned in *De Regno* save a passing reference to the courage of the soldier (I.9.69).

In short, the regime of nature reveals not only the rule of one but also the rule of the rational one as the best regime. He will have knowledge of his end, and the zeal to pursue it for himself and his people. The person who can exercise judgment is in the first place a *liber*, because he is capable of ruling himself through reason toward his proper end. Having the great moral virtues, he can also rule other *liberi* because he knows the requirements of freedom and sees their directionality toward God.

This passage illuminates Aquinas's awareness of the difference between the order of execution and the order of justification, which is to say between practical and theoretical reason. For Foucault, this passage illustrates the "theological-cosmological continuum in the name of which the sovereign is authorized to govern and which provides models in accordance with which he must govern."[7] In that "continuum," governance is nothing more than the "extension and uninterrupted continuity of the exercise of [the king's] sovereignty."[8] But we have seen two critical discontinuities between the rule of God and of the king: that between God as creator and the human person as creature; and here between metaphysics and ethics.

Similarly, Eschmann writes that the "methodical principle" of turning to the regime of nature "should not be considered as St. Thomas' last word in the matter," referring to *ST* II-II.47.10–13, which questions relate to prudence in legislation. Yet prudence plays a leading role in *De Regno*, as well. Indeed, whereas *De Regno* I.1–2 draws from metaphysics to justify monarchy as the best government, here Aquinas emphasizes the practical nature of the reason required for politics. The king must not only know the end but pursue it in practice and through the moral virtues. Aquinas means for the analogy to challenge the king, not simply to justify his rule: it is a standard against which to measure the ministry of a king insofar as he aspires to live out his position in the God-king analogy.

Thus, when Aquinas states at the opening of II.1 that the duties or office of the king are to be learned from the regime of nature (II.1.93), he does not propose a deterministic politics with no space for human agency or rationality. Aquinas states that the reason within man is to govern the polity, and he clearly distinguishes it from instinct of animals. And he suggests that in nature is revealed human reason: human nature is itself rational. Thus, the "regime of nature" here does not reduce politics to metaphysics. In fact, the king is exhorted to seek justice through prudence. This

---

7. Foucault, *Security, Territory, Population*, 232.
8. Foucault, *Security, Territory, Population*, 234.

reference to *iudicium* at the chapter's end, then, should only amplify what is already clear: the teleological foundations of Aquinas's political theory do not deny but reinforce the prudential nature of political rationality.⁹

II.1 offers a hope that the God-king analogy will deepen our understanding of the king's practical role. The king as *minister Dei* receives his reward from God, and imitates God's rule, but Aquinas has not specified how the king's "particular" government aligns with that of God's "universal" government. We know from I.7 that the king's rule is to conduce to the beatitude of his people. Does that mean that the king himself secures beatitude for his people? And while Aquinas emphasizes the analogy between divine and human rule in II.1, he also underlines two differences between the king and God: the first is the king cannot simply instantiate an imitation of God's rule, but must achieve it in practice, and so can be judged on that activity, and the second is that the king's rule is never more than "particular," always falling short of the "universal" government of God. In short, Aquinas needs to explain what role human governance plays in securing the ends of divine governance.

The Politics of Creation: II.2

II.1 informed the king that his duties can be discerned by considering God's governance of the world. II.2 now spells out of what that governance consists:

---

9. In a footnote, Eschmann writes that the "methodical principle" of turning to the regime of nature "should not be considered as St. Thomas' last word in the matter," and he refers the reader to *ST* II-II.47.10–13, which questions relate to prudence in legislation (*On Kingship*, introduction, 53, n. 2). The several albeit scattered references to practical reason in this chapter suggest that Aquinas's current method is not something he discards in later works.

In general two works of God in the world must be considered. One by which God created [*instituit*] the world, the other by which God governs [*gubernat*] the created world. These two works are furthermore performed in the body by the soul. First, by virtue of the soul the body is formed, and then by the soul the body is ruled [*regitur*] and moved (II.2.97).

God's two great activities in the world brought it into being and then have provided for its subsequent preservation (*ST* I.104.1–2). Aquinas compares God's creation and governance of the world to the soul's activity toward the body, although the difference in language is striking: God created (*instituit*) the world; the body is formed (*informatur*) by the soul. While the soul is the form of the body, the soul does not call the body out of nothingness.[10] At best, it forms and shapes it, as the Demiurge of Plato's *Timaeus* takes what already is and gives it form.[11]

Given that the soul cannot conjure something out of nothing, we would be surprised were a king able to do so. Indeed, Aquinas follows the above statement with an argument that "the second [activity] more properly pertains to the office of a king" (II.2.98). Aquinas then explains how the creation of the world illumines the creation of a kingdom. Creation involves production and distinction: bringing something into existence, and distinguishing orders of beings such that they are in harmony with each other. Aquinas cites the Genesis 1 account of the seven days of creation as an example: God not only brings the world into being but also orders it "fittingly" into heaven and earth, day and night and water and land (II.2.99). In like manner, a king must provide for a suitable site for his kingdom, establish where best can be placed the various

---

10. Étienne Gilson, *Christianisme et Philosophie* (Paris: Vrin, 1936), 168–88.
11. *ST* I.44.2. See Mark F. Johnson, "Did St. Thomas Attribute a Doctrine of Creation to Aristotle?" *The New Scholasticism* 63 (1989): 129–55.

The Politics of Revelation

offices and depots that will make the regime run, and shape his people for their flourishing (II.2.100).

The scope of this parallel between God and king has a clear limit, Aquinas writes: "Of course the founder of a city and kingdom cannot produce anew men, places of habitation and other necessities of life, but inevitably must use those things which pre-exist in nature" (II.2.100). Thus, the king is a kind of craftsman. Rather than creating *ex nihilo*, he identifies and selects the necessary elements of the city that "pre-exist in nature" through God's gift, and then orders them appropriately.

Aquinas's treatment of Moses in this section is telling. While many works before and after *De Regno* praise Moses as an exemplar of legislators, on par with Lycurgus, Theseus, and Romulus, Aquinas invokes Moses less as a legislator than as a witness to divine legislation: "But Moses has minutely and carefully expressed this plan [*rationem*] of creation" (II.2.99). What makes Moses praiseworthy is not his activity as such but rather its character as an imitation of God's activity in the world. By contrast, in *The Prince*, Machiavelli treats Moses as little less than a god. While calling Moses "a mere executor of things that had been ordered for him by God" (*The Prince* VI.22), Machiavelli praises Moses for distinctly earthly virtues: he uses arms well, unlike the unarmed Savonarola (VI.24). Machiavelli portrays Moses as a human liberator, for which the servitude of Israel was no tragedy but a great pretext to assert his will over them. Moses shapes his people, moreover, through a law of God that Machiavelli hints was invented by Moses for his own purposes. What Moses is not, however, is a virtuous leader who gives his people God's law. In the framework of *De Regno* II.2, Machiavelli casts Moses as a kind of creator. Through that "creation," Moses comes to a position of great power, almost omnipotent as far as the beleaguered Hebrews are concerned. For Aquinas, however, Moses is firmly a governor leading God's people to God's ends. What makes him a formidable legislator is that he strives to be a *minister Dei*. Thus, Moses in *De Regno* is presented as a prophet, one who can discern the pattern of God's wisdom in the world.[12]

To be sure, Aquinas argues at II.2.98 that even kings who do not establish kingdoms must nonetheless envision this act of founding as they govern, for to govern properly entails knowing the end for which something was founded. But the true foundation of being itself, not just the shaping of this or that bit of being, came to pass because of God's creation. Thus, even those kings who "found" kingdoms in the conventional sense must envision themselves as governors, not as founders, to the extent that they take their bearings from God's founding action. Again, Aquinas invokes teleology for practical purposes: political prudence must be understood as the virtue that supplies means to God-appointed ends, not as a cunning that invents ends for political power.

This chapter sets up a distinction between creation and governance, perhaps an abstract theme for a *speculum principum*. Yet the theme was not unknown to medieval political thought, influenced as it was by the *Timaeus* and its account of nature as an "entire ordered complex ... of secondary causes."[13] Moreover, Aquinas puts the distinction to a critical purpose: to clarify how human rule does and does not mirror that of God.[14] Founders of kingdoms are, indeed, the preeminent kings, but what they do is best done as an imitation of God, an imitation undertaken in the recognition that the human foundation of a kingdom must always

---

12. Cf. *ST* I-II.105.
13. Oakley, *The Mortgage of the Past*, 79.
14. Quentin Lauer, review of Max Seckler, *Das Heil in der Geschichte*, *Theological Studies* 26, no. 2 (1965): 317.

be derivative of God's foundation of the world. We learned in I.8, after all, that kings must govern their kingdoms in conformity with the human person's final end: beatitude. It would stand to reason, then, that such kingdoms were founded for that purpose, and that the very being constitutive of such kingdoms was created by God. In invoking these seemingly abstract categories, then, Aquinas has connected man's origins with his end.

This humble and God-fearing legislator could not form a sharper contrast with the tyrant of I.3–6. The tyrant, far from taking God as his exemplar, arrogates to himself the power of life and death over his subjects and remakes the political order to achieve such power. And he might even seem radically distinct from Machiavelli's founder, for the tyrant ruins and perverts rather than creates and orders. Yet when we consider the cult of founders, for example, Romulus, Theseus, or Ninus, it can seem that they founded their cities for the purpose of achieving honor and fame throughout the ages. This is certainly the strong suggestion of Machiavelli: that they build lasting cities whose prosperity redounds to the benefit of each citizen is a happy consequence. But if in some sense the founder secures the peace and prosperity of his people instrumentally, that is, only or primarily as it serves his glory, we can wonder what circumstances lead such founders to seek glory and honor in a way that benefits others, and what would lead them to trespass on the goods of others if it would bring them similar glory. What finally separates a tyrant from a founder?

If these concerns seem distant from modern politics, we would do well to remember the pervasive influence of social contract theories in our time. According to those accounts, humans must create out of nothing the social contract to remedy the deficiencies of the state of nature, not to perfect men's God-given virtues. Even Rousseau, who envisions a rich prepolitical human community, says of his law-giver in the *Social Contract* that he must create an artificial society in which coercive power can shape humans into something new, often despite of their nature.[15] Whether this stunning hubris will give rise to a founder or to a tyrant is an open question, but the account of *De Regno* argues that man does not create, and so he must govern in that humility. Society and its authority are natural, and the human person is made to live for and with others, not in spite of others, for with others he can become a most noble animal. The world is something given to man, and so his knowledge of it requires receptivity, not mastery.

In taking the measure of II.1–2, it is possible to see it as a recapitulation of I.1–2: both sections confirm that the human person is political and that his political rule mirrors patterns of government found in nature. But if I.1–2 proceeds according to some species of political naturalism, then II.1–2 proceeds according to the Christian doctrine of creation. Thus, the political naturalism of I.1–2 receives a divine seal from creation, much as political activity itself receives its reward from the divine: the king of I.1–2 must rule justly, and II.1–2 specifies that part of that justice means ruling not as God. He is a *minister Dei*, not *Deus*.

The doctrine of creation takes us beyond the scope of the medieval debate between partisans of Aristotle and Augustine, even granting that parts of II.1–2 comport with the thought of both thinkers. But this should not be surprising: as a Christian theologian, Aquinas's interests finally concern the truth about God, not human wisdom. Further, insofar as *De Regno* is a *speculum* and a pedagogical work meant as a gift from a theologian to a Christian

---

15. *Social Contract* II.7.3, in Jean-Jacques Rousseau, *"The Social Contract" and Other Later Political Writings*, Cambridge Texts in the History of Political Thought, ed. and trans. Victor Gourevitch (Cambridge: Cambridge University Press, 1997). On Machiavelli, see Harvey Mansfield, *Machiavelli's New Modes and Orders: A Study of the "Discourses on Livy"* (Chicago: University of Chicago Press, 1996), 62–66.

The Politics of Revelation

prince, to recall the language of the *prooemium*, perhaps Aquinas means for the education of this prince to be guided ultimately by Christian principles, not by disputes between the schools. Thus far, the greatest fruit of that approach is to have situated the king within salvation history as *minister Dei*.

The Politics of Revelation: II.3

II.2 lays out a distinction between creation and governance to explain how the king can serve as *minister Dei*. In II.3, Aquinas investigates the nature of that governance further. As he has told us that governance more properly relates to the royal office than does creation, we can expect this chapter to have more to say about the duties of kingship than did II.2.

Aquinas begins to address this question by stating that "It must first be considered [*praeconsiderandum*], however, that to govern is to lead [*perducere*] that which is governed fittingly to its proper end [*debitum finem*]" (II.3.103). Dondaine and Eschmann wonder if this "preconsideration" diverts Aquinas from his stated purpose in II.3: uncovering how the earthly city should be governed on the basis of the divine governance of the world.[16] As we will see, however, this preface to II.3 sets up a powerful distinction in II.3 that clarifies the task of politics, which Aquinas lays out more fully in II.4 and II.5–8.

Aquinas explains that there are two kinds of ends: an end beyond the thing governed, and one whose end is in itself. An ocean-going ship, for instance, has an end beyond itself, namely the port. Yet the ship also has an internal end: to be a ship. Among those things that must be directed to an external good, they must in some cases be ruled by two or more governors: one charged with

---

16. Dondaine, *De regno ad Regem Cypri*, préface, 423–24; Eschmann, *On Kingship*, introduction, xix.

the internal end of preserving it, and another with the office of conducting them to their extrinsic end. For instance, one might think of a carpenter as tasked with maintaining the being of the ship, and the pilot with conducting the ship to the port. This is the case with man:

> But there is a certain good extrinsic to man so long as he lives mortally, namely final beatitude [*ultima beatitudo*], which is looked for in the enjoyment of God after death... Therefore the Christian man, for whom that beatitude was purchased through the blood of Christ, and who has received the pledge [*arrham*] of the Holy Spirit in order to attain it, needs another, spiritual care through which he is directed to the port of eternal salvation. This care is held forth to the faithful by the ministers of the Church of Christ (II.3.105).

Aquinas packs a great many lessons into this short text. The human person has an end beyond himself: final or ultimate beatitude, which is to say, perfect happiness. Thus, the "aforesaid cares," referring to those of the leader of a regime, are not sufficient to lead man to that end. His attainment to that end requires the direction of the church. It is, moreover, a church guided by the supernatural both in its activity and in the very revelation of this truth. Thus, man would seem to have two masters: an earthly ruler and a spiritual one. Aquinas does not, however, move on to say that men in society act for external good X, and so should be governed by some power with care for their direction toward it. Rather, he pushes the question of what internal end men seek in society. Aquinas has already called the end of politics *unitas pacis* (I.2.17), but now he further specifies that the life of virtue is good for humans and an intrinsic end of society: "Therefore, virtuous life [*virtuosa vita*] is the end of human society [*finis humanae congregationis*]" (II.3.106).[17]

---

17. Dondaine here cites Aristotle, *Politics* VII.

This section seems to recapitulate I.1–2, but urges a more robust Aristotelianism than I.1–2, which we noted seemed more Ciceronian than Aristotelian. That man must live in society to attain to his virtue is an essential aspect of the teaching that man is a political animal. Aquinas thus speaks of the good life as *secundum virtutem*, according to virtue. Here he seems to have in mind no particular virtue, only general human excellence. While Aquinas argues at I.1 that the city arises to remedy human deficiencies in securing survival, he clarifies here that such remedy is not the only reason for the city. We note also that this section contains Aquinas's first reference to human law in *De Regno*. It might seem a minor reference, but Aquinas notably mentions it with regard to the virtue of citizens. Like political community itself, law arises from necessity but also seeks to instruct the citizens in living well, and thus is only as good as a regime's knowledge of and service to the human end of virtuous living.

Aquinas's sense of man as a political animal is so robust that it requires little explanation for him that society is also ordered to man's supernatural end: "It is therefore not the ultimate end [*ultimus finis*] of an assembled multitude to live according to virtue, but through the virtuous life to arrive at divine enjoyment [*fruitionem divinam*]" (II.3.107). Man, like the ship sailing to port, seeks not only an end internal to himself but also one external to himself, namely beatitude. Society is similarly ordered to this end.

We might pause here for two questions. First, why is it only in II.3 that Aquinas state that politics seeks virtue? Second, what is the relationship between the person's internal and external ends: virtue and beatitude? As for the first question, we can give two possibilities: one historical and one pedagogical. It is historically possible that Aquinas had spent more time with the text of Aristotle by the composition of II.3, and that he was less under the sway of Cicero than he was when he wrote I.1–2. On that account, he has in II.3 the need to state plainly Aristotle's teaching that living virtuously is the end of politics, whereas when he wrote I.1–2, he still hewed to Cicero's less ambitious teaching. This explanation would not explain, however, why Aquinas did not have I.1–2 corrected after his self-correction in II.3. It also assumes that a considerable time elapsed between the composition of book I and book II, which is a difficult assumption given our knowledge of Aquinas's work habits and his prodigious output.[18]

Pedagogically, it is possible that Aquinas wishes to underline the supernatural reward of politics before he articulates its full temporal goal. This would complement two other strategies of Aquinas in *De Regno*: to emphasize the supernatural reward of the natural activity of politics, and to diminish the natural reward of politics. Further, we might note that this Aristotelian naturalism comes after the creation-based account of II.1–2. Perhaps Aquinas wishes to draw the king's attention not only to the divine reward of politics but also the divine origins of the natural excellence of politics.

The pedagogy of such a strategy is simple. Given that Aquinas writes for a Christian king, perhaps he offers beatitude as a surer or more concrete teaching for the king than political naturalism. Political naturalism is, after all, a theoretically sophisticated teaching, and its practical implications are not always obvious. On the other hand, beatitude, while a teaching of tremendous importance, is rather simple: God loves man and wishes for man to be with him for eternity. Beatitude, then, is perhaps a more effective way to secure adherence to virtue in politics, a greater and clearer reward. The pursuit of beatitude would also, at least on Aquinas's terms, conduce to the pursuit of the natural end of politics, virtue.

---

18. Torrell, *Saint Thomas Aquinas*, 183.

Readers of *De Regno* who find such pedagogical sophistication far-fetched might recall that *De Regno* is a *speculum principum*. Aquinas displayed throughout his works a nuanced grasp of all the genres in which he worked. Further, this strategy speaks directly to Aquinas's explanation of the role of revelation in the *Summa Theologica:*

> Even as regards those truths about God which human reason could have discovered, it was necessary that man should be taught by a divine revelation; because the truth about God such as reason could discover, would only be known by a few, and that after a long time, and with the admixture of many errors (*ST* I.1.1 *respondeo*).

On the account of the *Summa*, Aquinas would be using revelation in *De Regno* to point out what should be known by nature, namely that man's reward is had from natural activity: man is naturally political, and his virtue is an intrinsic reward of that political activity, rightly exercised. By extension, Aquinas's procedure here might be useful in regimes in which human final ends of man are not known or are contested. I return to that theme in chapter 5.

Curiously, in book I, Aquinas emphasizes the material losses of tyranny (I.10) before detailing its spiritual loss of beatitude (I.11). Perhaps Aquinas inverts the order of spiritual and material here because he is writing for the king rather than for a tyrant. Indeed, we saw the description of tyranny at I.3–6 was written less as a warning to tyrants to reform their ways than as an encouragement to the would-be tyrant, the king, to take his task seriously. Perhaps, then, Aquinas first discusses the material losses of the tyrant because they correspond to the difficulties of politics that chasten the king's expectations for politics. Those difficulties are then sealed with divine punishment of the tyrant.

So much for our first question. As for our second: what is the relationship between this virtue and beatitude, and, moreover, between the authorities that secure each of them? Here Aquinas could say more. If we turn to the *Summa Theologica*, for instance, it is clear that the theological virtues, those God-given virtues that dispose one toward God, perfect the natural virtues. Thus, Aquinas goes beyond the classical account of virtues as simply natural. Yet for Aquinas, the natural virtues really are virtues, *pace* Augustine, even though they be defective without charity.[19] Similarly, while Aquinas argues that man has one final end, the ordering of man's intermediate ends to his final one gives those intermediary ends a new integrity (*ST* I-II.1).

We should not be surprised that in *De Regno* Aquinas's argument lacks the precision and specificity of a treatise, and for that reason it is difficult to compare it to the *Summa Theologica*. But note that *De Regno* contains a similar dynamic to the argument of the *Summa*: beatitude represents the fullness of human fulfillment, but the human person's natural end is far from inconsequential. Given the structure of *De Regno*, Aquinas seems to urge the king that politics should be consonant with the desire for beatitude. The immediate goal of politics, however, is not beatitude but virtue. It seems from II.3.107, moreover, that virtue is not an end merely instrumental to the final end of beatitude: man attaining to the virtue of man, after all, fulfills what it means to be man, much as the ship must be a ship. This was the point of I.1-2 and II.1-2. But virtue does somehow conduce to the attainment of beatitude, for "through living according to virtue" the person is "ordered" to beatitude. Aquinas seems to be suggesting that somehow the life of virtue pursued in politics is complementary to the external good of beatitude.

But what about the authority that secures virtue and beati-

---

19. *ST* II-II.23.6-8. See Robert Sokolowski, *The God of Faith and Reason* (Washington, D.C.: The Catholic University, 1982), 31-40, 69-87.

tude? This is another way of inquiring further into the task of the *minister Dei*. Does the king as minister of God also govern humans to beatitude? Aquinas takes up this question next. He explains that the king would govern his subjects toward beatitude "if this end could be attained by virtue of human nature," but, in fact, it cannot (II.3.108). For the loftier the end of government, the loftier that government is. And when one government serves a final end, then other governments that serve ends conducing toward that final end are subordinated to that final government. Note that Aquinas does not argue here that any government higher than another directs that lower one in all things: rather he argues the more restricted proposition that the higher one "commands those who execute the things that are ordained to that end." The government that tends to man's final end, however, is not that of the king but of the God-man king, Christ:

> Therefore the ministry of this kingdom, that spiritual things might be distinguished from earthly things, was committed not to earthly kings, but to priests, and especially to the chief priest, the successor of Peter, the vicar of Christ, the Roman pontiff, to whom all kings of the Christian people are to be as subject [*esse subiectos*] as to Lord Jesus Christ Himself.[20] Therefore to him to whom pertains the care of the ultimate end [*finis ultimi*] should be subject those to whom pertains the care of antecedent ends [*antecedentium finium*], and be directed by his command [*imperio*] (II.3.110).

This passage emphasizes the need to avoid confusing "the spiritual and the earthly." This distinction is necessary because they correspond to different human ends. The earthly king cannot fulfill man's final end of beatitude, because grace is required to do so. Thus, the church has been given the grace to govern man toward

---

20. Dondaine offers *subditos* as a variant of *subiectos* in some manuscripts (Dondaine, *De regno ad Regem Cypri*, préface, 466).

beatitude. For that reason, kings do not govern this spiritual kingdom; rather, priests are entrusted with this mission, and all kings are subject to the head priest, the pope.

The king is not only set below the pope but among "all kings of the Christian people." The *populus Christianus*, Eschmann notes, is a powerful concept for Aquinas, and one to which he adverts in several other writings. This *populus* is that over whom the pope rules. For this reason, antipapist writers like John of Paris will criticize, if only implicitly, Aquinas's treatment of that *populus Christianus*.[21]

But Aquinas has no use for such ideas here. To style the subjects of a king as "Christian" is to remind the king of his essentially Christian rule, but it also relativizes his service: there are many kings of the Christian people, but only one Christian people and only one Christian pope. The source of unity of that people is the pope rather than their kings. Indeed, Aquinas notably makes no mention of the empire here, which by Aquinas's time had long been seen as a source of unity for Christendom and was championed by later theorists like Dante and Marsilius as just such a source of unity.

Further, the king is not only one king among many, but he is also not the governor of his subjects toward their heavenly end. Indeed, Aquinas has seen fit in *De Regno* to leave indeterminate the exact relations between the virtue secured by politics and beatitude. Aquinas has thus denied to the king any pretensions to sacral monarchy. Indeed, this distinction between the king and the priesthood is a disanalogy between the king and God: the king

---

21. Eschmann notes the *Summa Contra Gentiles* IV.76 and the famous passage from the *Scriptum Super Libros Sententiarum* II.44 (Eschmann, *On Kingship*, introduction, 62, fn 15). See also Manent, *An Intellectual History of Liberalism*, 3–9, and Étienne Gilson, *Dante the Philosopher*, trans. David Moore (London: Sheed & Ward, 1952), 171–91.

imitates God only in the natural order, not in the supernatural order.

Given that the ministry of man's spiritual end is secured by the priesthood rather than by the ruler, perhaps the question of the best regime is less urgent. Here we return to Kraynak's thesis: while the sweep of Christian political thought recognizes monarchy as the best regime, other regime forms are legitimate, as well.[22] Presumably, other regime forms could also serve alongside the Christian priesthood, each governing in their respective spheres. Perhaps this explains, at least in part, why Aquinas does not enter into great detail as to the relationship between natural virtue and beatitude: he does not wish to specify the relationship between monarchy's provision for virtue in such a way that the king believes monarchy to be the only regime compatible with the church and the quest for beatitude. Indeed, Kraynak rightly claims that regimes need the legitimacy of the church more than the church need legitimacy from regimes. Certainly, as a child of vassals of the Hohenstaufens, Aquinas had seen princes seek to claim the support of the church. Thus, Aquinas might not have wished for monarchy to be too closely identified with the pursuit of beatitude.

The most curious aspect of this section, however, is Aquinas's procedure. He does not start by asking why the temporal and spiritual powers are separate and distinct, nor does he begin by asking which power is superior. He does not begin, in other words, with the "church and state" question, or the "papacy and empire" question, or the "Regnum and Sacerdotium" question.[23] Nor, to

---

22. Kraynak, *Christian Faith and Modern Democracy,* xiii.
23. I owe much in the following discussion of II.3.111–113 to Gilson, *Dante the Philosopher,* 209–216. Gilson points to the necessity of a comparative study of *De Regno* and the *De Monarchia* of Dante.

belabor the point, does he engage in a polemical attempt to justify some current state of affairs.[24] Aquinas begins, rather, by inquiring into human ends. The powers subsequently arise out of those ends, an inquiry that Aquinas began at I.1. We can see, then, how the entirety of *De Regno* has been building to this moment. And the superiority of one power over another is not based on that power as such but on the end that it serves. In fact, for most of *De Regno*, Aquinas has spoken of only one end of man and has argued that ends matter to politics. This was his sleight of hand at I.7, when he showed that what one would want to get from politics, even what the tyrant would want, would be incomplete without considering what fulfills man's end. He has, in turn, said little more about its governance other than that it belongs to the king to direct man to his end. And this would be all that need be said "if man were not ordered to another, external good" (II.3.105). He thus avoids the tired polemics over institutional jurisdictions between church and state that dominated the medieval and early modern period in the works of Dante, Marsilius of Padua, Aegidius Romanus, and even Hobbes, Locke, and Rousseau.

Nevertheless, what practical arrangement does this doctrine on human ends prescribe for a regime? Aquinas opened II.3, after all, with a promise to discuss how a king ought to govern. Will he disappoint us yet again, as he seemed to at I.6 and II.1?[25] Perhaps not, as Aquinas next turns to the character of this priesthood.

Aquinas speaks first of the "priesthood of the gentiles" (II.3.111). That priesthood and "the entire cult of [their] divinities" served nothing more than acquiring temporal goods, all of which were ordered to the common good. Thus, that priesthood and cult were governed by kings. This discussion calls to mind Aquinas's

24. Gilson, *Dante the Philosopher*, 172.
25. Eschmann, *On Kingship*, introduction, xix.

discussion at I.9.72, in which he notes that ancient peoples often saw something godly or divine in their kings and singles out the Roman emperors' appellation *Divus*. Aquinas's point there was to illustrate the testaments even in pagan societies to the likeness between king and God that he wants to advance within a Christian teaching. Now if we take Aquinas's further suggestion here that many ancient kings had cultic duties and were in some sense at the head of the priests, then we can see all the more why a king would seem god-like to his people. After all, these cults were chiefly dedicated to the temporal advancement of the kingdom. The head of the cult, therefore, would naturally be that society's prince.

Besides ancient peoples praying in earnest for fair weather, good crops, and peace, we know that many such cults evolved into "civil theologies" whose purpose increasingly became to grant legitimacy to rulers and laws, to bind the people to the land and their ruler by a set of mythic norms that some rulers were at times rather cynical about propagating. Rousseau argues in the *Social Contract*, for example, that lawgivers attribute laws to divine origins so that what the people lack in rational apprehension of his wise dictates, which in any event may not be so wise, they may gain in awe and respect for their authority (*Social Contract*, II.7.9–12). Thus, "at the origin of nations the one [religion] serves as the instrument of the other [politics]," (II.7.12). Whatever their sincerity, Aquinas here recognizes that such cults were instituted for natural human needs and to satisfy the most pressing concerns of life and death. They are also ergo fittingly directed by the leader of man's community.

Aquinas then turns to the "*lex vetera*," or Old Law. This was the law that God gave to the ancient Hebrews, especially to form their community in Palestine (*ST* I-II.98–105). The priests of the Old Law were also subject to the Hebrew rulers, whether judges or kings. The Old Law, after all, promised to secure the peace and prosperity of the Hebrews. It promised to educate them, in other words, in "earthly goods." This was a salutary provision, and, indeed, divine instruction. But with this law, the community was directed to goods they could attain by their own reason, even if God's word was helpful to pointing out what they needed and specific contingent formations of their society (*ST* I-II.114.10.1). Thus, in this respect, the regime of Moses was, indeed, earthly.

As went the Old Law, though, so went its customary modes of governance. For "in the New Law there is a higher priesthood by which men are carried [*traducunter*] to celestial goods" (II.3.111). Aquinas's language here is telling: he uses not the active verb *duco, ducere* to speak of man's direction or governance but rather *traduco* in the passive voice to underline that in heavenly matters, humans do not govern but are governed. Indeed, the priests mediate grace so that man can do what he could not do by his own natural faculties, namely, attain to beatitude. The primary element of this dynamic, then, is that man is given this grace and is rendered capable of acting on it, not that he accepts this grace and acts on it. Instead of the priests serving the earthly needs of the city, these priests grant human access to an end beyond the earthly one. Thus, "in the law of Christ, kings must be subject to priests." The king retains a special office in ordering the earthly to this heavenly end, but he must take direction from those with care for man's final end. The great shift in this priesthood, then, is not one of subordination to superiority but of the human person to God. The shift thus represents a change but not an inconsistency between Christian and pre-Christian modes of politics.

This section of II.3 contains three themes worth bringing out: its historical character; Christianity as its *telos* of that history; and the abuse of Christianity as *telos*.

As Gilson notes, at play in this section is the principle of coordinating ends and authorities: "to him to whom pertains the care of the ultimate end should be subject those to whom pertains the care of antecedent ends," but as Gilson might have made clearer, Aquinas illuminates this principle through a historical progression. Aquinas's understanding and use of history cannot be settled here, but we know that if he lacked a theory of history, he nevertheless at times thought historically. Moreover, while he did not regard history as a *scientia*, he argued that historical data could be taken up by a *scientia*, including by theology. Most notably, Aquinas takes up historical data in his discussion of the New and Old divine laws in the *Summa Theologica* (*ST* I-II.98–108).

In II.3, Aquinas uses history to develop the unfolding of Gilson's principle. To be more precise, the pagan, Hebrew, and Christian cases are not just isolated or arbitrarily chosen case studies but reflect a development toward full clarity about that principle. Aquinas clearly argues for Christianity as the *telos* of that history: it is not an open-ended, ever-evolving history. He does not, however, argue for how Christianity is the fullness of this history, but perhaps as a Christian theologian writing for a Christian king, he did not think that necessary.

Operative in his historical account, however, is something like the Gelasian tradition of dualism. As the work of John Courtney Murray and Gilson make clear, the Christian tradition of dualism makes two distinct but related points: the distinction of powers and the primacy of the spiritual. While the distinction of human ends has an Aristotelian ring to it, the primacy of the spiritual depends on the Christian answer to the question: what is the person's final end?[26] Christianity's unique answer to this

26. Gilson, *Dante the Philosopher*, 192–93.

question leads to a unique political arrangement: "That is why, in Christianity, and in Christianity alone, princes are subject to the priesthood in that the Pope, *qua* Pope, has supreme authority over princes *qua* princes."[27] Gilson argues that "nothing could be more lucid" in making this point than this section of *De Regno* II.3.

Murray argues that Gelasian dualism is a delicate and rare achievement, and Aquinas's history in *De Regno* helps to explain why. Civil religion has existed for millennia and has effected salutary arrangements in other times. Civil religion, in fact, was at the core of many "founding myths" against which Aquinas argued in II.2. The Christian effort to place religion above politics, much like the subsequent liberal effort to politically neutralize religion, is a novel approach to public religion that has never been completely successful: civil religion is an enduring feature of human community.[28] Even by 2017, more than 80 countries had established or provided for religion at some constitutional level.[29] What Aquinas proposes, however, is the sweeping away of these ancient and pervasive orders: distinguishing clearly these two activities by identifying and ordering the two human ends, and, in turn, identifying and ordering the two governments that lead man to those ends based on the hierarchy of their respective ends.

But in acknowledging that such civil religions exist in many times and places, and have existed to such benefit, Aquinas seems to admit that the Christian innovation is novel and historically rare, and that the civil religions Christianity aims to sweep away are

---

27. Gilson, *Dante the Philosopher*, 209.

28. See Ronald Beiner, "Machiavelli, Hobbes, and Rousseau on Civil Religion," *Review of Politics* 55, no. 4 (1993): 617–638, and Ronald Beiner, *Civil Religion: A Dialogue in the History of Political Philosophy* (Cambridge: Cambridge University Press, 2011).

29. "Many countries favor specific religions, officially or unofficially," Pew Research Center, http://www.pewforum.org/2017/10/03/many-countries-favor-specific-religions-officially-or-unofficially/.

quite common. For that reason, perhaps they are likely to endure after the arrival of Christianity. Perhaps Christian regimes themselves will be apt to lapse back into pre-Christian civil religions.

Indeed, in his history of civil religion, Aquinas assumes that religion and politics are discretely separate activities governed by distinct authorities for distinct ends. But he himself acknowledges that in pre-Christian dispensations, political and religious activities served temporal ends. There is thus some risk of anachronism in Aquinas's account: religious and political activities are conceptually distinct in the light of the Christian distinction between them, but it is not obvious that all pre-Christian civilizations would have seen them as such, particularly given, as Aquinas himself avers, that politics and religion served the same temporal ends in such societies. For if Christianity alone directs religious activity to a supernatural end, then the dualism of *De Regno* depends on Christian revelation.

From a purely earthly point of view, then, we might add another reason as to why this new priesthood of Christianity ought to be separate from the political order: the New Law will not be accepted in all places and all times, and in some cases, political power will have a vested interest in maintaining older forms of religion that serve under Caesar, or in retooling Christianity as a civil religion, one serving no more than the temporal benefit of the political authority. Aquinas's fear has been born out, of course, with Christian civil religions ranging from a conservative "Crown and Altar" or divine-right-of-kings vision, as with de Maistre, to a liberal one in which a simplified church or religion legitimizes certain visions of a tolerant and egalitarian society, as with Spinoza. Christianity has been a source of civil religion in the United States, as well, from the classical liberal creed to liberal Protestant progressivism and conservative evangelicalism.

The reception of this New Law, then, is critical to the political success of Christian dualism. It is through this revealed teaching that man is shown to have two ends and, moreover, that man's final end lies beyond politics. As we saw at I.8, one might be able to sense through unaided reason that no reward on earth is adequate to man's highest faculties, but Christianity alone, Aquinas says, has true knowledge of the end that is so adequate. It is, furthermore, through this law that the governor toward this end is revealed: the church. We might not know the precise arrangement of the king and the church, but we do know the necessity of such an ordering. In other words, the king needs to know that his rule does not extend to the spiritual. The king must know rather that the church supplies the government, and that somehow their diverse ends must be reconciled. These teachings can only be had from the revealed teaching of Christianity.

As sharply as Aquinas distinguishes between Christian and pre-Christian theological-political orders, however, he closes II.3 with two historical examples that emphasize the commonalities between the pagan and Christian. Aquinas's two examples are fraught cases: Rome and France. Ending II.3.111 with, "Consequently, in the law of Christ, kings must be subject to priests," Aquinas continues:

> Because of this, Divine Providence wonderfully provided that in the city of Rome, which God had foreseen would be the principal seat of the Christian people, the custom [*mos*] was gradually established that the rulers of the city should be subject to the priests. For as Valerius Maximus relates: "Our city always placed religion before everything else, even those things in which it aimed for the splendour of the highest majesty to be seen. For this reason the imperial did not hesitate to serve the sacred [*non dubitaverunt sacris imperia servire*], considering that they would thus hold the rule of human affairs if faithfully and constantly they attended to the divine power (II.3.112).

France, the Elder Daughter of the church, figures as the second example. It is again the condition of the country prior to Christianity that interests Aquinas: "Since, however, it was to be that the religion of the Christian priesthood should especially thrive [vigeret] in Gaul, God permitted that among the Gauls the gentile priests, whom they called Druids, should prescribe the law of all Gaul (II.3.113)." As we see, both examples are pagan: imperial Rome and Celtic France. Why does Aquinas present these pre-Christian examples? The chief reason seems to be to underline the natural virtue of religion: both examples show that these deeply Christian places had a sense of the importance of religion long before the advent of Christianity. With Rome, this awareness of the preeminence of religion was strong enough to arise even in a city for which religion was tightly fused with politics.[30] The primacy of the pope in Rome, then, represents a development from pagan Rome, not an innovation. France's ancient precursors, the Gauls, saw the wisdom in a priestly solicitude for their laws. The claim is relatively modest, then: not that gentile priests were theologian-kings or undisputed in temporal authority, or even that such ancient societies clearly distinguished between temporal and spiritual matters. Yet, however inchoately, the relation of priest to ruler in Celtic Gaul foreshadows the Christian teaching on the superiority of the spiritual to the temporal, a claim made on the basis of wisdom rather than power.[31]

Aquinas presents these pre-Christian examples of religion not only to underline the natural virtue of religion but also to underline it precisely as natural. As Kries explains, for Aquinas, the "distinction between politics and religion is not coterminous with

30. Cf. Machiavelli, *Discourses* I.11–15, 19.
31. See Jan Assman, *The Price of Monotheism*, trans. Robert Savage (Stanford, Calif.: Stanford University Press, 2009), 31–56.

the distinction between nature and grace."[32] It is not the case for Aquinas, as it is for Dante or John of Paris, that religion and politics can be divided neatly between humans and nature. Politics and religion, rather, are both natural to man. Even if the revealed religion of Christ is supernatural, the virtue of giving to God due as man's end is, in fact, natural, as Aquinas argues in the *Summa Theologica* at great length, for example, *ST* II-II.81–100. Aquinas quotes the definition of religion offered by Cicero, Kries observes, in full and with no qualifications: "offering service and ceremonial rites to a superior nature that men call divine."[33]

With these examples in *De Regno*, Aquinas clearly means to signal a similar teaching. Were the king willing to accept the force of these examples, then he would see that Christianity, although it offers something new, offers something that nonetheless corresponds to human nature and has been acknowledged by most pre-Christian regimes. This would make it difficult for the king to argue that politics precedes religion and so religion has no claim to it, or that Christianity invents new obligations for man with the purpose of manipulating politics. In other words, the king would know that politics even on natural terms cannot turn away from its obligations to religion.

This strategy of presenting religion as fundamentally natural contextualizes the king's service as *minister Dei* within human history. "Natural reason tells man that he is subject to a higher being," Aquinas argues in the *Summa*, "and whatever this superior being may be, it is known to all under the name of God."[34] So the king's Christian role as *minister Dei* has been preceded by millennia of kings serving natural religion. It would also be a gloss

---

32. Kries, "The Virtue of Religion," 104.
33. Kries, "The Virtue of Religion," 105.
34. Kries, "The Virtue of Religion," 105.

on II.2, in which the king learned to imitate the God by governing according to God-created ends, not by creating his own ends.

When Aquinas chooses to discuss pagan rather than Christian Rome and France, he could mean to avoid polemical controversies about which the king might already have hardened opinions. This could well be the case for the Roman example, and particularly à propos controversies surrounding the pope's temporal power. One intervention in those polemics comes from John of Paris, or Quidort, who is sometimes said to be the first Thomist.[35] Most relevantly to *De Regno*, it does not occur to Quidort that even in pre-Christian cultures, the problem of how the spiritual relates to the temporal was also an important aspect of political arrangements, as Aquinas has pointed out.

As for the king's native France, Aquinas's procedure perhaps has the effect of directing the king's attention to polemical controversy indirectly. In the time of Aquinas and our royal reader, France was a hotbed of anti-Roman sentiment. As the Holy Roman emperors became increasingly weaker, the French kings took up the mantle of temporal power, claiming the right to appoint and control bishops of French dioceses, farm revenues from church properties, and had little truck for papal objections. In other words, the French came close to founding a Christian civil religion. Yet here, Aquinas assures the king that the French have long understood the importance of religion and the deference owed it by political rulers, thus giving the king a new way to think

---

35. Quidort joined in the defense of Aquinas during the heated debates shortly after Aquinas's death, but it is doubtful that his own work conforms to that of Aquinas. See Marc F. Griesbach, "John of Paris as a Representative of Thomistic Political Philosophy," in *An Etienne Gilson Tribute: Presented By His North American Students With a Response by Étienne Gilson*, ed. Charles J. O'Neil (Milwaukee, Minn.: Marquette University Press, 1959), 33–55. McCoy links Quidort to Marsilius of Padua and his *Defensor Pacis*. See Charles N. R. McCoy, *The Structure of Political Thought: A Study in the History of Political Ideas* (New York: McGraw-Hill Book Company, 1963), 123–26.

about that controversy. We can thus wonder about the effect this teaching would have had on the Cypriot king, coming as he did from a baronial family in western France with close ties to the Capets.

In short, this has been a rich chapter. In many times and places, humans have recognized some correspondence between themselves and what is beyond the merely terrestrial or temporal. This correspondence has some significance for their communal life, as well. Their search to understand this correspondence, therefore, has not been a private activity or individual hobby, but a public activity of the community itself. Philosophy can give flesh to this intuition, as Aquinas showed at I.8. Further, Christianity reveals this natural desire to seek our end as fulfilled in God. What is new with Christianity, then, is not just an identification of man's spiritual end but a government by which to govern humans toward it. A distinct spiritual government, the church, conducts man to a distinct end, beatitude.

This chapter has thus provided an elaboration on the significance of the *minister Dei* concept for the king's governance. Book II, we saw, finally turns to the practical considerations of a king's reign. II.1 distinguishes between God's creation and governance of the world for models of royal governance, and II.2 sets out how the former aides the king in his task. II.3 naturally follows with a promise to set forth how our king may learn to govern by studying the divine government of the world. We are then led to a consideration of the distinct human ends, and the distinct powers that govern humans toward those ends. II.3, then, consists not in teaching the king how to govern from a consideration of God's governance of the world but rather in distinguishing the ends of temporal and spiritual government: a lesson in Gelasian dualism, in other words.

For our king, then, II.3 offers not just a history lesson but a pedagogy: an explanation of how a regime can move toward a truly Christian structure of politics. The king must ask himself whether his regime, however putatively Christian, does, in fact, embrace a pagan understanding of politics, one in which religion is subordinated to temporal ends. Will the king mirror God's rule by instantiating such virtues, laws, and practices such that he draws his people to their God-given ends? And will he dispose them to accept not only the natural obligations of religion but even the supernatural ones?[36]

II.3 also confirms Aquinas's political naturalism, arguing as he does that the end of politics is to live according to virtue, and that the authority governing politics has a certain distinction from that governing spiritual things. Indeed, as II.1–2 proceeds according to the Christian doctrine of creation, so II.3 extends that reflection through the doctrine of redemption. As II.1–2 specifies that humans can govern with God by participating in his governance of creation toward its divine-appointed ends, and by accepting their own place within that creation as creaturely, so II.3 specifies that man's final divine-appointed end is beyond his governance. He thus must accept his role as distinct from and inferior to the church. At play, then is a dynamic between the ways in which Christianity hallows and elevates political activity, and yet also in the same movement reduces the city of man to below the City of God.

Finally, we cannot fail to note again that *De Regno* II.3 contains one of the most trenchant rejections of civil religion within Christianity, on par with that of Augustine and Erik Peterson.[37] With that rejection, Aquinas has argued not only that political

36. Lauer, review of Max Seckler, 317.
37. See Erik Peterson, *Theological Tractates,* trans. Michael Hollerich (Stanford, Calif.: Stanford University Press, 2012).

authority governs rather than creates but that it governs politics, not religion. That rejection also offers a fascinating case study on Aquinas's use of history. This section deserves further study on its own merits and should be of interest even for those with no concern for *De Regno*.

The Office of the King: II.4

Aquinas makes two points in II.4: how the king should govern, and the three-fold task of the king. While the former appears to be a merely negative point, in fact, Aquinas takes this occasion to confirm yet again the integrity of political activity, a teaching reinforced by his subsequent description of those three royal tasks.

Aquinas begins II.4 by synthesizing what he has argued throughout II.1–3. As earthly life is ordained to celestial life, so Aquinas now argues that the goods of earthly life are ordered to the common good of community. This point was discussed in I.1–6, where it was established that the person's goods cannot be used against the common good. This leads to an important basis of the king's temporal authority:

> If, then, as we have said, who has care of the ultimate end ought to take precedence over those who have care of things ordained to that end, and to direct them by his command, it is clear from what has been said that the king, just as he ought to be subject to the lordship and regime administered by the office of priesthood, ought to take precedence [*praeesse*] over all human offices, and order them by the command of his regime (II.4.114).

In II.3, Aquinas made a point that could be difficult for our king to accept, namely that his rule ought to be subordinate to that of the church. Yet the same principle grants the king responsibility over those earthly things that tend to the benefit of the common good: he rules them. If the priesthood rules the king, the king rules those below him. We might think that, being prepared by the great reward of the task at I.8–10, he is willing to accept this role. Indeed, as Boyle notes, this is a clear affirmation of the autonomy of the temporal.[38]

Aquinas explains this further. When one performs an activity whose end serves a higher end, one must ensure that one performs that activity or preserves that end in such a way as to conduce toward that further end or activity it serves. We have seen, moreover, that the end of the community is ordered to something beyond it, to beatitude:

> Therefore, since heavenly beatitude [*beatitudo caelestis*] is the end of that life we live well [*bene*] at present, it pertains to the duty of the king to procure the good life of the multitude in such that it suits [*congruit*] the attainment of heavenly beatitude [*caelestem beatitudinem*], that is, he should order those things which lead to the happiness of Heaven and, as far as possible, forbid their contraries (II.4.115).[39]

Here we see a confirmation of II.3.106 on the importance of virtue as the end of the king's rule. The rule of the king that secures the virtuous end of that regime, then, must be such as to conduce to beatitude. Aquinas states that task in the positive and in the negative, both to "lead" his subjects toward Heaven, and also "forbid" them from the opposite.

Aquinas next specifies what mode of virtuous living congrues with beatitude, and how the king is to know it: "From divine law is known the way to true beatitude and what are impedi-

---

38. Boyle urges that this passage is "in the best dualistic tradition," and notes that Eschmann, "St. Thomas Aquinas on the Two Powers," who develops a distinctly hierocratic interpretation of *De Regno*, makes no mention of this passage (Boyle, "The De Regno and the Two Powers," 6).

39. Eschmann renders "end of that life" as "end of that virtuous life," which is justified by the context but unnecessary given that Aquinas adds *bene* later in the sentence.

ments of it, the teaching of which pertains to the office of priests" (II.4.116). Divine law is needful for good governance, for the king learns through the priests' interpretation of the *lex divina* what leads to beatitude and what prevents it: "Instructed by this divine law, therefore, [the king] ought to attend to this principal concern, how the multitude subject to him may live well" (II.4.116). Although this is vague instruction, we do know one reason why kings must consult *lex divina*: to know what they must not do. Recall the teaching of II.3.111 according to which the traditional subordination of priests to kings must be reversed. Thus, the king, just like Aquinas himself, must consult the *lex divina nova*, the new divine law, for a principled justification of the division of political and spiritual authority.

The duty of the king to beatitude has been stated in ancillary terms: he is not to govern them to beatitude, but to govern them toward some kind of virtuous life that would conduce to beatitude. Thus, it may well be that the point of the king referring to the divine law is primarily negative: the virtue that Aquinas wishes the king to propagate among his people are intermediate or antecedent to beatitude, and it turns out to be Aquinas's great political teaching that the end of political activity is emphatically not beatitude. A ruler pursues intermediate goods as intermediate and knows that they are not final goods.

Moreover, the teaching is negative in the sense that Aquinas emphasizes the negative as well as the positive side of law, for example, the king "should order those things which lead to the happiness of Heaven and, as far as possible, forbid their contraries" (II.4.115). This is in keeping with his account of law in the *Summa Theologica*, where he argues that law must restrain as well as enjoin (*ST* I-II.90.1).

Through this negative emphasis, Aquinas has also yet again

hallowed the political with theology. Just as Aquinas urged in II.1–2 that political rule fits within God's cosmic rule, now Aquinas argues in II.4 that political rule fits within the church's rule. That primacy of the spiritual, in other words, does not negate the relative integrity of the political sphere. Thus, while the Christian innovation of the primacy of spiritual authority over temporal authority cannot be confused with pre-Christian political naturalism, it still coheres with the principle that human nature requires fulfillment through political activity.

Perhaps the surest sign of this divine approbation of political naturalism comes in what follows. Having reasserted his political naturalism, Aquinas explains how a king can govern a regime whereby "the multitude subject to him may live well" (II.4.116). Aquinas takes the task to be threefold: to establish virtue among the multitude; to preserve that virtue; and to improve on it. A description of these tasks occupies II.4.118–121.

The first, to establish virtue among the citizens, is the great task of founding. And it is not easy work: "Yet the unity of man is caused by nature, while the unity of multitude, which is called peace, must be procured through the industry of the ruler" (II.4.118). The king may take his direction from the regime of nature, but his own work is a product of human intelligence. This *unitas pacis*, discussed at I.1, must be such that men are directed to acting well. This unity, Aquinas explains, has a two-fold nature: it has a material basis in the necessities that permit life in the first place, for example, food and shelter, but also in the kind of harmony that permits men to share a common life.

Recalling II.1–2, we know that the task of the king is not literally to create but to cultivate what God has created. That task requires knowledge of man's end. That task, we also see now, requires the virtues of "human intelligence" that allow him to execute his own work toward the *unitas pacis*. Thus, the task of the king is not only theoretical but also practical. This reinforces the lessons of II.1.95, wherein Aquinas articulated the need for moral virtues like prudence and clemency. While Aquinas's political theology rests on a knowledge of ends, then, it could never be executed in practice without a practical dimension. This attention to the distinction between practice and theory suffuses *De Regno*.

The second consideration is more recognizably Christian. To preserve this life of virtue requires a consideration of what can harm this *unitas pacis*: mortality, perversion of wills, and external attack (II.4.119). Even the most virtuous regime must reckon with mortality. To preserve the immortality of the regime, as it were, humans must be replaced, meaning raised well to virtue and then assume their offices in the community. The second concern is the "perversity of the wills of men." This perversity can lead to lazy omissions of duty, or active transgressions of justice in the form of violence and usurpations of power. This was the kind of tyranny that came to characterize the Romans after they overthrew their kings, although at least for a while, they enjoyed the bounties of republican liberty. There is, finally, attack from external enemies, by which a city, Aquinas dramatically notes, can be "completely blotted out [*funditus dissipatur*]." The ability to fend off such attacks, again, was the reason for the superiority of the *provincia* to the city at I.1.

We might find Aquinas's explanations for each of these factors obvious and mundane. But it is first extraordinary that external attacks come last in this list, for they are the most obvious threat to a community. Then again, we might wonder if external enemies are distinct from the second cause, the perversity of wills. Most obviously, citizens with little love for their country render it vulnerable to external attack, making it difficult to assay whether the country was finally brought down by internal sloth and decadence or external invaders who sense such weakness. But consider the ideal case, when one's city is perfectly virtuous but overcome by a hostile opponent with greater force of arms than one's own. In such a case, the root cause remains perversity of will, but that of others.

The *provincia*, we recall from I.1, has an advantage over the polis in its ability to defend itself from external attacks. External attack, we see here, is a great threat to the community, yet the city that protects itself from external attacks is not necessarily a city that seeks to order itself according to virtue. Thus, we wondered if the development of the *provincia* ultimately represents an unfortunate compromise between virtue and necessity. To be clear: a community ought to defend itself. As Aquinas argues in the next paragraph: "it would be useless to prevent internal dangers if the multitude could not be defended against external dangers" (II.4.120). But a citizenry that sought no higher end than bare life would be stunted. There could be something self-defeating to the military end of the *provincia*, then, should it end in tyranny because of a lack of virtue among its citizens.

It would be difficult to articulate this concern about the *provincia* in book I: as Aquinas was at times vague about the end of political life in I.1–2, it was unclear if he saw a need to assert for politics an end beyond necessity and security. Now that Aquinas has vigorously promoted political naturalism and the life of virtue in book II, it is clear that the life of virtue stands as a challenge to the military excellence of the *provincia* and is, moreover, the solution to the perversity of will that troubles Aquinas in this section: "by his laws and precepts, punishments and rewards [praemiis], he should restrain the men subject to him from wickedness and induce them to virtuous works, following the example of God, Who gave His law to man, and handing out reward [mercedem] to the observant, punishment to the transgressors (II.4.120)."

We already know that the king must lead his people toward virtue and thus away from vice. We have also seen that Aquinas takes the negative or restraining dimension of politics seriously. Aquinas also states this task in terms of an imitation of God in this, laying down laws and punishing and rewarding men as the case calls for it. This latter concern speaks to the king as *minister Dei* and might be another reason for the king to turn to divine law: to study how God made His law known and how such punishments and rewards have been meted out. We might press the point further and say that it is in many of those interactions between God and men that we see the full display of man's perversity. Thus, perhaps another teaching the king can glean from the divine law concerns the cause and character of man's perversity. If one must know the moral condition of citizens to know what sort of laws is appropriate for them, then a teaching on the concrete condition of men is a very practical one.

This is also only the second reference to "law" in *De Regno*, and the only one directed to our king. Aquinas's political thought is generally thought to hinge crucially on law, especially the natural law.[40] If the natural law is in some sense the foundation of Aquinas's political theology, why is it largely absent from *De Regno*? Answering this question would require revisiting the fraught question of the role of law in Aquinas's political thought, which we cannot do on the basis of *De Regno*, but we have at least seen herein that the question of law within the pedagogy of *De Regno* arises as a function of the *minister Dei*. Aquinas introduces the concept of law within the relationship he lays out between king, God, and

---

40. Guerra, "Beyond Natural Law Talk," 14, n. 2.

church. But perhaps this is not so different from the "Treatise on Law" arising in the *Secunda pars* of the *Summa Theologica*.

So much for the second task: preserving virtuous living among his people. We noted above that there is an Augustinian flavor to Aquinas's consideration of that task, and it perhaps recalls the content of I.3–6. There is this great difference, however, between I.3–6 and II.4: whereas Aquinas could provide no immediate solution to the problem of the tyrant in I.3–6, he now offers the cultivation of virtue as a direct response to the problems that beset a community, whether internal or external. In this way, this part of II.4 completes I.6 on the task of avoiding tyranny. One can reform mild tyranny, as noted in I.6, according to the advice of II.4 to govern by virtue.

The third task of the king toward the virtuous life, namely seeking to improve it, serves as a seal on the previous two duties. Maintaining the virtue of his life as best he can, he should seek always to identify what ails it and improve it. Aquinas thus quotes from 1 Corinthians 12:31: be "zealous for the better gifts." The king, in other words, should govern knowing that he serves something beyond him or his kingdom.

A consideration of these three tasks confirms our suspicion that Aquinas has not defined the king's task in great detail because Aquinas does not mean anything particularly novel or radical by those tasks. Politics is difficult, and Christianity wants to support that task insofar as politics can provide the sort of virtue that can dispose people toward beatitude, but Aquinas has never suggested in *De Regno* that Christianity radically changes the activity of politics.[41]

What is unique, however, is how the political task is under-

41. See James V. Schall, SJ, "Fides et Ratio: Approaches to a Roman Catholic Political Philosophy," *Review of Politics* 62, no. 1 (2000): 49–75.

stood within the horizon of the *minister Dei*. We called II.3 an "ambivalent confirmation of Aquinas's political naturalism," but II.4 is more direct. Not only does man's political rule fit within God's cosmic rule (II.1–2), but man's political rule coheres with and complements its autonomy vis-a-vis the church's rule. Just as I.7–11 strengthens the end of politics by linking it to man's supernatural reward, so II.4 strengthens the natural character of politics by linking it to God's governance through the church.

This strategy is perhaps pedagogical as much as theological: for a Christian king with little understanding of classical political philosophy, the teaching of I.1–2 might seem abstract and irrelevant, never mind philosophically dense. To be told that royal rule has a definite and unique place within God's government, however, would be far more direct and concrete a teaching for him. II.4 thus confirms what we saw in II.3: Aquinas at times uses revelation in *De Regno* to point out what should be known by nature. Whereas earlier in II.1–2 uses the Christian doctrine of Creation to reinforce philosophical political naturalism, in II.3–4, he uses the doctrine of Redemption or the Resurrection to reinforce that naturalism within Christendom. Just as the final reward of I.7–9 reinforces the end of politics, so in II.3–4 that reward complements the activity of politics.

Eschmann worries that II.3–4 is a digression,[42] but the section has, indeed, answered quite directly how the king is to rule: as a *minister Dei*, ruling for virtuous living with a view toward the person's supernatural end. As we noted in II.4, the challenge of the Christian in politics for Aquinas is not to name the basic activities of politics, which thinkers identified hundreds of years before Christianity. It is rather to struggle toward those ends within the

42. Eschmann, *On Kingship*, introduction, xix; Dondaine, *De regno ad Regem Cypri*, préface, 423–24.

horizon set by the still-scandalous truth of Christianity. In this sense, II.3–4 could not be more apt to the task of instructing the king in his royal office, and it is every bit befitting a gift of a theologian and priest.

Conclusion: *De Regno* II.1–4

Book II.1–4 has much to offer its reader, both the Cypriot king and us. Most obviously, it offers answers to the two questions with which we opened chapter 4, questions for which our king might also desire answers: what is the practical significance of the analogy between the king-in-his-kingdom and God-in-his-creation, and can politics reach man's end? We have seen that the answers to these questions are related. Political activity has a discrete end, namely virtue, but that end is also antecedent or intermediate to a superior end. In other words, the *minister Dei* imitates God not by securing man's final end but by securing his intermediate, temporal end. As we noted of II.3, Aquinas thereby elevates politics as an intrinsically good activity, and yet also in the same movement delimits it by subordinating it to the City of God.

Book II.1–4 has effected this program through a twin movement of desacralizing politics even as Aquinas elevates it as a ministry of God. As Murray and Gilson note, Gelasian dualism and the primacy of the spiritual are central elements of Christian thought on politics, and we saw both teachings play a great role in Aquinas's rejection of civil religion in II.3. That rejection, in turn, was based on the critical distinction between creation and governance, a distinction which, in its own turn, depends on the distinction between Creator and creature.

We see now, as well, the close connection between tyranny and sacred monarchy. The tyrant of I.3–6 shares with the sacred monarch of II.3 a denial of God's sovereignty, the tyrant through a denial of the goods of politics set by God and the sacred monarch by a denial of the goods of religion set by God beyond politics. Thus, on Aquinas's terms, much of divine right theory of monarchy misunderstands the relationship between the temporal and the spiritual and is, indeed, a tyrannical arrogation of the latter by the former. More broadly, we see Aquinas in the first half of book II confirm a central tradition of Christianity, namely its tendency to set limits on political and temporal activity.[43]

In a related vein, two topics that are not often treated in Thomistic political thought play outsized roles in this text: civil religion and the natural virtue of religion. While the virtue of religion and its practices are natural, civil religion is not natural. Or, more precisely, civil religion might be natural to a certain period of human development. With Christianity, however, civil religion becomes impossible: humans must confront the Christian challenge that humanity's final end transcends politics and the temporal.

Finally, we can see that Aquinas has never made the relationship between church and state depend on any particular regime form. While Aquinas argues philosophically for the superiority of monarchy as the best regime, he has made clear that political regimes do not secure beatitude for their subjects, and so the regime form can only be of indirect importance for beatitude. Further, Aquinas has argued that the source of unity of the Christian *populus* is not a grand king or emperor but the pope. Thus, the beatitude of Christendom does not depend on the ability of a monarch to secure the temporal unity of Christians.

This may frustrate some, as Aquinas in *De Regno* does not move much beyond the generality of *Scriptum Super Libros Sententiarum*. Aquinas does, however, confirm in *De Regno* the basic

---

43. See James V. Schall, SJ "Transcendence and Political Philosophy," *The Review of Politics* 55 (1993): 247–65.

The Politics of Revelation

principles of the *Scriptum*, particularly the centrality of the *populus Christianus*; the common derivation of temporal and spiritual authority from "the divine power," that is, God; and the unity of the Christian people in the pope. Thus, I agree with Boyle against Eschmann in the essential complementarity of *De Regno* and Aquinas's *Sentences* commentary.[44]

The Structure and Teaching of *De Regno*

Beyond such particular claims about book II, we can see that it has brought to light a new way to understand the structure of *De Regno*, a structure in which such claims emerge. That structure can be represented in the table below:

Doctrine	Initial Elaboration	Recapitulation
Creation	I.1–2	II.1–2
Fall	I.3–6	I.10–12
Redemption	I.7–9	II.3–4

This structure synthesizes several features of *De Regno* that we have already observed: Aquinas advances through book I with a treatment of political naturalism, the destruction of sin and vice, and the reward of the king. In book II, we see those philosophical elements elevated by theological doctrines: creation, Fall, and Redemption. A weak thesis would merely note these structural parallels, and there is much to be gained from observing those parallels, but I will advance a bolder thesis about four themes that this structure reveals about *De Regno*: the integrity of *De Regno*, Thomistic naturalism, the pedagogical nature of the text, and the teleological unfolding of the *minister Dei*.

---

44. See Boyle, "The *De Regno* and the Two Powers," and Eschmann, "St. Thomas Aquinas on the Two Powers."

First, this structure reveals the integrity of the text. For some interpreters, *De Regno* is a patchwork of fragments with no coherent order, with opinions ranging from Eschmann's hyperbole to Dondaine's cool concern. While my proposed structure cannot resolve all those concerns, which also rest on paleographic considerations, understanding *De Regno* according to this structure at least offers reason to think that the units of the text, in fact, cohere in a rational order. As we have noted, Aquinas argues for political naturalism in I.1–2 and then turns to tyranny in I.3–6. He does not abandon that naturalism but, in fact, solidifies this teaching with his invocation of the doctrine of Creation in II.1–2. His subsequent discussion of vices and sins in I.3–6 are completed in I.10–12, when he details the suffering and loss of the tyrant. Finally, where Aquinas spells out the end of the human person in I.7–9, at II.3–4, he shows how the political securing of that natural end finds its place within the economy of governments. In each of these three cases, as we have perhaps noted to the point of tedium, Aquinas uses divine revelation to buttress the claims of reason.

The confirmation of nature through revelation therefore not only structures the text but undergirds the teaching of the text. This dynamic of Creation-Fall-Redemption thus offers a subtle grounding to a second theme, what I call "Thomistic naturalism." This is not the naturalism of Cicero or Aristotle but rather a political naturalism rooted in reason but extended through Christian theological truths, especially Creation and Redemption. Aquinas confirms the person's political nature so as to unite it with the person's supernatural end. *De Regno* on this account would not be a "political theology," or at least not of the sort often associated with Carl Schmitt, which is to say the theological prescription of particular political orders.[45] But it certainly is a "theology of

---

45. Jordan, "*De Regno* and the Place of Political Thinking in Thomas Aquinas."

politics," that is, a vision of politics guided by theological reflection on man's ends.[46]

The structure of *De Regno* offers a teaching in Thomistic naturalism, which is to say that it is pedagogical, as befits a *speculum principum*. We have seen that this genre crucially structures the teaching, as suggested by Chenu, Roguet, and Dondaine. But *De Regno* has reaffirmed the pedagogical nature of civic relations, not just of the text. This is the third theme articulated in the Creation-Fall-Redemption structure. The point that Aquinas makes most clearly in II.3 is true of the text writ-large: man's community grows as it grows in knowledge and instantiation of its ends. Aquinas has in many places emphasized that this political order does not spontaneously spring into existence but urges instead that it must be developed over time. For Aquinas, politics depends on the interplay of man's knowledge of his ends and his practical instantiation of that knowledge in the institutions and practices that serve those ends. The king himself must live out that interplay as he grows into his own place within the God-king analogy.

This developmentalism is nowhere clearer in *De Regno* than in Aquinas's discussion of civil religion. What Aquinas proposes is three-fold: distinguish the "political" and the "spiritual"; order those ends to one another in a hierarchy of ends; and lay out principles for the ordering of those ends in the activity of man. With this analysis in place, we can examine not only how Christianity depends on the natural virtue of religion but also how Christianity has changed and been resisted by political activity.[47] Attempts within the Christian age of Europe to resurrect civil theology have

---

46. See Matthias Riedl, "Clarifications concerning the Concept of Political Theology: Carl Schmitt and Augustine," paper presented at the annual conference of the American Political Science Association, Philadelphia, August 28–31, 2003.

47. See especially Robert N. Bellah, "Civil Religion in America," *Daedalus* 96, no. 1 (1967): 1–21.

thus born this double aspect: a rejection of the Christian teaching and a return to pre-Christian ways of thinking about politics and religion. Other political philosophies, most notably those of Locke, have appropriated the distinction between the temporal and spiritual posited by Christianity but not the hierarchical ordering of the two.[48] At the core of this contest between Christianity and civil religion is a conceptual question about how the human person's spiritual end bear upon his natural end. Practically, that contest concerns how the very desires that lead men to civil religion are instantiated by a community in the development of a Christian regime.

The fourth theme revealed by this structure is the role of the *minister Dei*, a role that has evolved with the regime of *De Regno*, and a role that moreover corresponds to human persons in general as political beings. Aquinas has shown us at least four different cities in *De Regno*: the naturalistic city of I.1–2, the tyrannical city of I.3–6, the just city of II.1–2, and the supernaturally directed city of II.3–4. One might also, however, conceive of *De Regno* as exhibiting distinct moments in the life of the same city, in its progress toward its perfection. Aquinas prefaces the articulation of each moment or developmental level of this city with an account of how the city can be advanced to the next stage. Most strikingly, in I.7 he calls for the conversion of citizens toward justice. The citizens of I.6 are exhorted to *fortitudo* in the name of justice: to discern what would be best for the city, not to dispose immediately of a ruler who does not suit their interests. They are urged to reform themselves in the name of a better regime. If the

---

48. See J. Brian Benestad, *Church, State, and Society* (Washington, D.C.: The Catholic University of America Press, 2011), 35–47, on "dignity," but also Charles De Koninck, *De la primauté du bien commun contres les personnalistes,* (Québec: Éditions de l'Université Laval, 1943).

conversion of the people involves them seeing the human temporal end as intermediate to that final end, then conversion has a profoundly political dimension. One might think of this as the "magnanimous regime": the city whose end must be great and worthy of man's higher nature, even if its citizens are not yet clear on the precise nature of this end. What precisely this end should be is not discussed at any length, but it is at least clear that it is not tyranny. We might even think of this as Aquinas's "state of nature": humans naturally live in society and seek how best to secure virtue through it.

The pedagogical nature of this text intersects with its unfolding of the *minister Dei* role: *De Regno* is, after all, a means to educate the *minister Dei* himself. The king himself has not been called idolatrous (I.3), a hypocrite (I.5–8), a tyrant (I.2–6), desperately friendless (I.5), a thief (I.5), a murderer (I.9), a liar (I.9) or vainglorious (I.5). He has been shown, however, that such perils threaten the reader who does not heed Aquinas's teaching. Moreover, if the king thus comes to see himself as lacking in virtue, he sees it not under the aspect of a harsh law or of the critique of a political opponent but rather in the estimation of a theologian who shows him the means by which he might live out this *imitatio Dei*.

To be sure, this way of understanding *De Regno* as structured around Creation-Fall-Redemption is a speculative claim that I cannot fully prove, and one could glean much from *De Regno* without granting it. But note that this dynamic of Creation-Fall-Redemption complements another way of thinking about Aquinas's thought: the *exitus-reditus* scheme associated with the *Summa Theologica*.

Some have described the logic of the *Summa Theologica* in terms of "*exitus*" and "*reditus*": Aquinas proceeds from God's nature to the going forth of all things from him through his creative activity and concluding with the salvific acts of Christ whereby man returns to God.[49] There are limitations to this model, including its difficulty in accounting for the *Tertia pars*, and I do not wish my interpretation of *De Regno* to stand or fall with Chenu's thesis. Yet if *De Regno* follows a trajectory of Creation-Fall-Redemption, then it is, indeed, of the order of an *exitus-reditus* model. Aquinas in *De Regno*, after all, paints the picture of a politics driven by ends, in which man must recognize his creaturely status and then embrace that his final end is both from and leads him back to God. Crucially, *De Regno* begins not with the theological doctrine of Creation but the philosophical teaching of political naturalism. Thus, one might argue that Aquinas builds toward the *exitus-reditus* model in *De Regno* rather than simply instantiates it.

I do not mean to argue that in *De Regno* Aquinas anticipates the *exitus-reditus* structure of the *Summa*. The comparison between these two hermeneutic principles reminds us, however, that fundamental Christian doctrines had a profound effect on Aquinas's thought. And were one sympathetic to the common claim that Aquinas was fundamentally never interested in politics, we might think that Aquinas's political thought would be guided less by political philosophy than by Christian considerations such as we have uncovered in *De Regno*.[50]

An objection to this construal of *De Regno* concerns a point I have already taken up, that one might insist on the fruit in conceiving of *De Regno* as a mediation of the Aristotelian and Augustinian traditions. Recourse to those traditions has at times illumi-

---

49. Brian Davies, *The Thought of Thomas Aquinas* (Oxford: Clarendon Press, 1992), 21; Oakley, *The Mortgage of the Past*, 106. For a critique of the model, see Brian Davies, *Thomas Aquinas's Summa Theologiae: A Guide and Commentary* (New York: Oxford University Press, 2014), 14@1-6.

50. Jordan, "*De Regno* and the Place of Political Thinking in Thomas Aquinas."

nated the themes of *De Regno*, but perhaps the best evidence we have seen in *De Regno* for his reckoning with those traditions are the ways in which Aquinas almost effortlessly transcends them. On Nederman's terms, the thought of Aristotle and Augustine are less ends than means for Aquinas: means to argue for political naturalism and man's fallen nature. Although many medieval theologians no doubt confused means for ends in the bitter disputes between the Aristotelian and Augustinian schools of medieval Europe, Aquinas has made no such mistake.

Postscript: *De Regno* II.5–8

Thus far, we have neglected the concluding chapters of *De Regno*, which Eschmann characterizes as "much neglected, sometimes even ridiculed."[51] In them, Aquinas presents the most prosaic teaching of *De Regno*. What interests the scholar of Aquinas in them will be less their teaching than their manner of presentation. Therein, Aquinas links the greatest glory of kings, founding a city, with the most mundane considerations. He thus provides an example of the political naturalism that suffuses *De Regno*.

Aquinas begins II.5 promising to treat on the "greatest glory" of kings: "the founding of a city or kingdom [*ab institutione civitatis aut regni*]" (II.5.123). Quoting Vegetius, a Roman writer of the late fourth century whose *De re militari* was a popular military guide in medieval Europe, Aquinas declares "the mightiest nations and most commended kings thought it their greatest glory either to found new cities or have their names made part of ... the names of cities already founded by others." Aquinas invokes *Ecclesiasticus* that "The building of a city shall establish a name," and the example of the greatest founder: "The name of Romulus ... *would be unknown today had he not founded the city of Rome*" (II.5.123).

51. Eschmann, *On Kingship*, introduction, xxxiii.

These invocations of royal glory and fame come at an odd time in the text. Aquinas has spent much of *De Regno* instilling in his royal reader a sense of humility in his governance. That humility, in turn, has a basis in the distinctions between creature and creator: God and not man rules universally (II.1); God and not humans establish the end of the person (II.2); God through the spiritual power and not political authority conducts humans to their final end (II.3); political authority must be ordained to the spiritual power (II.4).

Aquinas does not mean to undermine the school of humility he has created in *De Regno*; as in II.5–8, he links the king's desire for glory with quotidian foundations of the common good. Aquinas details the importance of choosing the right site, with particular reference to climate (II.5); to air, orientation to the sun and water (II.6); to food (II.7); and to the beauty (*amenitas*) of the site (II.8). This discussion gives flesh to II.1–2: the king in founding a city or kingdom must employ prudence in shaping God's creation so as to provide for his people.

Indeed, while mundane, these considerations have implications for the virtue that the king is to cultivate in his people. Particularly, food (II.7) raises the question of trade, and beauty (II.8) the question of pleasure. Cities should provide for their own food so far as possible, Aquinas argues, as it allows them to be self-sufficient (II.7.136–7). Further, as Aquinas argues in a direct reference to Aristotle's *Politics*, relying on trade opens a city to negative outside influences, which can be "particularly harmful to civic customs" (II.7.138). Indeed, the life of trade breeds many vices (II.7.139–140). Aquinas also worries that trade will cause a city to grow inordinately, when it is better that the citizens live primarily in the countryside (II.7.141).

Aquinas also extolls the importance of the beauty of the location of a founding. He notes that people will be more likely to move to and stay in such a place and describes beauty in natural terms that complement what else he has said about climate and fecundity: "a broad expanse of meadows, an abundant forest growth, mountains to be seen close at hand, pleasant groves and a copiousness of water" (II.8.143). Again, what is good is good because God made it so, not because a king fashions it out of nothing.

Yet too much beauty can lead to "indulgence in superfluous pleasure" that makes a people vicious, weak-minded, and lazy. These vices lead to poverty and crime. Aquinas does not state it explicitly, but by his logic, such indulgence could also lead to subjugation by others, and thus threaten the very self-sufficiency that is the mark of a good regime. The emphasis in this chapter is rather sober moderation. When Aquinas argues that "By thus avoiding any excess, the mean of virtue will be more easily attained" (II.8.145), he enjoins the king not only to prudent virtue but also to secure such for his people. The concluding words of the chapter are thus a seal on the whole of *De Regno,* an affirmation of the teaching for the king as well as the teaching he must impart on his regime: "However, in human intercourse it is best to have a moderate share of pleasure as a spice of life, so to speak, wherein man's mind may find some recreation" (II.8.148).

Aquinas in these final chapters presents the task of the king as humble but fundamental: he must secure those basic goods that make possible the virtue of his people. There is little mention in this section of the riches, honor, and pride that one might associate with the foundation of kingdoms. Aquinas has presented politics as created and delimited by God's divine activity and ordained to the church's supernatural governance. He has used II.5–8, however, to nonetheless remind the king of the goodness of the task of politics, a goodness grounded in the very nature of Creation.

Attention to that task, Aquinas argues, will secure for the king a name equal to that of Romulus.

    Chapter 4 ends our exegesis of *De Regno*. In its structured presentation of Thomistic naturalism, *De Regno* affords a pedagogy whereby the king as *minister Dei* can begin to assume his proper place in the world. One might wonder whether that model can be brought to bear upon times and places other than that of Aquinas. Chapter 5 will pursue that question.

CHAPTER 5

The Christian Structure of Politics

De Regno on Church and State

Thus far, *De Regno* might seem to lack an answer to the most pressing political matter of Aquinas's time: the church/state question. Indeed, for a scholar who so greatly prized clarity and distinction in his efforts toward universal or scientific knowledge, Aquinas has little direct to say of church/state relations in general. Aquinas's other references to church/state relations are brief and fleeting: in his *Commentary on the Sentences*, he famously but enigmatically refers to the pope as the apex of spiritual and temporal power, leaving one to speculate the precise ramifications of that claim; in the *Summa Theologica*, he discusses the possibility of the use of coercion for apostates. This vague state of the question has led many scholars to treat Aquinas's references to the church/state question like Rorschach tests, finding whatever they wish to discover in them. The argument between Boyle and Eschmann on church and state in *De Regno*, rich as it is, leans on the *Commentary*, itself an enigmatic teaching.[1] Keys asks meaningful questions but mostly voices misgivings about the illiberalism of

---

1. Eschmann, "St. Thomas Aquinas on the Two Powers"; Boyle, "The *De Regno* and the Two Powers."

Aquinas.[2] And Murray in his discussion of Bellarmine uses Aquinas at least in part to justify Murray's own notion of the secular state—one that does not clearly accord with that of Aquinas.[3]

Yet we can extract some principles on the matter from this text, and while those principles might seem a meager teaching, they have great power. As the material from *De Regno* on church/state relations is thin, so must this chapter be. It will nonetheless be worth doing. For while we could explore *De Regno* for its teaching on many topics, perhaps no topic would have been so momentous for his contemporaries, and *mutatis mutandis* for our own time, as the church/state question, which is to say, the nature and order of "Christendom," itself a contested term. Such an investigation will also help us to reexamine the place of Aquinas in the history of political thought, including in contemporary debates, for the church/state question has not disappeared: it has merely assumed new forms.

In this chapter, I sketch a set of principles of the relationship between church and state from the text of *De Regno*. By synthesizing numerous strands of the text of *De Regno*, we can elaborate guidelines by which to judge concrete relationships between particular temporal and spiritual authorities. To illuminate the challenge of these principles, I then compare them to two medieval and one modern model of church/state relations.

De Regno: The Church/State Model

Our analysis of *De Regno* has yielded valuable insights on church/state relations that together form a standard against which to judge any concrete church/state relationship. In this section of the

---

2. Keys, *Aquinas, Aristotle, and the Promise of the Common Good.*

3. Douglas Kries, "Defending Robert Bellarmine," in *Jerusalem, Athens, & Rome: Essays in Honor of James V. Schall, S.J.*, ed. Marc D. Guerra (South Bend, Ind.: St. Augustine's Press, 2013), 129–35.

chapter, I will condense those insights into five principles: Gelasianism; Thomistic political naturalism; a critique of civil religion and theocracy; ambivalence to particular regimes; and pedagogy. These principles could be distinguished and ordered differently, and they no doubt vary in their importance for church/state relations and their textual basis in Aquinas's *De Regno*. But I will argue and explain here that they each pick out important aspects of Aquinas's church/state teaching in *De Regno*. In the following sections, I further show their robustness by contrasting them with principles of other medieval as well as modern thinkers.

Gelasianism

Gelasianism forms the core of the Christian tradition on politics, what D'Entrèves calls "the most important factor of western civilization."[4] Its appearance in *De Regno* should therefore not be surprising, yet Aquinas articulates Gelasianism with rare delicacy.

Most tellingly, while Gelasianism is often rendered in terms of "dualism," careful observers, including Aquinas in *De Regno*, have noted that the teaching, in fact, bears on two concepts: dualism and primacy.[5] Specifically, Gelasianism argues not only for dualism in society between church and state but also for the primacy of the spiritual above the temporal. As Griesbach notes, a Gelasianism that does not account for this primacy would not be a Christian dualism.[6] On the other hand, the invocation of *libertas Ecclesiae* without reference to dualism might seem to misunderstand dualism's intimate connection with the primacy of the spiritual.

4. McCoy, *The Structure of Political Thought: A Study in the History of Political Ideas*, 100, quoting D'Entrèves.
5. John Courtney Murray, SJ, "Contemporary Orientations of Catholic Thought on Church and State in the Light of History," *Theological Studies* 10 (1949): 204, although at times Murray privileges dualism over the primacy of the spiritual.
6. Griesbach, "John of Paris," 38, n. 21.

This teaching thus strikes a subtle balance. On the one hand, each power has a dignity and integrity proper to the end it serves: the temporal end of the human person by temporal authority, and the spiritual end by spiritual authority. On the other hand, the spiritual end is the one ultimate end of the human person, and so temporal goods must be brought into alignment with the pursuit of that spiritual good. An authority attempting to arrogate the functions of the other would be undercutting its own basis of power: institutions serve ends, not the other way around.

The basis of this balance brings us to a second element of Aquinas's Gelasianism: it is not in the first place an argument about institutions but rather about human ends. It proceeds from knowledge about human ends, taking that knowledge as principles from which to analyze and judge institutional arrangements. If indeed institutions must serve ends, then one important way Aquinas's Gelasianism can go wrong is in the reversal of this priority, where ends come to serve institutions. As Oakley notes, this was a signal problem of the medieval period, when complex theological disputes were reduced to jurisdictional turf battles between *Sacerdotium* and *Imperium*, with kings jockeying in between seeking to bolster their nascent nation-states. Aquinas's principles in *De Regno*, however, should be applicable across time periods because they are not wedded to particular institutions.

The distinction between dualism and the primacy of the spiritual might seem pedantic, but it adds nuance to the differentiation of church/state theories. As we will see later in this chapter, some medieval theories of church/state relations prioritize dualism but not primacy; others prioritize the opposite. And when we turn to the fraught question of liberalism's relationship to Gelasiansim, this distinction helps us mark out ways in which liberalism's commitment to dualism is stronger than to the primacy of the spiritual. For if liberalism has at times adopted or even arisen out of the Christian distinction between the temporal and spiritual, it has not been so welcoming of its doctrine of the primacy of the spiritual.

Rejection of Civil Religion and Theocracy

Aquinas's rejection of civil religion and theocracy logically follows from his advocacy of Gelasianism. It is nonetheless worth treating separately, because it bears mention that while civil religion and theocracy are both forms of monism, they differ considerably in other respects.

The opposite of dualism is monism: the subjugation of one of the two powers to the other. Perhaps no one has analyzed this subject as thoroughly as John Courtney Murray, who details two distinct types of monism.[7] In its "hierocratic" form, theocracy, monism instrumentalizes political authority to religious authority. In its "regal" form, civil religion, monism instrumentalizes religious authority to political authority. Gelasian dualism, then, is a *via media* between these two kinds of monism: the two powers are seen in their autonomy, although they are ordered to one another as are man's ends.

We saw in chapter 3 that Aquinas presents a history of politics in terms of monism and dualism (*De Regno* II.3). While he clearly advocates for dualism, Aquinas acknowledges the subordination of religious authorities to political ones as the historical norm until Christianity, and indeed accepts this subordination as a relative good insofar as it cultivated the natural virtue of religion. Under the Christian dispensation, however, civil religion cannot obtain spiritual ends and cannot be subordinated to temporal ones.

---

7. See Murray, "Contemporary Orientations," 202, among other places.

Yet while temporal ends can be ordained to spiritual ones, those temporal ends are still preserved in a certain integrity that is not simply reducible to the spiritual, and so theocracy, both in its general, nebulous sense and on Murray's monistic account, is ruled out. We saw in chapter 4 that the duty of the king was stated in ancillary terms: he is to govern his people toward the kind of virtuous life that would conduce to beatitude. But note that virtue is in itself an infravalent end: it is an end as well as a mean to further happiness. And Aquinas invokes revelation in book II not to denigrate but to elevate politics: the political naturalism of I.1–2 receives what we called "a divine seal" at II.1–2.

To be sure, Aquinas's history emphasizes the rejection of civil religion more so than that of theocracy. Indeed, he probably fears civil religion more than he fears theocracy, which would seem to be rarer than civil religion. Further, given that civil authorities will have much to gain from civil religion, it is not surprising that ecclesial authorities should be more robust in their opposition to civil religion than to theocracy. In fact, the worry about civil religion could be understood as a worry about reversion: most pre-Christian regimes were civil-religious, and so any diminution of the Christian teaching could lead back to civil religion. Indeed, as Sokolowski observes, the very fact that man has a natural religious instinct means that Christianity must "continually differentiate itself" from it.[8]

While both theocracy and civil religion are violations of dualism, only civil religion also violates the primacy of the spiritual, for it not only denies dualism in subjugating one authority (the spiritual) to another authority (the temporal) but also denies the primacy of the spiritual authority over the temporal authority. As

---

8. Sokolowski, *The God of Faith and Reason*, xi.

such, civil religion is a peculiarly potent form of tyranny: the tyrant employing civil religion, perhaps in the guise of sacred or "divine right" monarchy, not only perverts the ends of politics but the ends of religion as well. We can see, then, why a Christian thinker would worry about civil religion more than theocracy.

Perhaps Aquinas ought to have been harsher on theocracy. After all, it is a serious rejection of Aristotelian philosophy, which understands the human person to be naturally political and is a rejection of the goodness of creation, particularly the goodness of man's created nature and community. More pragmatically, a blasé attitude toward theocracy does Christianity no favors among its critics, who are naturally more concerned about theocracy than are Christians. This dynamic will be familiar to students of twenty-first-century debates in which Christian critics of liberalism shrug off charges of theocracy or integralism as easily as their interlocutors lob them. In short, Christianity needs politics to be politics, much as revelation needs reason to be reason.

None of what we have said touches on a fraught practical question, which is the prudential judgment as to whether in a given set of circumstances civil religion or theocracy is a more fearful possibility. But it is fair to say that many students of the church/state question have implicit answers to this question, with ramifications for their theoretical work.

In any event, while both civil religion and theocracy clearly violate Gelasianism, they also trespass on Thomistic naturalism, as we shall see. For Thomistic naturalism offers the warrant of revelation for politics in ways that affirm both the primacy of the spiritual and the relative integrity of politics. Civil religion, however, seeks the warrant of revelation for politics without acknowledging that primacy, and theocracy reduces politics beneath the spiritual without affirming that integrity.

To restate, the impact of this teaching for church/state relations is primarily negative: Gelasianism demands that neither authority can instrumentalize the other for its own benefit. And while the history of civil religions, as we saw in *De Regno* II.3, puts regimes on guard against the eternal return of civil religions, it is clear that theocracy must also be avoided. Political realism, however, leads us to admit that partisans of the church will tend to worry more about civil religion, and partisans of the state will worry more about theocracy.

Thomistic Political Naturalism

What I have called "Thomistic political naturalism" is a variation on Aristotle's political naturalism. Aquinas uses divine revelation to reinforce the political nature of the person, but in so doing explicitly limits his temporal end within the horizon of his eternal destiny. It is thus a qualified but nonetheless robust iteration of political naturalism.

As we noted in the beginning of this study, Aquinas agrees with Aristotle that the end of politics is to live according to virtue, and thus, political activity fulfills something noble in humans. Indeed, while the human transtemporal end might seem to undercut politics, Aquinas uses it to the contrary: revelation offers an end beyond the temporal that buttresses politics.

For if man's political nature can be known through reason, as Aristotle and Cicero in different ways establish, revelation can nonetheless, to again invoke the language of the *Summa Theologica*, point out what humans could know by reason but often do not. Revelation also names why reason so often falls short of its own task, or perhaps why the will so often obstructs reason's task. While Aquinas never names the Fall in *De Regno*, the Fall contributes, of course, significantly to the vice and sin that prevents man acting according to right reason, as Aquinas exemplifies in his discussion of tyranny.[9]

This Thomistic political naturalism is in some sense not original to Aquinas, for it is nothing other than the ways by which Aquinas spells out the political ramifications of traditional Christian doctrine. *De Regno* is a very fresh and politically powerful statement of those ramifications, however, and with constant references to the political naturalism that characterizes so much pre-Christian political thought.

Thomistic political naturalism gives flesh to church/state relations. Just as Gelasianism promotes a duality of temporal and spiritual authority, so Thomistic political naturalism underwrites the harmony of that duality through insistence that the data of revelation and reason concur on the political nature of the human person. Again, it strikes a balance: revelation reinforces reason's argument for the naturalness of politics, but in so doing asserts the primacy of the spiritual.

This naturalism is profoundly pedagogical, for it relies on revealed teachings to instruct rational politics. More specifically, it is the teaching whereby Gelasianism can be instantiated in a community: the emergence of Christian revelation makes plain both Gelasian dualism and the primacy of the spiritual, and thereby the harmony between the two powers that is Thomistic political naturalism.

Ambivalence to Particular Regimes

The principle of ambivalence to particular regimes is two-fold. First, as per classical political philosophy, regimes can take a variety of forms: the best form for a given community at a given time

---

9. *ST* I-II.94.6; *ST* I-II.91.4; McCoy, *The Structure of Political Thought*, 152–54.

is a matter of prudence. Second, and more importantly for Christianity: all particular regimes fall short of the Kingdom of God.

The first point is not strongly represented in *De Regno*: Aquinas is vocal in his support for monarchy as the best regime and has little to say of the other regime forms. But I have argued that Aquinas's robust endorsement for monarchy is in part rhetorical, as he is, of course, addressing a king. Nowhere in *De Regno*, moreover, does he rule out the legitimacy of other just regimes. And the legitimacy of diverse regime forms is a strong feature of the Christian and classical political traditions, as Kraynak persuasively argues.[10] So, in the absence of clear evidence to the contrary, we should not assume that Aquinas disagrees with it.

As for the second point, that all particular regimes should be handled with indifference as short of the Kingdom of God, we have noted that Aquinas clearly distinguishes the two powers in terms of ends: spiritual government for spiritual ends, and temporal government for temporal ends (*De Regno* II.3). While the two authorities can overlap—these are formal distinctions, not material distinctions—the temporal government cannot provide for spiritual ends, and Aquinas clearly means to caution Christians who would have the state exercise the role of the church. As we saw, the distinction between the king and the priesthood is a disanalogy between the king and God: the king only imitates God in the natural order, not in the supernatural order. Nowhere in *De Regno* does Aquinas explicitly prescribe a relationship between the church and the Cypriot's state. This not only allows Aquinas to valorize the integrity of politics for the king but also to emphasize the superiority of the church to any political eventuality. As Tocqueville puts it: "But when religion wishes to be supported by

---

10. Kraynak, *Christian Faith and Modern Democracy*, 97–98.

the interests of this world, it becomes almost as fragile as all the powers on earth. Alone, it can hope for immortality; bound to ephemeral powers, it follows their fortune and often falls with the passions of a day that sustain them."[11]

This ambivalence bears greatly upon church/state relations. This principle speaks to the asymmetry between spiritual and temporal authorities: whereas temporal authorities come and go, the spiritual authority of the church will endure until quite literally Kingdom come. Moreover, while distinct approaches and efforts toward temporal goods are worthy, none of them should be confused with the end beyond time. The spiritual authority should engage with temporal authority with a spiritual freedom in pursuit of the great end of the Kingdom of God, a principle that theocracy runs afoul of as much as does civil religion.

Another way to put this principle is the "Kraynak Dilemma" to which we adverted in chapter 4: political regimes need the legitimacy of the church more than the church needs legitimacy from regimes. In Aquinas's day, it was monarchical regimes that sought the church's warrant. In the twentieth century, it was democratic regimes that sought the church's warrant. And often enough, the church sought support from those regimes, too.[12] But Aquinas in *De Regno* insists that the spiritual authority should not rest its legitimacy or activity on the temporal power. Moreover, the church will have to possess the historical consciousness to which Aquinas adverts in *De Regno* II.3: while a particular set of relations between church and state might obtain for some time, even good relations should be viewed with an eye toward their mutability and mortality.

---

11. Alexis de Tocqueville, *Democracy in America*, vol. 1, trans. and ed. Harvey C. Mansfield and Delba Winthrop (Chicago: University of Chicago Press, 2000), pt. II, chap. 9. See also Kraynak, *Christian Faith and Modern Democracy*, 269.

12. Kraynak, *Christian Faith and Modern Democracy*, xii–xiii.

The Pedagogy of Politics

De Regno as a *speculum principum* is pedagogical: as one would expect of this genre, its content is structured with a concern for teaching the reader. More substantively, the model of politics it presents is itself pedagogical: humans come to know more about the nature of themselves, human community, and God through political activity, and political activity, like all human activity, is embedded in a salvation history through which humans come to know more about God and themselves. Given that politics is a practical activity, full knowledge of engaging it can only be had through doing it. In this broad sense, then, politics, like all practical activity, has a pedagogical element.

Beyond this general sense of pedagogy, however, I argue that in our study of *De Regno*, we have seen two further senses in which this text is pedagogical: a teleological element and an eschatological element. As for the teleological element, Aquinas makes clear in *De Regno* that human societies must advance communally to the kind of knowledge about human ends that allow them to legislate intelligently and prudently. This Aristotelian dictum seems to guide Aquinas in *De Regno*: the city of survival becomes the excellent and virtuous city as the ends of man are discerned and pursued. In this sense, then, it might appear that "pedagogy" means that man is a political animal, and he discovers himself through politics.

As for the eschatological element, Aquinas argues in *De Regno* that the final end of man is a gift in the hands of God, not something that man can sure by his own efforts. The complete possession of that gift, moreover, eludes man in this life: he can only see it "through a glass darkly," in the words of Saint Paul. Thus, even as man directs his actions teleologically, he must place his faith in God to bring about finally the attainment of that end. That faith in a divine power beyond human agency, in turn, makes history more mysterious, which is why, Kraynak argues, history must be deeply ambiguous for Christians.[13]

It would be well to note, too, obstacles to these pedagogical elements, although Aquinas is less systematic in his reflection on this than in the general pedagogical structure. Theoretically, they include a lack of knowledge and the darkened intellect after the Fall. Practically, those obstacles include a lack of practical knowledge, which can only be developed over time through experience, and the weak will after the Fall.

As we cannot fail to observe, this fusion of the teleological and eschatological is also a synthesis of Aristotle and Augustine, or more broadly, classical political thought and Christian theology. For Aquinas has by Christian revelation extended the teleological ethics of Aristotle to encompass man's supernatural end, while also revealing through Christian revelation the limitations of man's pursuit of the good.

Thus, *De Regno* presents not only a pedagogy toward politics; politics itself is educative, an activity of learning. As we noted of the Creation-Fall-Redemption structure, Aquinas has in many places emphasized that this political order does not spontaneously spring into existence but must be developed over time. Politics depends not only knowledge of human ends but a practical instantiation of that knowledge in institutions and practices. That instantiation, in turn, must somehow match growth and change in knowledge of both those ends and how those institutions and practices function in history.

This pedagogy can be understood in light of what we might call the "teleological institutionalism" of Aquinas's Gelasianism:

13. Kraynak, *Christian Faith and Modern Democracy*, 270 et seq.

institutions follow ends, not the other way around. Thus, humans must conduct any political arrangement with a freedom toward institutions. Just as the church must be ambivalent toward temporal arrangements, to recall the Tocqueville quotation above, so, even within political life, humans must approach political forms with the prudence and humility of a student, acknowledging that they, both legislators and communities, always have more to learn.[14]

This naturalism calls for a prudence, the virtue that builds from means to ends, or from lower ends to higher ends. As we noted at II.1, *De Regno* suggests that Aquinas wants the king to learn prudence along the way with justice and other virtues, for prudence allows one to reckon with the contingent and the changing, hallmarks of politics.[15] And, to repeat, *prudentia* is not just the application of knowledge but requires humans to discern the proper ends of action and pursue the means to achieve them: to be a virtuous person who knows and seeks the good in his activity.

This principle bears upon church/state relations in all the ways that Thomistic naturalism bears upon those relations. Considered thematically, perhaps the greatest consequence of this pedagogy arises from the basic fact that while regimes, strictly speaking, must all be ordered to the same end, namely beatitude, they must progress in an understanding of that end, and in the instantiation of what that means for their practices and institutions. While communities will not always agree on the final or ultimate moral commitments of their political activity, a healthy regime will build from those basic or intermediate ends toward the final end. In other words, a "social contract" or "democratic charter" or any other decision to limit *a priori* the ends of political life is hereby

---

14. On law as pedagogue, see Cathleen Kaveny, *Law's Virtues: Fostering Autonomy and Solidarity in American Society* (Washington, D.C.: Georgetown University Press, 2012).

15. Aristotle, *Nicomachean Ethics* VI; cf. Aquinas, *Commentary on "Nicomachean Ethics,"* bk. VI, lects. IV and VII.

ruled out.[16] For our king, Aquinas's concern would be less for him to articulate precise institutional commitments and more for him to take stock of the moral health of his rule and community, and from there to question how he can promote their health further.

Today, for instance, we might think we need to choose between a thin, *modus vivendi* dispensation and a "comprehensive" doctrine. In fact, Aquinas's pedagogy urges us to build community where we already find ourselves and examine where growth in moral knowledge ought to take us. Perhaps this pedagogy is the most helpful way of engaging our conditions of pluralism. Instead of accepting pluralism as a simple brute fact about the world, we might interrogate it more probingly: what do we agree on as a pluralistic community? What do we not? On what basis do we agree, or not? Where are we headed in terms of agreement? Are there ways in which, at least on Christian terms, we are moving away from monism and toward dualism? If the primacy of the spiritual cannot be respected, can it at least not be trampled?

Toward a Thomistic Politics

At the risk of becoming tedious, I will emphasize again that these principles do not amount to a full picture of the relationship between the temporal and spiritual powers. This does not seem, however, to have been Aquinas's goal. Aquinas does not lay out a fuller theory of church/state relations, but what he does give us has been of considerable substance.

On the other hand, we can take this lacuna as one of the surest confirmations of Aquinas's political naturalism. As we noted in chapter 4 of II.4, Aquinas does not take the activity of politics to be mysterious. People have been practicing it for millennia, and

---

16. See Thaddeus Kozinski, *The Political Problem of Religious Pluralism: And Why Philosophers Can't Solve It* (Lanham, Md.: Lexington Books, 2010).

Christianity provides no easy recipes to simplify it. Indeed, Aquinas has emphasized that politics is noble but difficult. Perhaps one might here invoke Father Schall's tongue-in-cheek claim that there is no such thing as a Catholic political philosophy.[17] From the data of *De Regno*, Schall's statement seems profoundly true but also incomplete: politics begins with reason and experience, but revelation can return politics to that task if politically active citizens are willing to recognize the horizon of the spiritual beyond all temporality.

Three Rival Versions of Church/State Models

These five principles from *De Regno* are challenging to the ways Westerners think through spiritual-temporal relations. Having synthesized those principles, let us turn to three other models of church/state relations. I hope with these comparisons to flesh out what Aquinas is trying to do—and not do—with his own model of church/state relations in *De Regno*, and to place Aquinas's *De Regno*, and thus Aquinas himself, in the history of political thought.

The purpose of the first goal is obvious, but the second might be less so. My point will be simple: Aquinas is unique among medieval political thinkers. As Maritain argues, it is simply not the case that he is "representative" of the thought of his time: no great thinker would be. For that reason, we should be suspicious of claims that Aquinas champions or promotes any one dominant strain of medieval political thought.

As for Aquinas's place vis-a-vis modern political thought, we must avoid two tendencies in modern political theory: first, to make Aquinas palatable to moderns by domesticating his thought, as the "Whig" line of Thomism has done, and second, to make

---

17. Schall, "*Fides et Ratio*," 49.

him so alien to modernity that we do not even try to explore how his thought might speak to our own time.[18] As Garnett argues of medieval thought on religious liberty, it is hard work to translate Aquinas's politics into terms meaningful to our own day, but it is possible, and it is desirable.[19]

In what follows, we will consider two medieval models and two modern ones: Aristotelian and Augustinian, and rational and pluralist liberalism.

Medieval Church/State Theory

It is cliché to argue that the intellectual debates of medieval Europe were riven between partisans of Aristotle and Saint Augustine. Yet the saying has some force: the Stagirite and the bishop exercised tremendous influence on Western thought of the time, and their legacies were prima facie not easy to reconcile. Indeed, partisans of their traditions often advocated diametrically opposed teachings on the human person, political communities, and the temporal/spiritual question. We have already seen Aquinas seek in *De Regno* to synthesize Aristotle's political naturalism with the postlapsarian politics of Saint Augustine.

In this section, I will argue that Aquinas's principles follow a principled *via media* between the tendencies of scholars influenced by Aristotle and Augustine. As spokesmen for those schools, I will select John of Paris (Quidort) and Giles of Rome (Aegidius Romanus).[20] The point here is not to determine precisely the thought

18. For instance, Michael Novak, "Aquinas and the Heretics," *First Things* 58 (1995): 33–38, or Finnis, *Aquinas*.

19. Richard W. Garnett, "'The Freedom of the Church': (Towards) An Exposition, Translation, and Defense," *Journal of Contemporary Legal Issues* 21 (2013): 54.

20. Murray, "Contemporary Orientations" singles out these two very thinkers for comparison with Aquinas. Murray finds Quidort's thinking consonant with that of Aquinas, however, whereas I do not. And where Murray finds the thought of Giles of Rome far removed from that of Aquinas, I find Giles agrees on at least one point with Aquinas that

of these thinkers but to contrast broadly the approaches of these two thinkers with each other and with Aquinas. I conclude that medieval thinkers tended to oscillate between dualism and the primacy of the spiritual, Aristotelians the former and Augustinians the latter, and that Aquinas remarkably incorporates both into his theory, attaining the unusual goal of preserving both dualism and primacy.

John of Paris and the Aristotelian Tradition

John of Paris, or Quidort, was a student of Thomas Aquinas and has been called the first Thomist. Although his views were controversial even within his own lifetime, few commentators have noted his striking departures from Aquinas in his political thought. Here, those departures will take center stage.

Quidort fittingly begins his work *On Royal and Papal Power* with the Aristotelian claim that "It happens sometimes that a person wishing to avoid a certain error falls into its opposite." The "truth about the power" of popes, he argues, "holds a middle position between two errors": those who deny the pope any temporal power, and those who grant him total temporal power.[21]

He grounds his *via media* in a series of arguments intended to show that the temporal realm is autonomous from the spiritual. Griesbach argues persuasively that, for Quidort, "the entire order of politics ... is separated from ecclesiastical jurisdiction" and "is not only distinct, but separate and self-sufficient apart from the ecclesiastical authority."[22]

Quidort begins his inquiry by distinguishing the origins and

Quidort does not. McCoy also pairs these two thinkers, making of them a troika with Marsilius of Padua. I am more sympathetic to his reading (McCoy, *The Structure of Political Thought*, 122–31).

21. John of Paris, *De Potestate Regia et Papali*, prologue, 1–5.
22. Griesbach, "John of Paris," 40–41.

ends of *regnum* and *sacerdotium*. He then works out their relationship based on those ends and origins. That relation, he argues, hinges in large part on the question of temporal priority: kingship emerged prior to the priesthood and was therefore perfect without it. While the priesthood has a superior dignity, that dignity does not supersede the perfection of the power of kingship.

While Quidort argues that inferior causes ought to be subordinated to superior causes insofar as the inferior cause bears upon the superior cause, he denies that the temporal power ought to be subordinate to the spiritual.[23] This is first because, as we have already seen, he thinks the superiority of the spiritual is merely one of dignity, not of power. But Quidort also denies that the end of temporal life has any direct bearing on spiritual ends, such that he takes it as a matter of indifference whether Christians live under tyrants or kings. Quidort not only denies that grace is necessary to perfect the natural virtues, as Aquinas would argue in the *Summa Theologica*: he also denies that matters of religion can themselves be a part of the natural virtues, as Aquinas argues in *De Regno*, and therefore that earthly virtues ought to conduce to beatitude.

Recall that while Aquinas concedes in *De Regno* II.3 that Christian priesthood temporally proceeds political communities, he also argues that the Christian priesthood nevertheless brings to their *telos* earlier religious authorities that have been with man from the beginning of history. Because the spiritual and temporal ends of man are related for Aquinas, the development of the spiritual authority has temporal consequences for him. Thus, the subordination of religious authority to political authority becomes the subordination of the political to the religious. Quidort, however, makes a sharp distinction between the Christian and pre-Christian priesthood. Even "if priesthood is taken broadly

---

23. John of Paris, *De Potestate Regia et Papali*, XVII.23.

and improperly" to include pre-Christian religious authority, Quidort argues, the "priesthood and kingship arose and fell concurrently," and so priesthood still cannot claim temporal priority.[24] The unfolding of revelation, Quidort argues, has one primary impact on the relation between the spiritual and temporal powers: to separate them.

The *temporalia* of political life did not depend in any way on the spiritual before Christianity, Quidort argues, so there is no reason why they should under Christianity. Quidort thereby reflects a tendency of Christian Aristotelians, in whose company one might include Dante and Marsilius of Padua, to embrace Aristotle's political naturalism so as to emphasize dualism but deny the primacy of the spiritual. Quidort thus comes close to denying Gelasianism. He certainly parts company with Aquinas, who can both acknowledge the naturalness of politics and affirm the primacy of the spiritual.

We see that Quidort also departs from Thomistic political naturalism. Aquinas agrees that political authority has a certain autonomy, but one that depends on its end. As we saw, Aquinas also thinks that man's revealed end can strengthen man's natural end. Quidort has no such interest: human reason has devised human law since time out of mind, and divine law has no relevance, either in limiting it or guiding it.

For that matter, Quidort and other Christian Aristotelians also arguably part company with Aristotle himself, who, after all, knew that politics had a certain incompleteness to it. The aim of the contemplative life, to be the philosopher, might always depend on political life, but it has a certain divinity to which quotidian political life cannot pretend to attain. Moreover, as Nichols notes, for all of Aristotle's political rationalism, he sees a vital role for

---

24. John of Paris, *De Potestate Regia et Papali*, IV.

piety and religion in even the best regime.[25] Quidort and others, however, close off the polis from such questions, turning Aristotle's teleological speculations into institutional questions.

Quidort would seem to agree with Aquinas's critique of civil religion and theocracy. His notion of the material distinction between religion and politics seems to ground what Griesbach calls "a genuine separation of Church and State."[26] There is certainly no danger of theocracy on his account. And yet one can wonder how thoroughly civil religion can be prevented if the spiritual has no role in limiting the temporal: spiritual authority would seemingly be powerless to protest the ever-present threats of tyranny afforded by civil religion and sacred monarchy.

Quidort would have no objections to Aquinas's principle of ambivalence, and perhaps takes it too far: Quidort's assertion that politics has nothing to do with the spiritual gives the Christian, as we noted above, precious few resources for understanding politics in the light of faith.

What Quidort would have particular difficulty with, however, is Aquinas's notion of pedagogy. One gets the impression that, for Quidort, politics and religion can be treated in metaphysical terms without recourse to any practical science. There is little sense in which human community develops and grows toward moral ends. Politics, as it were, has had justice as its end from time out of mind, and Christianity has added nothing to knowledge of communal living. Indeed, his refusal to see pre-Christian religious authority as "priesthood" is a refusal to see how religious life develops out of natural faculties, and to see how religion exists on the plane of nature, not just grace.[27] Quidort seems willfully blind

---

25. Nichols, response to Robert C. Bartlett, 152–60.
26. Griesbach, "John of Paris," 46, n. 55.
27. Kries, "The Virtue of Religion."

of the profoundly Aristotelian dynamic at play here, teleology, in his effort to establish that Christianity lacks any temporal priority to politics. McCoy can be forgiven for doubting the good faith of Quidort's arguments.[28]

Thus, Quidort has little truck for Aquinas's teleological understanding of pedagogy. As for the eschatological, Quidort so severs grace from nature that it is hard to see how he does not reject Augustine's Two Cities and the fundamental ambiguity of history. Humans seem to be capable of full justice in politics without grace.

Quidort's theory expertly preserves dualism and the autonomy of the temporal from the spiritual, but he preserves the primacy of the spiritual by reducing it to an ineffectual "dignity." Indeed, his concern seems to be not reconciling man's ends and the authorities that govern him toward them but rather safeguarding political institutions. Quidort's hyper-Aristotelian commitments cause him to deny the incredible impact of Christianity on political culture.

Giles of Rome and the Augustinian Tradition

Giles of Rome, also known as Aegidius Romanus and Egidius Colonna, has a reputation for political Augustinianism matched only by Pope Boniface VIII.[29] Political Augustinianism, a prominent thread in medieval Christian political thought during and subsequent to Aquinas's time, interpreted Augustine's "Two Cities" doctrine in sharply institutional terms, calling for the total absorption of the temporal power by the spiritual power.[30] As noted

---

28. McCoy, *The Structure of Political Thought*, 123–26.

29. McCoy greatly informs my reading of Giles. See his rich summary in *The Structure of Political Thought*, 122–23. I use the English translation of R. W. Dyson, *Giles of Rome's On Ecclesiastical Power. A Medieval Theory of World Government.* (New York: Columbia University Press, 2004).

30. Bruno, *Political Augustinianism*, 1; Oakley, *Empty Bottles*, 123, 127.

earlier, the linkage of this line of thought to St. Augustine himself is quite weak.[31] Further, this tradition of theocracy was only one of two strains of Augustinianism, the other emphasizing the early Augustine's flight from the city.

Like many Augustinians of his time, Giles was a canonist, and he trained his legal sights on the construction of a thoroughly hierocratic vision of Christian politics. Whatever else we can say, Giles reflects a tendency of political Augustinians to embrace an interpretation of the primacy of the spiritual at the cost of the Christian teaching on dualism. In his *De Ecclesiastica Potestate*, Giles argues that all power derives from the pope, including the temporal power of kings. Therefore, kings receive their authority by delegation from the pope. Giles bases his argument on the *plenitudo potestatis*, or the claim that the pope's office carries all power on earth. Giles sees human affairs as a simple unity, in which "the parts have no function independently of the whole."[32] To say that the temporal power derives from this *plenitudo potestatis*, then, means to collapse the temporal into the spiritual power. Aquinas also subscribes to something like the *plenitudo potestatis*, but he has a more sophisticated understanding of the social metaphysics at play. For Aquinas, as McCoy argues, Christendom is a unity of order: the temporal does not cease to govern itself because it is ordered to the spiritual, and is therefore not subsumed.[33] Moreover, Aquinas agrees with Quidort that political authority has a temporal priority to the Christian priesthood. Aquinas takes that priority to mean less than does Quidort, but more than does Aegidius. On Aquinas's account, that temporal priority shows that man would be political even were the priesthood never to arise,

---

31. Bruno, *Political Augustinianism*, 39–42.
32. McCoy, *The Structure of Political Thought*, 123.
33. McCoy, *The Structure of Political Thought*, 53.

but also that in the Christian dispensation, the two authorities require ordering and harmonization.

Giles' notion of political power leads him to violate Gelasian dualism, although he advocates a robust version of the primacy of the spiritual. He deploys the "principle of the hierarchy of ends to a *Respublica Christiana* viewed as a *simple unity* under the hegemony of the Pope," in McCoy's language.[34] Giles' relationship with Thomistic naturalism is more complicated. Giles, like Aquinas, appreciates the pedagogy of revelation: he is very clear that the proclamation of Christian truth has a tremendous impact on politics, such that humans must learn from and adapt to it in their political activity. Thus, while Giles could not be further away from civil religion, his theory defines theocracy for the Western tradition. Because of this radical subordination of politics to religion, Giles argues that man's spiritual end instrumentalizes politics rather than relativizes it. Whereas for Aquinas beatitude should strengthen the pursuit of man's temporal end, for Giles, beatitude reduces politics to an auxiliary role, as though the facilities department of the church.

Giles is promonarchy, like Aquinas, but without his ambivalence toward regime form. He rather links temporal regimes closely to the church, which makes the question of the best regime a fraught question: monarchy is not only the best regime but also the only regime suitable for the proper relationship between church and state. Further, Giles exhibits little concern that joining the fortunes of the church to the fortunes of political governance could be disastrous for the church itself, as Tocqueville warned later.

As for pedagogy, Giles shares with Quidort a strongly metaphysical approach to politics and the church/state question. Like Quidort, he does not distinguish between the theoretical order,

---

34. McCoy, *The Structure of Political Thought*, 123.

whereby exemplary relations between the ends of man are identified, and the practical order, wherein the institutions seeking such ends are instantiated and in time and space perfected. Rather, Giles reduces the ends of the person to an institutional problem: how to subordinate the state to the church. In this, he shares a similar institutional focus with Quidort, rather than the teleological focus that concerns Aquinas.

Aquinas Between Aristotelian and Augustinianism

From what we have collected on Quidort and Giles as broadly representative of the Christian Aristotelian and Augustinian traditions, it is not difficult to position Aquinas as a *via media* between these two traditions. Aquinas agrees with Quidort on the integrity of the political against Giles, but with Giles on the primacy of the spiritual against Quidort. Indeed, variation in Christian political thought can be understood in large part as varying emphases in the Gelasian tradition. An emphasis on dualism without the primacy of the spiritual, as we see in the case of Quidort, seems to adopt a Christian teaching on the distinction between the spiritual and temporal, while also denying the force of Christianity itself, or rather try to accommodate Christian teaching without disruption to the temporal. An emphasis on primacy that collapsed dualism, however, such as that of Giles of Rome, simply does not take seriously the deliverances of reason on man's nature, and perhaps does not even take seriously the deliverances of revelation, which also insists that man is social and political.

For all their important differences, both traditions make a choice between dualism and the primacy of the spiritual. Perhaps this choice is inevitable: the Gelasian teaching calls for a difficult reconciliation of dualism and primacy of the spiritual. It is little more common in theory than in practice.

This choice to prefer one part of Gelasiansim over the other, however, leads them to prioritize institutions over ends. They choose different institutions—Quidort the city over the church, and Giles the church over the *regnum*—but both employ the preservation of an institution to guide their reflection rather than human ends. Again, perhaps this is not surprising: reflection on human ends is difficult, drawing as it does on both speculative and practical questions, and not easily determinative of political arrangements. The temptation to simplify the problem of human ends to one of juridical formation is therefore understandably quite strong in the tradition of Christian political thought, a temptation naturally, or rather unnaturally, reinforced by the *libido dominandi* of those seeking to control those institutions.

There is a certain irony in this emphasis on institutions. A key claim of early modern thinkers, as we have already noted, is that prior political thought focused on the attainment of unrealistic ends: Machiavelli's "imagined republics." While our analysis of Giles and Quidort is not dispositive of this question, it at least suggests that many premodern forms of politics, in fact, focused on institutions rather than ends: just like those very critics. But for Aquinas in *De Regno*, politics cannot stop meditating on the question of human ends. Institutional relationships between the spiritual and temporal, moreover, must not be separated from that meditation, but must rather reflect it, for those institutions and their relationships grow out of human understandings of those ends.

The teachings of Quidort and Giles remind us that Aquinas's teaching is a delicate balance. For Gelasianism is a two-fold teaching and implies a linkage between speculative and practical thought that is theoretically demanding and practically frustrating. It thus offers at least two characteristic ways to go wrong.

Here, too, we have seen some of the limits of the "Aristotle versus Augustine" cliché in medieval political historiography. Quidort uses Aristotelian methodology to advance a strikingly anti-Aristotelian teaching, proceeding from first principles to argue for the fundamental discontinuity between the ends of man. Giles' "Augustinian" analysis, we saw, reduces the supernatural realities of the Two Cities to two earthly institutions: kingdoms and the church. While many think of Aquinas as an Aristotelian, we have seen yet again that Aquinas resists easy classification. If he is an Aristotelian, he is not of the tradition of John of Paris, Dante, or Marsilius. But if he is an Augustinian, he is certainly not of the tradition of Giles or Boniface VIII.

A strong case can be made that Aquinas has a better grasp of Aristotle than do the Christian Aristotelians, and of Augustine than do the radical Augustinians. This does not render him, however, either an "Aristotelian" or an "Augustinian" but rather Thomas Aquinas.[35] We might emphasize again that Quidort and Giles represent two traditions into which Aquinas is often subsumed, but we can see that he fits comfortably in neither. Again, the difference between him and these schools is not just on the level of institutions but also on the level of teleology, for in *De Regno*, Aquinas privileges human ends over institutions, and thus can emphasize both primacy and dualism.

On a yet more speculative level, the tendency of Gelasianism to collapse into monism raises a question: has Gelasianism ever been practiced? If not, then its rejection by modern political thinkers is

35. For Manent (*An Intellectual History of Liberalism*, 11–12) and Ernest L Fortin, AA, *The Birth of Philosophic Christianity*, vol. 1 of *Collected Essays*, ed. J. Brian Benestad (Lanham, Md.: Rowman and Littlefield, 1996), 199–222, Aquinas fundamentally breaks with Augustine in his use of Aristotle. For Radical Orthodoxy scholars, Aquinas is the Augustinian *par excellence*. See John Milbank, *Theology and Social Theory: Beyond Secular Reason* (Oxford: Blackwell, 1990) and Tracey Rowland, *Culture and the Thomist Tradition* (London: Routledge, 2003).

little short of tragic. Then again, Gelasianism has survived in modern times, at least on some accounts, through the legacy of medieval constitutional pluralism. I will next take up this question.

Liberalism: Rationalism and Pluralism

Quidort and Giles were medievals like Aquinas, but what of more modern thought? In this section, I compass liberalism to consider its relation to *De Regno*. Specifically, I offer an account of rationalism and pluralism as twin strands of liberalism, following Levy and Muñiz-Fraticelli. I then consider each of the two strands vis-a-vis Aquinas's Gelasian dualism and pedagogy. I conclude that Aquinas's thought is deeply opposed to rationalism but has important points of connection with pluralism that can bolster pluralism. As the church has long been an agent of pluralism in West, it accordingly has been a *bête noire* of liberal rationalism but has buttressed and benefited from liberalism's pluralist instincts.

In his *Rationalism, Pluralism, and Freedom*, Levy describes liberalism in terms of two "two broad patterns": "one inclined toward the use of state power to protect individuals from local group power, one inclined to see groups as the results of individual free choice and the protectors of freedom against state power."[36] The first pattern is the "rationalism" associated with the social contract tradition. The second is pluralism.[37] Historically, pluralism arises from a variety of premodern sources, and rationalism preeminently takes the form of social contract theory, which as a systematic body of reflection has a distinctly modern vintage. More theoretically, Levy argues, these trends arise from differing "ways of looking at the triadic relationship among individual persons,

36. Levy, *Rationalism, Pluralism, and Freedom*, 27.
37. In this study, we are primarily interested in political pluralism, as opposed to meta-ethical and ethical pluralism. See Victor Muñiz-Fraticelli, *The Structure of Pluralism* (Oxford: Oxford University Press, 2014), 9–30.

intermediate groups, and states."[38] While pluralism tends to look positively on such intermediate groups as "sites where free people live their diverse lives," rationalism views those groups "as sites of local tyranny that the liberal state must be strong enough to keep in check." Thus, pluralism tends to value the diversity and particularity of customs, traditions, and groups in which people find themselves. Rationalism, on the other hand, tends to value the "progress, universalism, and equality before a unified law" that protects people from the arbitrary domination of "local tyrannies" and thus "looks to the importance of free persons' ability to transform or transcend those current lives."[39] Put differently, whereas pluralism tends to accept multiple spheres of authority in a society, rationalism seeks to rationalize them under the aegis of the liberal state, which alone can secure the liberty of persons.

Rationalism thus emerges as the more ambitious of the two stands. A primary form of rationalism, and one exemplary of its reformist ambitions, is contractarianism. Levy offers a helpful summary of social contract theory: "Social contract theory imagines political societies as resting on a fundamental agreement, adopted at a discrete moment in hypothetical time," a decision "that both bound individual persons together into a single polity and set fundamental rules regarding that polity's structure and powers."[40] A key word here is "imagines." As Levy argues, the contractarian tradition rests on an abstraction from history in favor of the hypothetical contract model: its image of constitution-making, he writes, "flattens and distorts" real constitution-making. Social contract theory, he says, misses that constitution-making happens in a context of "ongoing societies," mediating between "preexist-

---

38. Levy, *Rationalism, Pluralism, and Freedom*, 2.
39. Levy, *Rationalism, Pluralism, and Freedom*, 2.
40. Levy, *Rationalism, Pluralism, and Freedom*, 192.

ing laws and legal systems, political organizations, cultural and linguistic and religious divisions, and norms and mores."[41] Constitutional orders have to "appropriate, incorporate, and channel the histories and divisions of the societies they govern," Levy argues, whereas social contract theory implies that constitutions rather emerge *in vacuo*, as with Thomas Paine's suggestion that the American Revolution returned the colonies to the state of nature, or Rawls' reliance on the "veil of ignorance."[42]

Many of contractarianism's critics have characterized it as "monistic."[43] Pluralism calls for something different:

> Against monism, the pluralists assert that, in any society, there are multiple sources of legitimate political authority personated in various groups and associations, of which the state is but one; none of these has inherent precedence over the others. Groups—e.g. churches, unions, universities—exercise sovereignty in their own right, and it is only this dispersion of authority that secures freedom against the state.[44]

Pluralism is descriptive, Levy argues, in that it recognizes "that the sources of social organization are many, not one," but it is also prescriptive, for it holds that these various bodies and groups should be allowed "to follow their own various norms" rather than be held to some external standard, for example, those of rationalism.[45]

As Levy emphasizes, pluralism is a premodern source of liberalism and constitutionalism more generally. Aquinas is part of that tradition, even if saying much more than that leads to anachronism. After all, for all the talk of medieval society as fundamentally "pluralistic," it also seems to be dualistic as well. How, then,

---

41. Levy, *Rationalism, Pluralism, and Freedom*, 192.
42. Levy, *Rationalism, Pluralism, and Freedom*, 204 and 196.
43. Mark Bevir, "A History of Modern Pluralism," in *Modern Pluralism*, ed. Mark Bevir (Cambridge: Cambridge University Press, 2012), 2.
44. Muñiz-Fraticelli, *The Structure of Pluralism*, 18.
45. Levy, *Rationalism, Pluralism, and Freedom*, 27.

are we to relate this pluralism to the duality of the spiritual and temporal authority?

Crucially for our engagement between liberalism and the teaching of *De Regno*, religious liberty is a "core commitment" of Western liberalism for both rationalism and pluralism.[46] Religious liberty has historically been a great goal of liberalism, a goal shaped in part by the medieval clashes between empire and papacy, but rationalism and pluralism tend to understand religious liberty in different ways, and in manners characteristic of their divergent view of intermediate groups more generally. For while pluralism tends to promote religious liberty as vital to the flourishing of persons in the religious bodies that help to animate social life, rationalism typically promotes religious liberty as a protection from religious bodies, groups that rationalism views as illiberal and thus inimical to the rationalist agenda.[47]

In what follows, I will consider rationalism and pluralism vis-a-vis two principles of Aquinas's *De Regno*: Gelasianism (both dualism and primacy) and pedagogy. I hope through this comparison to deepen our understanding of Aquinas's place in the history of political thought and to uncover possibilities for contemporary engagement between the liberal and the Christian political traditions.

Rationalism: Gelasianism and Pedagogy

Let us consider the rationalist tradition in terms of Aquinas's Gelasianism. While there can be no question that liberal rationalism encompasses nothing like primacy of the spiritual, does it perhaps make some room for dualism?

---

46. Levy, *Rationalism, Pluralism, and Freedom*, 31, 87.
47. Levy, *Rationalism, Pluralism, and Freedom*, 29–31. See Victor Muñiz-Fraticelli, "The Distinctiveness of Religious Liberty," in *Mapping the Legal Boundaries of Belonging: Religion and Multiculturalism from Israel to Canada*, ed. Rene Provost (New York: Oxford University Press, 2014), 99–120.

Contractarianism posits the radical reformulation of society along the lines of the liberal state. As Levy points out, in the rationalist tradition of liberalism, very little "survives" the contract: "social, civil, legal, and political institutions are all coeval with sovereign statehood."[48] As such, contractarian "civil society" refers to "the self-contained and unified political society" that excludes all other authoritative public bodies, including free cities, feudal powers, and "coercive religious jurisdiction."[49] It is, in other words, a sphere of "freedom from group power, secured by a publicly accessible and rationally determined system of state law."[50]

This scheme logically opposes dualism. Rationalism as a monistic vision of authority comprehends all other social and political bodies as precisely "substate": existing beneath, as it were, the state. There is no room in its vision for a nonstate actor that also exercises sovereignty. Thus, although the church predates any social contract constituting the liberal state, Aquinas's church can only be the church of Locke's "individualistic, anticorporate" voluntary association.[51] For rationalists, the church is but one private association among many. The *libertas Ecclesiae* possible under rationalism would not be grounded on a recognition of the public character and mission of the church, as would be the case in Gelasian dualism, but rather as a grant of or concession from the contractarian state and under the "publicly accessible and rationally determined system of state law" in Levy's description above. Rationalism thus appears as a kind of monism, introducing a pre-Christian state of affairs in which religion is subordinate to the political.

As religious bodies are but one of many substate actors in

---

48. Levy, *Rationalism, Pluralism, and Freedom*, 136.
49. Levy, *Rationalism, Pluralism, and Freedom*, 18.
50. Levy, *Rationalism, Pluralism, and Freedom*, 21.
51. Levy, *Rationalism, Pluralism, and Freedom*, 139.

the rationalist tradition, religious liberty is "nothing special" on the rationalist account: it is a matter "indifferent" for politics, in Locke's language.[52] Or, if it is special, it is special in a negative way, in the sense that religious liberty is understood primarily as freedom *from* religion.[53] Further, because of rationalism's individualism, it tends to understand religious liberty as grounded in the rights of conscience of the individual, and not in the corporate body that transcends any individual, that is, the church. Thus, even my earlier suggestion of a *libertas Ecclesiae* is misleading; that sort of language has been replaced by the civil liberties of the individual. While there is some overlap between the two concepts, they are not the same.

To be merely one of many associations under the contract raises the question of whether the church should be subject in its internal activity to the same standards of justice and fairness as the liberal contractarian state. Rationalism tends to hold that substate groups ought to be held to liberal standards precisely so that they do not become sites of tyranny and domination, and thus pockets of resistance to liberalism.[54] Further, the rationalist understanding of the church as a private voluntary association under the aegis of the contractarian state encounters great difficulties in the church's transnational membership and activity.[55] Such activity can be construed as a rejection of the claim of the social contract to contain all social life.

52. Micah Schwartzman, "What if Religion Is Not Special?" *The University of Chicago Law Review* 79: 1351–427.
53. Levy, *Rationalism, Pluralism, and Freedom*, 29–31.
54. Levy, *Rationalism, Pluralism, and Freedom*, 53–5, 68–70, 267.
55. Levy, *Rationalism, Pluralism, and Freedom*, 65–66. See also Susanne Hoeber Rudolph, "Introduction: Religion, States, and Transnational Civil Society," in *Transnational Religion and Fading States*, ed. Susanne Hoeber Rudolph and James Piscatori (Boulder, Co.: Westview Press, 1997).

Rationalism's monism excludes any kind of Thomistic dualism. It also rejects Thomistic pedagogy. Recall Levy's claim that the contractarian tradition rests on an abstraction from history in favor of the hypothetical contract model.[56] Social contract theory assumes a particular agreement predicated on a particular reason or set of reasons for humans' entrance into political community, in turn reflecting a certain consensus about citizens based on what they know and believe as they enter. The state thus imagined, in other words, has a specific set of ends and a relatively static outcome.

Our talk of "image" and "imagination" reminds us that the social contract is a metaphor, and that its attendant visual imagery need not be in every respect fully instantiated in reality. No doubt, in other words, the state under the social contract can and does changes. Yet anyone concerned about how a regime might account for change in the knowledge and beliefs that bind citizens would have to worry about the ability of the social contract theory to allow for the constitutional development of the regime to match the moral and epistemic development of its people, and the negative effects of such images and metaphors on the possibility for such development. Indeed, it would seem to arrest the moral and political development of its people.

Thus, rationalism would seem to rule out the pedagogy at work in Aquinas's *De Regno*. As we noted above, part of Aquinas's pedagogy is rooted in Aristotle's claim that "though [the city] originates for the sake of staying alive, it exists for the sake of living well" (*Politics* 1252b27). In light of that claim, social contract theory would not seem to differentiate between those basic ends that bring man into political community and the more excellent ends that man comes to seek as his life in community becomes more

---

56. See also Jacob T. Levy, "Not So Novus an Ordo: Constitutions without Social Contracts," *Political Theory* 37, no. 2 (2009): 192.

rational. To this, one could respond that the contractarian regime has the goal of satisfying necessity, not Aristotle's excellence. That low goal, moreover, arose out of the reflection of thinkers like Hobbes and Machiavelli, who judged the premodern tendency toward political excellence to be a terrible failure, what Machiavelli dismissed as "imagined republics." The social contract is a low but solid affirmation of that on which a society can agree, and other, more contentious matters are set aside.

Here we might note two things. First, Aquinas's pedagogical element makes *De Regno* more responsive to the conditions of pluralism than one might expect from popular assumptions about Aquinas's politics. A pluralistic society, after all, would exhibit considerable change over time in its moral and political commitments. But a contractarian regime that consciously sets truth-and-morality markers would precisely not be sensitive to such shifts. Aquinas's pedagogy in *De Regno*, however, would be.

Second, as we have noted, many early modern thinkers argued against premodern traditions of politics on the grounds that they were hopelessly teleological or utopian. Our analysis of Giles and Quidort, however, suggests that many premodern forms of politics actually focused on institutions rather than ends. In other words, modern forms of politics only reinscribe the premodern polemics over institutional jurisdictions. Perhaps it would be more useful to "get behind" the institutions toward human ends.

Part of this effort to get behind institutions would be a new appreciation for intellectual humility. Social contract theory, like the "Aristotelian" and "Augustinian" traditions we discussed above, displays breathtaking confidence about how political institutions are to be configured. This is in marked contrast to the humble pedagogical model of politics adumbrated by Aquinas in *De Regno*. While this confidence might be justified in a society marked by high degrees of cohesion and homogeneity, it is precisely what a fragmented, pluralistic society does not need. Perhaps, then, political theory and practice would do well to embrace the humility of the student and shed the theoretical confidence of the teacher. I argue, then, that contractarianism would be better were it to embrace Aquinas's understanding of politics as pedagogical.

In short, liberal rationalism bears little in common with the text of *De Regno*: rationalism is monist where *De Regno* is dualist, and rationalism is antipedagogical where *De Regno* is pedagogical. We see here, then, a correspondence with arguments that early modern political thought represents a critical departure from medieval thought. But this is not the end of Aquinas's dialogue with liberalism. We have seen Levy's argument that liberalism has two strands, and so we must now turn to an encounter between Aquinas and that second strand: pluralism.

Pluralism: Gelasianism and Pedagogy

While liberalism's rationalist tendencies militate against the totality of Aquinas's teaching, pluralism complements crucial aspects of that teaching. Indeed, Gelasian dualism and pluralism share much in common, such that much of medieval political thought has been labeled pluralist. But if dualism and pluralism share a similar commitment to limiting the power of the state, and even credit great agency to the church toward that effort, they nonetheless do not accord the same status to the church and to religious liberty. This difference in status, in turn, has important implications for how pluralism comports with Aquinas's pedagogical element in *De Regno*.

As we noted, pluralism tends to see groups as "sites where free people live their diverse lives."[57] This attitude alone should secure

---

57. Levy, *Rationalism, Pluralism, and Freedom*, 2.

plural sympathies for the Catholic Church, but the church is not just any intermediary body for the pluralist tradition. As illustrated by the dramatic events of Canossa, it has played a central role in defining and limiting the power of political authority in the West.[58] For its historical role in making possible nonstate authority in the West, then, pluralism cannot but regard religious liberty as important. Pluralism's interest in the church, however, is not simply antiquarian, for insofar as pluralism is committed to the autonomy and life of nonstate groups, the Catholic Church continues to play an outsized role in the pluralist imagination. Thus, it should come as no surprise that the Catholic Church continues to figure in debates surrounding the limits of the state, the rights of conscience and the moral implications of politics, concerning, for example, marriage and sexuality, the rights of immigrants and refugees, abortion and the death penalty, and end-of-life ethics.

Indeed, the church is in many ways for pluralism the intermediate group *par excellence*, with a vast transnational membership and elaborate governance structure, and with motivations and ways of proceeding that are systematically distinct from modern liberalism. A religious body like the church is not just a "culture," as Muñiz-Fraticelli demonstrates, but an authority.[59] This means that the church makes normative claims on its adherents, claims that at times can limit the role of the government. And this is part of the distinctiveness of religious liberty: that liberty has robust institutions speaking in its defense. The presence of such institutions, in turn, means that the church can counterbalance the state.[60]

---

58. Levy, *Rationalism, Pluralism, and Freedom*, 29–31. See Paul Horwitz, "Freedom of the Church Without Romance," *Journal of Contemporary Legal Issues* 21 (2013): 59–132, who claims that scholars' emphasis on Canossa distorts the historical record and obscures theoretical issues.

59. Muñiz-Fraticelli, "The Distinctiveness of Religious Liberty," 107–15.

60. Garnett, "The Freedom of the Church," 41–43.

In short, both pluralism and Gelasianism see a unique role for the church. They both reject the state as omnicompetent or monist. They both see religious liberty as important to limiting that monism, and the institutional role of the church as vital in promoting those limitations. For these reasons and more, in the pluralist tradition, religious liberty is understood not just as liberty *from* religion, as for rationalists, but *for* religion. There thus seem to be possibilities for pluralism to respect primacy of church in ways that rationalism does not. As Garnett notes, there is even room for something like the *libertas ecclesiae*.[61]

On the basis of such similarities, scholars have argued that pluralism is a natural advance of Christian dualism, even placing Thomas Aquinas and medieval political thought as the *fons et origo* of pluralism, as when John Courtney Murray, SJ, argued that "the Religion Clause of our First Amendment "codified" the freedom of the Church."[62] Similarly, some even argue for the benefits of applying this pluralism to the Holy See.[63] Indeed, it was precisely when the papacy was deprived of the papal states that it "could be reconstituted as the core of a transnational religious regime."[64]

While Aquinas's *De Regno* reveals deep complementarities between dualism and pluralism, there are crucial differences between them, which are wide enough, in fact, that any claim that

---

61. Garnett, "The Freedom of the Church," a most thoughtful piece, whose tenor is less optimistic.

62. Garnett, "The Freedom of the Church," 63.

63. Monica Duffy Toft, Daniel Philpott, and Timothy Samuel Shah, *God's Century: Resurgent Religion and Global Politics* (New York: W.W. Norton & Company, 2011), 20–39. See also Daniel Philpott, "Explaining the Political Ambivalence of Religion," *American Political Science Review* 101, no. 3 (2007): 505–25.

64. José Casanova, "Globalizing Catholicism and the Return to a 'Universal' Church," in *Transnational Religion and Fading States*, ed. Susanne Hoeber Rudolph and James Piscatori (Boulder, Colo.: Westview Press, 1997), 121.

pluralism is an advance on dualism is, in fact, a claim of preference for pluralism over dualism, not a simple observation about dualism's development. I do not wish to contest the historical claim that the church's struggle for *libertas ecclesiae* against the empire has influenced what we now think of as liberal pluralism. In what follows, however, I will consider two significant differences between dualism and pluralism: the metaphysics of social bodies and the politics of religious liberty. In grasping the differences between dualism and pluralism, I hope to make clear that these are differences not only between dualism and contemporary pluralism but also between dualism and medieval pluralism.

To begin with their metaphysical differences, the lexical distinction between "dualism" and "pluralism" is telling: whereas dualism attests to the two powers on earth that govern man's two ends, "pluralism" admits to multiple powers. Dualism, then, is a species within the genus of pluralism, the sort in which social life is normatively guided by two powers. On this account, dualism is a species of pluralism historically associated with Christianity.

The sense in which medieval Europe was pluralistic and dualistic, however, is far more ambiguous. Consider this seemingly simple historical observation by Muñiz-Fraticelli: "The later medieval world was characterized by many overlapping jurisdictions, of which the pope and the Holy Roman Empire were the most prominent."[65] Encoded in this observation is an ambiguity that cuts across much scholarly reflection on the practice and discourse of medieval Europe, and *a fortiori* on that practice and discourse itself. For while some scholars see medieval Europe as primarily pluralistic, others characterize it as dualistic. Scholars emphasizing medieval Europe's differences from the rationalism of the modern

---

65. Muñiz-Fraticelli, "The Distinctiveness of Religious Liberty," 105.

nation state, or its commonalities with modern pluralism, for instance, often argue that medieval society was characterized by plural sovereignty, but that same society is also often said to have been characterized by the struggle between the papacy and empire, between the *Sacerdotium* and *Regnum*.[66] That struggle found expression and normative guidance, moreover, in a substantial tradition, one associated with Pope Gelasius I, according to which human society ought to be directed by two powers, one temporal and one spiritual, with the temporal under the spiritual.

Thus, any account of medieval society must balance two facts: the plurality of authorities at play in medieval society, with its kings, bishops, princes, abbots, barons, guilds, families, and so forth; and the fundamentally dualistic dynamic in which two authorities contended for the power to coordinate that plurality of authorities, their struggle conditioning how other authority could be instantiated and exercised. In short, medieval society was never simply "dualistic": it was fundamentally pluralistic in important ways. But if that is true, then Gelasian dualism, a tradition of which Aquinas was a part, was never simply a description of Christian society. It was an aspiration of how society ought to be and a critique of mediaeval pluralism, which was far from perfect. As Murray himself notes, pluralism always inclined toward monism and denied the primacy of the spiritual. This tendency is just what Aquinas confronts in his critique of civil religion at *De Regno* II.3.

One could object that I am dancing around a central issue: the distinct justifications for dualism and pluralism. And here we can say that, on that account, dualism is not a species of pluralism, but that, at least in the medieval European case, it is more useful to see them as in distinct genera distinguished by their foundations:

---

66. Oakley, *The Mortgage of the Past*, 4.

pluralism is a political theory of the diversity of authorities, but dualism is a meta-political ("theologico-political") theory of how those authorities ought to relate and be configured. The basis of that metapolitics, again, is theological ethics: human ends.

Contemporary pluralism, however, takes a more utilitarian approach: it sees the church as a historically helpful partner in its campaign against rationalism. This means the church does not gain any authority or liberty because it guides humans to their final end but only insofar as that end happens to be transpolitical and therefore helps limit the authority and power of the state. In other words, contemporary pluralism recognizes the distinction between temporal and spiritual power insofar as spiritual power is not temporal, but it does not accord the spiritual power a place of primacy vis-a-vis the temporal.

To recapitulate: medieval Europe could be both pluralistic and dualistic because, at least in aspiration, its many powers were coordinated by two powers: the spiritual and the temporal in abstract, and the papacy and the empire *in concreto*. While the contemporary West has aspects of pluralism, it falls decidedly short of anything like Gelasian dualism.

In addition to their metaphysical differences, pluralism and dualism are also distinct in their conceptions of religious liberty. Modern religious liberty, we said, is typically grounded in the conscience of the individual. Can that liberty be extended to groups? For the church's argument is metaphysical and about the social body of the church: all human beings have a right and obligation to follow the truth, an exercise that is fundamentally communal. As Schragger and Schwartzman have it, the problem with contemporary applications of *libertas ecclesiae* is that society has changed dramatically since the days in which the concept emerged and flourished. Specifically, we are pluralistic—there is no longer "the church" but "the churches." For this reason, any explicitly theological justification for *libertas ecclesiae* would have to be more "ecumenical" and less specific to the Catholic tradition: "freedom of the church must be reformulated—or translated—to account for the pluralism and fragmentation of religion in modern democratic states."[67] Then again, many societies are characterized by nonbelief as well as religious pluralism, such that *libertas* would also have to be reformulated, they argue, into secular terms.

Garnett's observations are helpful. While agreeing with scholars that the invocation of the *libertas ecclesiae* in the modern liberal state requires a great effort of "translation," he argues that the "most formidable" obstacle to such efforts of translation is "the lack of interest in translating."[68] Moreover, that effort will depend in part on seeing *libertas ecclesiae* less as one idea or doctrine than as an "animating value, even mood."[69] For instance, Garnett sees some hope in the "church autonomy doctrine" for preserving the liberty of religious groups. But he argues that such a doctrine could only be part of such an approach.

Here we have moved far from pluralism, but perhaps Garnett here speaks for the pluralist tradition: whereas rationalism might demand that the church find secular ways of arguing for its liberty, pluralism might value different authorities advocating for their own political and ethical convictions, and in their own languages. And we can further recall Levy's claim about tension.[70] It is probably good for liberalism that the church's understanding of its liberty conflicts with that of political authority in the liberal state. If Western history is any guide, such conflict will redound to the

---

67. Richard C. Schragger and Micah Schwartzmann, "Against Religious Institutionalism," *Virginia Law Review* 99 (2013): 16.
68. Garnett, "The Freedom of the Church," 54.
69. Garnett, "The Freedom of the Church," 38.
70. See Muñiz-Fraticelli, *The Structure of Pluralism*, vii.

benefit of the liberty of many groups and persons in society. That tension can only be maintained, however, if the strong monistic impulses of rationalism are resisted.

Pluralists should therefore welcome the dualist conception of *libertas ecclesiae*, even if only prudentially, as an ally against overweening rationalism. Indeed, we might be so bold as to wonder if pluralism needs dualism more than dualism needs pluralism. As such, this is an important note on the place of dualism within the history of political thought: its continued vitality is a matter of some interest to liberalism, alongside pluralism and despite rationalism.

So much for dualism and pluralism. Let us now turn to pluralism and pedagogy. Pluralism in its various forms understands that an important part of political activity is to facilitate the liberty of associational life: to recognize and cultivate what emerges largely naturally from human social interactions. This understanding of politics has important consequences for its response to something like Aquinas's pedagogy. First, pluralism has no contractarian notion of a discrete moment in time in which reasons and purposes for entering into political community are crystallized. This brings us to a simple point: few ways of thinking about constitutions and regimes are as antipedagogical as is contractarianism.

Second, pluralism's fundamental commitment to the liberty of groups means that pluralism respects the autonomy of groups to chart their own course.[71] As Levy notes, pluralism respects that groups have life before the state and very well perhaps after the state. Pluralism is a fundamentally more modest and more humble account of politics and society than is rationalism. It is more open to accepting political life as it is than is rationalism and is less con-

---

71. David Nicholls, *The Pluralist State: The Political Ideas of J. N. Figgis and his Contemporaries* (London: Palgrave, 1994), 18–37.

cerned than the latter to advance a "project" of reshaping society after its own image. To the extent that pluralism finds a society of societies open to change and development, then it is open to pedagogy. As pluralism sees the church as but one among many groups, however, it denies the church the kind of authority to influence and direct that growth as in dualism.

Pluralism respects that such growth and development can have effects on the state. For instance, Figgis argued that the British state must acknowledge that British society was no longer fundamentally Christian.[72] Against those who fought for the continued constitutional establishment of Christianity in Western Europe, Figgis argued that toleration of religious diversity, and state neutrality toward those bodies, should be the order of the day. Similarly, we saw in *De Regno* II.3 that Aquinas thinks the political structures of a society should account for the regime coming to see the truth of Christian revelation.

To be sure, pluralism must face the consequences of this openness to change. These changes often lead to conflicts, and it is famously difficult to adjudicate these conflicts. It is probably best on pluralism's own terms that change leads to conflict, however, as such conflict suggests that groups are healthy enough to protect their interests and members robustly, much as did the *Sacerdotium* and *Imperium* in the medieval period.[73]

Although these are good reasons for a pedagogical approach to politics in pluralism's terms, we should, however, be clear that the basis of this pedagogy is distinct from that of Aquinas. As we noted, Aquinas's pedagogy is distinctly teleological: human societies must advance communally to the kind of knowledge about hu-

---

72. Nicholls, *The Pluralist State*, 96–110. Figgis' thoughts on secularism deserve far more attention than I can give them in this study.

73. Nicholls, *The Pluralist State*, 34, and Levy, *Rationalism, Pluralism, and Freedom*, 71.

man ends that allow them to legislate intelligently and prudently.

As a strain of liberalism, modern pluralism is committed to liberty for individuals and for groups. As such, modern pluralists would like to see that change be a development toward greater liberty. To the extent that Aquinas's notion of virtue depends on a conception of liberty, then the two are on the same page. To the extent that Aquinas would want that liberty directed to the pursuit of holiness, however, many pluralists would find his pedagogy too thick in its object. Or, rather, they would encourage him to pursue that object through the church, not the state, because they see the church as one among many bodies.[74]

Even this is too simple, however. Perhaps one might have no wish for the church to have any coercive influence in society, but nonetheless wish the church to exercise a role in society such as to encourage the virtue of its citizens. In this case, that person might very much desire that the church engage a pedagogical role in disposing citizens to political virtues and even holiness but would object to the church being given an authoritative role in governing humans toward those ends.

Pluralism does not simply exist as a form of government, however: as Levy notes, it exists entangled with rationalism. Thus, where pluralism hits the limits of pedagogy is likely where pluralism runs into rationalism. And we cannot deny that the state will have a legitimate interest in preventing certain injustices, even if interventions might seem to raise questions about the autonomy of nonstate groups, for example, child abuse in the Catholic Church.

In short, there is much room for agreement between Aquinas's *De Regno* and pluralism on the matter of pedagogy. Pluralism respects group life in a polity, and so it makes a space for groups like the church to influence society. To the extent that pluralism sees

---

74. Nicholls, *The Pluralist State*, 97.

the church as but one among many groups, however, it denies the church the kind of authority recognized in it by dualism.

On some accounts, this pluralistic approach is the true way that the church ought to so influence society, but we have surmised that Aquinas would have understood pluralism as a second-best state of affairs to dualism. What must be explored further, then, are the ways in which pluralism can be open to the presence of teleologically oriented bodies like the church.

Aquinas and Liberalism: Conclusions

Levy offers an account of Western liberalism that rests on the tension between rationalism and pluralism, an account with profound implications for religious groups like the Catholic Church. What are we to conclude about Aquinas's *De Regno* and those liberal traditions?

First, in any analysis of the complementarity between liberalism and Christian political thought, including that of Aquinas, the distinction between rationalism and pluralism must be attended to. Several thinkers are at least aware of this problem. Maritain and other Catholics have made that distinction with reference to "Anglo-American" and "Continental" liberalism, often with allusions to the difference between the American and French Revolutions.[75] But many Catholic critics of modernity speak as though liberalism were only rationalist.[76] Perhaps this is because they deny the vitality of the pluralistic tradition, in which case an argument should be produced to justify that conclusion. Perhaps, too, they are unaware that pluralism is not simply a holdover of medieval

---

75. Perhaps most famous are the popes and Leo XIII.
76. Levy notes that many critics of liberalism treat it as exclusively rationalist, usually by treating Hobbes as the protoliberal. Levy, "From Liberal Constitutionalism to Pluralism," in *Modern Pluralism*, ed. Mark Bevir (Cambridge: Cambridge University Press, 2012), 21–39. He singles out Strauss, Pettit, and McPherson.

political thought but a vital part of liberalism. In such case, it might be necessary to show more explicitly that the work of Tierney, Berman, and others are not simply of antiquarian interest but continue to animate modern liberalism.[77] On the other hand, some Catholic supporters of *rapprochement* between Catholicism and liberalism perhaps obscure the difficulties of such a project when they identify liberalism as synonymous with pluralism, rather than recognizing its rationalist twin.

Second, granting that distinction, Gelasian dualism finds more support in the pluralist tradition than in the rationalist tradition. Where rationalism seeks to reduce all group life under a monistic state, pluralism seeks to limit the role of the state so as to cultivate associations. Where rationalism sees the church as a great opponent of monism, pluralism sees the church as a powerful partner in the effort against statism. Further, where rationalism only apprehends religious liberty as a matter of rights of individual conscience, there is some hope that pluralism can cognize the corporate liberty of the church.[78] Finally, while rationalism's contractarian element militates against Aquinas's pedagogy, pluralism in its embrace of the independence of groups seems at least open to the ways that changes in group life could change society broadly.

Third, even the pluralist tradition offers only an attenuated support for dualism. Pluralism recognizes the rights of the church to exist as a group, but it is not clear how far that right equates to the *libertas ecclesiae*, nor how settled it is in different nations' jurisprudence. Moreover, pluralism sees the church as but one social body among many. To be guarded, then, the church's status must be somehow "unique" or "distinctive," a status that must reflect

---

77. Brian Tierney, *The Crisis of Church and State: 1050–1300, with Selected Documents* (Toronto: University of Toronto Press, 1988).
78. McCoy, *The Structure of Political Thought*, 100.

contemporary needs as well as the historical record. Further, while pluralism has a certain openness to pedagogy, it would not understand that pedagogy to be directed toward man's spiritual ends but rather to the kind of liberty that allows multiple visions of the good to flourish.

This leads us to our fourth point: in practical terms, the relationship between dualism and pluralism depends on the relationship between rationalism and pluralism. To restate Levy's thesis: pluralism always exists alongside rationalism, and while their tension might be good for liberalism, as he claims, rationalism is not good for the church. The pluralist openness to dualism, in other words, counts for little if in the *longue durée* rationalism vitiates pluralism. Levy argues that the tension between pluralism and rationalism in liberalism is deep and not likely to be resolved. In particular, new developments in rationalism always produce "countermovements" of pluralism.[79]

One might reject Levy's argument for the tension between pluralism and rationalism, however, as he notes of Charles Taylor, whose "Long March" is the story of pluralism increasingly giving way to rationalism.[80] Earlier, I concluded that the contractarian state does not easily "grow" in the pedagogical sense of Aquinas, but for Taylor, the fear is not that the contractarian state simply refuses to grow. Rather, Taylor's concern amounts to a worry that the liberal state would indeed grow but in a contractarian, monistic direction, and thus at the expense of groups like the church. For even if the two traditions are in tension, that tension would seem to hold only if both traditions are healthy. At the very least, the presence of rationalism means that pluralism cannot be tak-

---

79. Levy, *Rationalism, Pluralism, and Freedom*, 289.
80. Levy, *Rationalism, Pluralism, and Freedom*, 285–88. See Charles Taylor, *A Secular Age*. (Cambridge, Mass.: Belknap Press, 2007), 211.

en for granted. Weak pluralism will be destroyed by rationalism, or rationalism will deploy pluralism for its own benefit: forcing groups, for example, to adhere to the congruence theory, pitting groups against each other that oppose one another on that count.

Conclusion: *De Regno* in the Canon

In this chapter, we have come to five main conclusions. First, the five principles we adumbrated in the first half of the chapter are a substantive guide to church/state relations and one at least as rich as anything else in Aquinas's *opera*. While *De Regno* does not provide a treatise on the relationship between temporal and spiritual authorities, it nonetheless can help guide a polity toward salutary arrangements and help avoid negative ones. I would particularly note that these principles include more than just dualism and the primacy of the spiritual: pedagogy, ambivalence, and the rejection of civil religion and theocracy all deserve study and application.

Second, we have seen that Aquinas does not fit easily into the history of political thought. Aquinas strikes a *via media* between "Aristotelian" and "Augustinian" traditions and offers a balanced compromise between two regnant schools of medieval thought on church/state relations. Against the oscillation within Christian political thought between reducing temporal authority to a function of spiritual authority, and reducing spiritual to a seal of legitimacy for the temporal, Aquinas argues for an affirmation of both the spiritual and the temporal.[81]

Third, Aquinas's theoretical achievement would seem in practice to be fragile, perhaps indicating why so few thinkers have followed his lead—and why it has never been fully practiced. Indeed, we ought to remember that the specific thinkers to which we compared Aquinas, John of Paris and Giles of Rome, came quite

---

81. Sokolowski, *The God of Faith and Reason*, 99.

shortly after him. In other words, the teaching of *De Regno* was abandoned by the very first generation of Thomists. His Gelasian dualism easily lapses into monism, either civil religion in pursuit of political power or theocracy in pursuit of ecclesiastical control.

This brings us to the fourth conclusion, about Aquinas's relationship with liberalism. Liberalism contains strains with widely varying orientations toward Aquinas's politics and to Christian dualism more generally. The correspondences between contemporary pluralism and Aquinas's dualism must be articulated with some nuance lest they obscure real differences between them.

Our fifth and final conclusion will be less substantiated but no less weighty, namely that the modern tradition of politics does not escape the medieval orientation toward institutions. The Augustinian and Aristotelian traditions abstracted from questions of human ends to establish the perfect theoretical formulation of institutions. They thus bear a surprising similarity to modern traditions of politics, particularly the contractarian tradition. This fact could lead to a new evaluation of early modern philosophy in light of the question: does the early modern rejection of teleology distinguish it from medieval political philosophy that had also abandoned teleology?

In short, Aquinas's greatest challenge for all these traditions is a humble pedagogy. Aquinas does not pretend to have all the answers, nor does he claim his theory to be a substitute for the good, honest hard work of everyday politics. To that challenge we now turn.

Conclusion

On Actions and Words

Pierre Manent argues in *Metamorphoses of the City* that Christianity introduces a "disparity between actions and words" in public life.[1] This "unmanageable gap" has been "impossible to master," offering in words the promise of a reality far beyond the mundane, but not, in fact, delivering this communion "for which it has awakened the desire."[2]

While Manent does not analyze this gap in detail, he seems to have at least two distinct but related issues in mind. First, this divorce between actions and words points to a standard of good and evil that stands independent of the human person and judges his actions. Second, this divorce points to a distinction between the world in which we live and act and the world we look forward to in hope: Augustine's Two Cities.[3] This moral dimension is not unique to Christianity: many thinkers and communities have set a standard of goodness beyond convention, utility, or pleasure. The eschatological dimension, however, distinguishes Christianity

---

1. Pierre Manent, *Metamorphoses of the City*, trans. Marc LePain (Cambridge, Mass.: Harvard University Press, 2013), 9–10. The phrase "unmanageable gap" comes from his article "City, Empire, Church, Nation" in *City Journal*, Summer 2012, https://www.city-journal.org/html/city-empire-church-nation-13487.html.
2. Manent, *Metamorphoses of the City*, 5.
3. Manent, *Metamorphoses of the City*, 274–303.

from other faiths: it promises a realization of the City of God that must remain invisible within history.

These two dimensions come together in an ethics that appears to hate the present, the natural, and the love of one's own in favor of the supernatural, the future, and the stranger. Christianity "requires men to love what they naturally hate (their enemies) and to hate what they naturally love (themselves)."[4]

For critics of Christianity like Rousseau, this gap limits the effectiveness of man's life in common, which is to say politics: "action ordered and implemented." The Greek *polis* was "the first complete implementation of human action, the ordering of the human world that made action possible and meaningful." The Christian chasm between word and action, however, became a chasm within the *polis*: between the Kingdom of God and the earthly city, frustrating the ability of humans to deliberate and formulate "projects of action."[5]

Thus, as Manent has it, modern politics starting with Martin Luther has sought to reduce or eliminate this gap between words and actions, to create a "perfect equation between action and word."[6] Machiavelli, for example, proposes to attend to what men do rather than what they say, to observe "the effectual truth of the thing" rather than "imagined republics" and standards of good and evil that for Machiavelli have no real reference to political reality.[7] Machiavelli wishes to set aside that standard in the interest of offering meaningful counsel to rulers who would wrestle with Fortuna.

To make matters worse, Manent argues, the church has not

---

4. Manent, "City, Empire, Church, Nation."
5. Manent, "City, Empire, Church, Nation."
6. Manent, *Metamorphoses of the City*, 311–13.
7. Manent, *Metamorphoses of the City*, 7.

Conclusion: On Actions and Words

been an effective source of unity. For this reason, the West has sought new bases for bridging the divide between word and action, now seeking hope for unity in "humanity."[8] Manent also says that the theory of one of the greatest theorists of this gap, St. Augustine, is not very "useful."[9] He describes the theory as "neither practical nor theoretical" but rather "an intermediary perspective" that cultivates a certain disposition that "incites us to desire to enter into the city of God", but does not "orient ourselves in the cities of people."[10]

But exactly what is Augustine's thought supposed to be "useful" for? While Manent seems ambivalent about Christianity's gap between word and action, Aquinas and Augustine are not. If one thinks that this theory should be useful for closing the gap between the Two Cities, then it indeed surely does not do that. If a theory should be useful for living this tension, however, then here I think we are on the right track. To restate the problem: the gap between words and actions is crucial to maintain, because it reflects not only the division between right and wrong knowable by reason but also between the earthly city and the City of God laid out in God's revelation.

We have seen *De Regno* present a teaching of politics deeply riven by this divide between words and action. The five principles we laid out each specify an aspect of this tension between reality as we know it and reality as it will become. Gelasianism is the distinction and coordination between the two powers that themselves reflect how earthly power can conduce toward but never attain beatitude. The rejection of civil religion and theocracy is the rejection of any attempt to flatten out or eliminate that es-

---

8. Manent, *Metamorphoses of the City*, 323–27.
9. Manent, *Metamorphoses of the City*, 280.
10. Manent, *Metamorphoses of the City*, 290.

chatological dimension. Thomistic naturalism indicates that the person is good by nature but fallen in his will in a way that can be repaired only at the end of history. It would be vastly simpler to argue that the person is by nature good or bad, but that would betray this gap between the promise of a new reality and the arrival of that reality.[11] Ambivalence toward regime forms is the principle that the earthly city cannot be confused with the City of God. Finally, pedagogy adverts to the fact that we hope to move toward something better but always fall short.

Manent's insight is valuable, for he invites us to ask how a given regime lives out that gap practically. After all, if this divorce between word and speech can only be partly reconciled this side of the *eschaton*, then we must ask how a regime in its lived reality respects or attempts to transgress that divorce. Further, how do Christians individually and ecclesially give witness to the necessity of attending to this gap in a society that knows next to nothing of that gap or the promise of the *eschaton*? For that matter, how will Christians resist the lure of ideologies that promise to instantiate that *eschaton* in the here and now?

A key task of Christianity for politics must be to determine ways to live that tension. *De Regno* can be read as such an education in the practical dynamic Manent describes. A pathos pervades the text, one that orients the king toward a difficult but noble goal. In fact, Aquinas nowhere promises his royal reader that he will attain to that goal, but in offering a pedagogy toward virtue, the king has come to see himself as a *minister Dei* who pursues a peace that conduces toward the beatitude mediated by the church. That beatitude, it has been made abundantly clear, is a gift of God, not of the king, who is a mere man and not a divine figure.

---

11. Manent, *Metamorphoses of the City*, 280.

Conclusion: On Actions and Words 259

In these ways, *De Regno* reveals Manent's gap between actions and words: politics in the Christian dispensation looks forward in hope to the City of God but does not instantiate it and, indeed, must rest content in the humility that the church and not political authority mediates the fullness of God's grace. As Aquinas's account of civil religion reveals, the temptation to close this gap is strong. Further, in *De Regno,* Aquinas sets virtue and beatitude as the good of humans, not honor, glory, or pleasure. Indeed, the centerpiece of *De Regno*, the much-misunderstood "The Reward of the King" (I.7-12), orients the entire text around the question of the good of man as the true reward of the virtuous king. We might think of this divorce between words and actions as a practical heuristic for all the principles we found in *De Regno*. And while we might see those principles as a theory of politics, they also point toward the pathos of political life: a spirituality of politics as much as a theology of politics.

Understanding this gap as a practical matter raises the question of obstacles to maintaining it. Several obstacles to accepting this gap feature in *De Regno*. First and foremost, the king might see his reward as something other than the good of his people. Second, he will especially be inclined to do so if he sees that reward as something other and less than beatitude, for example, honor, glory, or riches. Third, the king might see himself as God. In all these ways, he might be tempted to see himself as simply matter satisfied by a material reward, or simply spiritual, satisfied by a purely spiritual reward and even God Himself.

These obstacles, for all of their variety, are clarified in the light of this problem of the gap adumbrated by Manent. Tracey Rowland offers another view of it: "The pathos of the moral life is generated by the constant struggle of the person to cooperate with the Holy Spirit and the work of grace and thereby grow in the likeness of Christ, against the double temptation to self-idolatry and self-subjectification."[12] The "double temptation" Rowland presents is a temptation to opt out of the challenge of being human, to close the gap of Manent by denying its challenge or by pretending to have transcended it. By warning the king against finding his end in material things or in self-deification, Aquinas offers the king the opportunity to grow in virtue and to serve his people not despite of the gap, but because of it.

When one asks what *De Regno* has to say about religion and politics in our own time, one might say that it offers an ethical attitude for living out this tension, a spirituality of politics. *De Regno* does not supply the answers to all of our problems, but it does offer a precious and urgent gift: a spirituality of politics for living in the "gap" between the world promised by Christian revelation and the world in which we now live. And in the face of ever-growing political, social, economic, and ecological problems that have no immediate solutions, we might see this spirituality as a gift to be brought into dialogue with the whole world.

If that gap has indeed been "unmanageable," it is perhaps because we have not availed ourselves of that spirituality. And while that spirituality has always been necessary, it is perhaps more so in our own time. If the need for it be great, however, we may hope the receptivity for it will be as well.

---

12. Tracey Rowland, "Vatican II, John Paul II, and Postconciliar Theology," in *Called to be the Children of God: The Catholic Theology of Human Deification*, ed. David Meconi, SJ, and Carl E. Olson (San Francisco: Ignatius Press, 2016), 245–62. Rowland notes that Aristotle anticipates this line of thought with his claim that man is neither beast nor god (Rowland, "Vatican II," 250).

BIBLIOGRAPHY

Aquinas, Thomas. *De Regno, ad regem Cypri*. Edited by R. M. Spiazzi. Turin: Marietti, 1954. Available at "De Regno," edited by Roberto Busa, http://www.corpusthomisticum.org/orp.html.
———. *On Kingship*. Translated by I. Th. Eschmann. Toronto: Pontifical Institute of Mediaeval Studies, 1949.
———. *Du Gouvernement Royal*. Translated by Claude Roguet. Paris: Librairie du Dauphin, 1931.
———. *Commentary on the "Nicomachean Ethics."* Translated by C. I. Litzinger, OP. Chicago: Henry Regnery Company, 1964.
———. *De regno ad Regem Cypri*. Edited by H.-F. Dondaine, OP. In *Sancti Thomae de Aquino opera omnia*. Vol. 42 of *Opuscula* III, 417–71. Roma: Editori di San Tommaso, 1979.
———. *Thomas Aquinas On Law, Morality and Politics*. Translated by Richard J. Regan. 2nd ed. Indianapolis, Ind.: Hackett Publishing Company, 2002.
———. *Aquinas: Political Writings*. Cambridge Texts in the History of Political Thought. Edited and translated by R.W. Dyson. Cambridge: Cambridge University Press, 2002.
Aristotle. *Nicomachean Ethics*. Translated by Robert C. Bartlett and Susan D. Collins. Chicago: University of Chicago Press, 2011.
———. *Politics*. 2nd ed. Translated by Carnes Lord. Chicago: University of Chicago Press, 2013.
Arnhart, Larry. "Statesmanship as Magnanimity: Classical, Christian & Modern." *Polity* 16, no. 2 (1983). 2632–83.
Assman, Jan. *The Price of Monotheism*. Translated by Robert Savage. Stanford, Calif.: Stanford University Press, 2009.
Augustine. *De Civitate Dei*. Vols. 47 and 48 of Corpus Christianorum Series Latina. Edited by Bernard Dombart and Alphonsus Kalb. Turnhout, Belgium: Brepols, 1955.
Barraclough, Geoffrey. *The Origins of Modern Germany*. Oxford: Blackwell, 1947.
Baur, Michael. "Aquinas on Law and Natural Law." In *The Oxford Handbook of Aquinas*, edited by Brian Davies and Eleanor Stump, 238–54. Oxford: Oxford University Press, 2011.
Bejczy, I. P., and Cary J. Nederman, eds. *Princely Virtues in the Middle Ages, 1200–1500*. Turnhout: Brepols, 2007.

Bibliography

Bellah, Robert N. "Civil Religion in America." *Daedalus* 96, no. 1 (1967): 1–21.
Beiner, Ronald. "Machiavelli, Hobbes, and Rousseau on Civil Religion." *Review of Politics* 55, no. 4 (1993): 617–38.
———. *Civil Religion: A Dialogue in the History of Political Philosophy*. Cambridge: Cambridge University Press, 2011.
Benestad, J. Brian. *Church, State, and Society*. Washington, D.C.: The Catholic University of America Press, 2011.
Bevir, Mark, ed. *Modern Pluralism*. Cambridge: Cambridge University Press, 2012.
Black, Antony. *Political Thought in Europe, 1250–1450*. Cambridge: Cambridge University Press, 1992.
Blythe, James M. Introduction to *On the Government of Rulers*. Translated by James M. Blythe, 1–59. Philadelphia: University of Pennsylvania Press, 1997.
———. *Ideal Government and the Mixed Constitution in the Middle Ages*. Princeton, N.J.: Princeton University Press, 2014.
Boyle, Leonard E., OP, ed. "The De Regno and the Two Powers." In *Facing History: A Different Thomas Aquinas*, 3–12. Louvain-la-Neuve: Collège Cardinal Mercier, 2000.
Breidenbach, Michael D., and William McCormick, SJ. "Aquinas on Tyranny, Resistance, and the End of Politics." *Perspectives on Political Science* 44, no. 1 (2014): 10–17.
Bruno, Michael J. S. *Political Augustinianism: Modern Interpretations of Augustine's Political Thought*. Minneapolis, Minn.: Fortress Press, 2014.
Carlyle, A. J. and R. W. *A History of Mediaeval Political Theory in the West*. Vol. 5. Edinburgh: W. Blackwood & Sons, 1936.
Casanova, José. "Globalizing Catholicism and the Return to a "Universal" Church." In *Transnational Religion and Fading States*, edited by Susanne Hoeber Rudolph and James Piscatori, 121–43. Boulder, Co.: Westview Press, 1997.
Celano, Anthony J. "The Concept of Worldly Beatitude in the Writings of Thomas Aquinas." *Journal of the History of Philosophy* 25, no. 2 (1987): 215–26.
Chenu, Marie-Dominique, OP. Book review. *Bulletin thomiste* (1928): 198.
Collins, Susan D. "Moral Virtue and the Limits of the Political Community in Aristotle's *Nicomachean Ethics*." *American Journal of Political Science* 48, no. 1 (2004): 47–61.
Coppleston, Frederick, SJ. *A History of Medieval Philosophy*. New York: Harper & Row, 1993.
Davies, Brian. *The Thought of Thomas Aquinas*. Oxford: Clarendon Press, 1992.
———. *Thomas Aquinas's Summa Theologiae: A Guide and Commentary*. New York: Oxford University Press, 2014.
Dawson, Christopher. *The Formation of Christendom*. San Francisco: Ignatius Press, 2008.

De Koninck, Charles. *De la primauté du bien commun contres les personnalistes.* Québec: Éditions de l'Université Laval, 1943.

Deneen, Patrick. *Why Liberalism Failed.* New Haven, Conn.: Yale University Press, 2018.

Dreher, Rod. *The Benedict Option.* New York: Sentinel, 2017.

Di Blasi, Fulvio. *God and the Natural Law: A Rereading of Thomas Aquinas.* South Bend, Ind.: St. Augustine's Press, 2006.

Dodaro, Robert. *Christ and the Just Society in the Thought of Augustine.* Cambridge: Cambridge University Press, 2008.

Eschmann, I. Th., OP. Introduction to *On Kingship.* Translated by I. Th. Eschmann, ix–xxxix. Toronto: Pontifical Institute of Mediaeval Studies, 1949.

———. "St. Thomas Aquinas on the Two Powers." *Mediaeval Studies* 20, no. 1 (1958): 177–205.

Faulkner, Robert. *The Case for Greatness: Honorable Ambition and Its Critics.* New Haven, Conn.: Yale University Press, 2008.

Finnis, John. *Aquinas: Moral, Political, and Legal Theory.* Oxford: Clarendon Press, 1998.

Fitzgerald, Laurence, OP. "St. Thomas Aquinas and the Two Powers." *Angelicum* 56 (1979): 515–56.

Folz, Robert. *The Concept of Empire in Western Europe from the Fifth to the Fourteenth Century.* Translated by Sheila Ann Ogilvie. London: Edward Arnold, 1969.

Foucault, Michel. *Security, Territory, Population: Lectures at the Collège de France, 1977–1978.* Translated by Graham Burchell. New York: Picador, 2007.

Fortin, Ernest L., AA. *The Birth of Philosophic Christianity.* Vol. 1 of *Collected Essays.* Edited by J. Brian Benestad. Lanham, Md.: Rowman and Littlefield, 1996.

Froelich, Gregory. "The Equivocal Status of *Bonum Commune*." *The New Scholasticism* 63, no. 1 (1989): 38–57.

Garnett, Richard W. "The Freedom of the Church." *Journal of Catholic Social Thought* 4, no. 1 (2007): 59–86.

———. "'The Freedom of the Church': (Towards) An Exposition, Translation, and Defense." *Journal of Contemporary Legal Issues* 21 (July 2013): 33–57.

Genicot, Léopold. "Le *De Regno*: Spéculation ou réalisme?" In *Aquinas and Problems of His Time*, edited by G. Verbeke and D. Verheist, 3–17. Leuven: Leuven University Press, 1976.

Gilbert, Allen. *Machiavelli's* Prince *and its Forerunners,* The Prince *as a Typical Book* De Regimine Principum. Durham, N.C.: Duke University Press, 1938.

Gilby, Thomas. *The Political Thought of Thomas Aquinas.* Chicago: University of Chicago Press, 1958.

Giles of Rome. *Giles of Rome's "On Ecclesiastical Power": A Medieval Theory of World Government.* Edited and translated by R.W. Dyson. New York: Columbia University Press, 2004.

Gilson, Étienne. *Christianisme et Philosophie*. Paris: Vrin, 1936.
———. *Dante the Philosopher*. Translated by David Moore. London: Sheed & Ward, 1952.
Gregory the Great. *The Book of Pastoral Rule*. Translated by George E. Demacopoulos. Popular Patristics Series. Crestwood, N.Y.: St. Vladimir's Seminary Press, 2007.
Griesbach, Marc F. "John of Paris as a Representative of Thomistic Political Philosophy." In *An Etienne Gilson Tribute: Presented by His North American Students with a Response by Étienne Gilson*, edited by Charles J. O'Neil, 33–50. Milwaukee, Minn.: Marquette University Press, 1959.
Guerra, Marc D. "Beyond Natural Law Talk: Politics and Prudence in St. Thomas Aquinas's *On Kingship*." *Perspectives on Politics* 31, no. 1 (2002): 9–14.
Habermas, Jürgen, and Joseph Ratzinger. *Dialectics of Secularization: On Reason and Religion*. Translated by Brian McNeil. San Francisco: Ignatius Press, 2006.
Halbertal, Moshe, and Stephen Holmes. *The Beginning of Politics*. Princeton, N.J.: Princeton University Press, 2017.
Hill, Geoffrey F. *The Frankish Period*. Vol. 2 of *A History of Cyprus*. Cambridge: Cambridge University Press, 1948.
Hittinger, Russell. "The Coherence of the Four Basic Principles of Catholic Social Doctrine: An Interpretation." Pontifical Academy of Social Sciences, XVIII Plenary Session (Città Del Vaticano), May 2, 2008.
Hobbes, Thomas. *Leviathan*. Edited by Edwin Curley. Indianapolis, Ind.: Hackett, 1994.
Holloway, Carson. "Christianity, Magnanimity, and Statesmanship." *The Review of Politics* 61, no. 4 (1999): 581–604.
Horwitz, Paul. "Freedom of the Church without Romance." *Journal of Contemporary Legal Issues* 21 (May 2013): 59–132.
Howland, Jacob. "Aristotle's Great-Souled Man." *Review of Politics* 64, no. 1 (2002): 27–56.
John of Paris (Quidort). *De Potestate Regia et Papali*. Translated by Arthur P. Monahan. New York: Columbia University Press, 1974.
Johnson, Mark F. "Did St. Thomas Attribute a Doctrine of Creation to Aristotle?" *The New Scholasticism* 63, no. 2 (1989): 129–55.
Jordan, Mark D. "*De Regno* and the Place of Political Thinking in Thomas Aquinas." *Medioevo* 18 (1992): 151–68.
Kalyvas, Andreas. "The Tyranny of Dictatorship: When the Greek Tyrant Met the Roman Dictator." *Political Theory* 35, no. 4 (2007): 412–43.
Kaveny, Cathleen. *Law's Virtues: Fostering Autonomy and Solidarity in American Society*. Washington, D.C.: Georgetown University Press, 2012.
Kern, Fritz. *Kingship and Law in the Middle Ages*. Translated by S. B. Chrimes. Oxford: Blackwell, 1939.

Keys, Mary M. "Humility and Greatness of Soul." *Perspectives on Political Science* 37, no. 4 (1996): 17–22.

———. *Aquinas, Aristotle, and the Promise of the Common Good*. Cambridge: Cambridge University Press, 2006.

Kozinski, Thaddeus. *The Political Problem of Religious Pluralism: And Why Philosophers Can't Solve It*. Lanham, Md.: Lexington Books, 2010.

Kraynak, Robert. *Christian Faith and Modern Democracy*. Notre Dame, Ind.: University of Notre Dame Press, 2001.

Kries, Douglas. "Thomas Aquinas and the Politics of Moses." *Review of Politics* 52, no. 1 (1990): 84–104.

———. "The Virtue of Religion in the Political Thought of Thomas Aquinas." *Proceedings of the PMR Conference* 15 (1990): 103–15.

———. "Defending Robert Bellarmine." In *Jerusalem, Athens, & Rome: Essays in Honor of James V. Schall, S.J.*, edited by Marc D. Guerra, 120–38. South Bend, Ind.: St. Augustine's Press, 2013.

Lauer, Quentin. Review of Max Seckler, *Das Heil in der Geschichte*. *Theological Studies* 26, no. 2 (1965): 317.

Lerner, Ralph, and Muhsin Mahdi, eds. *Medieval Political Philosophy: A Sourcebook*. Ithaca, N.Y.: Cornell University Press, 1972.

Levin, Yuval. *The Fractured Republic*. New York: Basic Books, 2016.

Levy, Jacob T. "Not So *novus an ordo*: Constitutions without Social Contracts." *Political Theory* 37, no. 2 (2009): 191–217.

———. *Rationalism, Pluralism, and Freedom*. Oxford: Oxford University Press, 2017.

Locke, John. *Two Treatises of Government*. Cambridge Texts in the History of Political Thought. Edited by Peter Laslett. Cambridge: Cambridge University Press, 1996.

Manent, Pierre. *An Intellectual History of Liberalism*. Translated by Rebecca Balinski. Princeton, N.J.: Princeton University Press, 1996.

———. *Metamorphoses of the City*. Translated by Marc LePain. Cambridge, Mass.: Harvard University Press, 2013.

Mansfield, Harvey. *Machiavelli's New Modes and Orders: A Study of the "Discourses on Livy."* Chicago: University of Chicago Press, 1996.

Maritain, Jacques. *An Essay on Christian Philosophy*. Translated by Edward H. Flannery. New York: Philosophical Library, 1955.

———. *Integral Humanism*. New York: Scribner's Sons, 1968.

McCoy, Charles N. R. *The Structure of Political Thought: A Study in the History of Political Ideas*. New York: McGraw-Hill Book Company, 1963.

Milbank, John. *Theology and Social Theory: Beyond Secular Reason*. Oxford: Blackwell, 1990.

Muñiz-Fraticelli, Victor. *The Structure of Pluralism*. Oxford: Oxford University Press, 2014.

———. "The Distinctiveness of Religious Liberty." In *Mapping the Legal Boundaries of Belonging: Religion and Multiculturalism from Israel to Canada*, edited by Rene Provost. 99–120. New York: Oxford University Press, 2014.

Murray, John Courtney, SJ. "Contemporary Orientations of Catholic Thought on Church and State in the Light of History." *Theological Studies* 10, no. 2 (1949): 177–234.

Nederman, Cary J. "Nature, Sin and the Origins of Society: The Ciceronian Tradition in Medieval Political Thought." *Journal of the History of Ideas* 49, no. 1 (1988): 3–26.

———. "Aristotelianism and the Origins of 'Political Science' in the Twelfth Century." *Journal of the History of Ideas* 52, no. 2 (1991): 179–94.

Nelson, Eric. *The Hebrew Republic*. Cambridge: Cambridge University Press, 2010.

Nicholls, David. *The Pluralist State: The Political Ideas of J. N. Figgis and his Contemporaries*. London: Palgrave, 1994.

Nichols, Mary. "Response to Robert Bartlett, 1995." *American Political Science Review* 89, no. 1 (1995): 152–55.

Novak, Michael. "Aquinas and the Heretics." *First Things* 58 (December 1995): 33–38.

O'Donovan, John, and Joan Lockwood O'Donovan, eds. *From Irenaeus to Grotius: A Sourcebook in Christian Political Thought*. Grand Rapids, Mich.: Wm. B. Eerdmans, 1999.

Oakley, Francis. *Empty Bottles of Gentilism: Kingship and Divinity in Late Antiquity and the Early Middle Ages (to 1050)*. Vol. 1 of *The Emergence of Western Political Thought in the Latin Middle Ages*. New Haven, Conn.: Yale University Press, 2010.

———. *The Mortgage of the Past: Reshaping the Ancient Political Inheritance (1050–1300)*. Vol. 2 of *The Emergence of Western Political Thought in the Latin Middle Ages*. New Haven, Conn.: Yale University Press, 2012.

O'Rahilly, Alfred. "Notes on St. Thomas. IV. *De Regimine Principum*. V. Tolomeo of Lucca, the Continuator of the '*De Regimine Principum*.'" *Irish Ecclesiastical Record* 31 (1928): 396–410.

Pakaluk, Michael. "Is the Common Good of Political Society Limited and Instrumental?" *The Review of Metaphysics* 55, no. 1 (2001): 57–94.

Peterson, Erik. *Theological Tractates*. Translated by Michael Hollerich. Palo Alto, Calif.: Stanford University Press, 2012.

Pew Research Center. "Many Countries Favor Specific Religions, Officially or Unofficially." October 3, 2017. http://www.pewforum.org/2017/10/03/many-countries-favor-specific-religions-officially-or-unofficially/.

Philpott, Daniel. "Explaining the Political Ambivalence of Religion." *American Political Science Review* 101, no. 3 (2007): 505–25.

Pinckaers, Servais, OP. *The Sources of Christian Ethics*. Translated by Mary

Thomas Noble, OP. Washington, D.C.: The Catholic University of America Press, 1995.

———. "The Sources of the Ethics of St. Thomas Aquinas." In *The Ethics of Aquinas*, edited by Stephen J. Pope, 21–23. Washington, D.C.: Georgetown University Press, 2002.

Ptolemy of Lucca. *On the Government of Rulers: De Regimine Principum*. Translated by James M. Blythe. Philadelphia: University of Pennsylvania Press, 1997.

Quetif, Jacques, OP, and Jacques Échard, OP. *Scriptores Ordinis Praedicatorum*. Paris, 1719.

Riedl, Matthias. "Clarifications concerning the Concept of Political Theology: Carl Schmitt and Augustine." Paper presented at the annual conference of the American Political Science Association, Philadelphia, August 28–31, 2003.

Rousseau, Jean-Jacques. *"The Social Contract" and Other Later Political Writings*. Cambridge Texts in the History of Political Thought. Translated and edited by Victor Gourevitch. Cambridge: Cambridge University Press, 1997.

Rowland, Tracey. *Culture and the Thomist Tradition*. London: Routledge, 2003.

Rudolph, Susanne Hoeber. "Introduction: Religion, States, and Transnational Civil Society." In *Transnational Religion and Fading States,* edited by Susanne Hoeber Rudolph and James Piscatori. Boulder, Co.: Westview Press, 1997.

Schall, James V., SJ. "Transcendence and Political Philosophy." *The Review of Politics* 55, no. 2 (1993): 247–65.

———. "Fides et Ratio: Approaches to a Roman Catholic Political Philosophy." *Review of Politics* 62, no. 1 (2000): 49–75.

Schragger, Richard C., and Micah Schwartzman. "Against Religious Institutionalism." *Virginia Law Review* 99, no. 5 (2013): 16.

Schwartzman, Micah. "What if Religion Is Not Special?" *University of Chicago Law Review* 79, no. 4 (2012): 1351–427.

Simpson, Peter. *A Philosophical Commentary on the Politics of Aristotle*. Chapel Hill: University of North Carolina Press, 1998.

Skinner, Quentin. *Liberty Before Liberalism*. Canto Classics. Cambridge: Cambridge University Press, 2012.

Sokolowski, Robert. *The God of Faith and Reason*. Washington, D.C.: The Catholic University of America Press, 1982.

Spiering, Jamie Anne. "*Liber est Causa Sui*: Thomas Aquinas and the Maxim "The Free is the Cause of Itself." *Review of Metaphysics* 65 (December 2011): 351–76.

Stoner, James R. "Was Thomas Aquinas a Republican?" Paper presented for the annual conference of the Southern Political Science Association, New Orleans, January 5, 2007.

Taylor, Charles. *A Secular Age*. Cambridge, Mass.: Belknap Press, 2007.
Thorndyke, Lynn, and Pearl Kibre. *A Catalogue of Incipits of Mediaeval Scientific Writings in Latin*. Cambridge, Mass.: The Mediaeval Academy of America, 1937.
Tierney, Brian. *The Crisis of Church and State: 1050–1300, with Selected Documents*. Toronto: University of Toronto Press, 1988.
Tocqueville, Alexis de. *Democracy in America*. Translated and edited by Harvey C. Mansfield and Delba Winthrop. Chicago: University of Chicago Press, 2000.
Toft, Monica Duffy, Daniel Philpott, and Timothy Samuel Shah. *God's Century: Resurgent Religion and Global Politics*. New York: W.W. Norton & Company, 2011.
Torrell, Jean-Pierre, OP. *Saint Thomas Aquinas: The Person and His Work*. Translated by Robert Royal. Washington, D.C.: The Catholic University of America Press, 1996.
Wallis, Jim. *God's Politics: Why the Right Gets It Wrong and the Left Doesn't Get It*. San Francisco: HarperSanFrancisco, 2006.
Wear, Michael. *Reclaiming Hope: Lessons Learned in the Obama White House About the Future of Faith in America*. New York: Thomas Nelson, 2017.
Weithman, Paul J., "Augustine and Aquinas on Original Sin and the Function of Political Authority." *Journal of the History of Philosophy* 30, no. 3 (1992): 353–76.
Winters, Michael Sean. *Left at the Altar: How the Democrats Lost the Catholics and How the Catholics Can Save the Democrats*. New York: Basic Books, 2008.
Wright, Matthew D. "The Aim of Law and the Nature of Political Community: An Assessment of Finnis on Aquinas." *The American Journal of Jurisprudence* 54, no. 1 (2009): 133–60.
Wyllie, Robert. "Reconsidering Tyranny and Tyrannicide in Aquinas's *De Regno*." *Perspectives on Political Science* 47, no. 3 (2018): 154–60.

INDEX

ambivalence, to particular regimes, 213–15
Aquinas, Thomas. *See Commentary on the "Sentences"* (Aquinas); *De Regno* (Aquinas); *Summa Theologica* (Aquinas)
Aquinas: Moral, Political, and Legal Theory (Finnis), 16
aristocracy, 41–42, 55, 79, 81–82
Aristotle: Aquinas commentaries on, 6; Cicero and, 35; *De Regno* and, 8–9; free men in, 38–39; glory and honor in, 103–4; heart in, 51n53; John of Paris and, 222–26; magnanimity in, 104–5, 105n11; in medieval political thought, 17; *Nicomachean Ethics*, 48, 104–5, 131n44, 136n47; political naturalism in, 33, 95, 147–48, 212, 224; *Politics*, 9, 12, 32, 41, 57, 65–66, 85, 131, 202; slavery in, 38; as source, 23; *speculum principum* genre and, 25–26; tyranny in, 84–85
Augustine: Cicero and, 35; *De Regno* and, 8–9; evil in, 40; family in, 67–68, 68n11; glory in, 104; government in, 66; in medieval political thought, 17; monarchy in, 114–15, 118–19; political authority in, 70–72; as source, 23; tyranny in, 65; virtue in, 103
authority, political: in Augustine, 70; causality and, 34; community and, 31; dualism and, 210–11; monarchy and, 32, 99, 111; monism and, 209; naturalness of, 27–37; priesthood and, 177; spiritual *vs.*, 186–87, 202; subordination of religious to, 223; tyranny and, 89–90, 136
Avicenna, 28n11, 29n12, 33, 33n21, 36, 119

beatitude, 134, 140, 148, 164–71, 185–86
Bellarmine, Robert, 206
Berman, Harold J., 251
Black, Antony, 32, 35, 44
Boniface VIII, 226, 231
Boyle, Leonard E., 13n30, 185, 185n38, 195, 205
Busa, Roberto, 87n27

causality, 31, 34, 136n47, 223
Chenu, Marie-Dominique, 14, 197, 200
Christian Faith and Modern Democracy (Kraynak), 17–18
church/state model, 206–32
Cicero, 17, 23, 60, 67; divinity in, 108n14; glory and honor in, 101–4; as mediator between Aristotle and Augustine, 73; political naturalism in, 33–35, 43, 47, 69, 95, 212
City of God, The (Augustine), 40, 65–66, 68n11, 71, 91–92, 103–4, 118–19
"City upon a Hill," 3
civil religion, 2, 21, 26, 176–77, 183–84, 197–98, 209–12, 228
clemency, 153–55, 188
Cold War, 3
Commentary on Aristotle's "Metaphysics" (Aquinas), 51n53
Commentary on the "Sentences" (Aquinas), 5, 35, 92, 194, 205
common good, 30–31, 95–96, 172–73
contractarianism, 21–22, 233–34, 236–40, 247, 251–52, 254
creation, 47, 136n47, 151–52, 157–63, 187–88, 196, 199–200, 202–3, 217
Crusades, 26, 44

269

Dante Alighieri, 180, 224
David, 41–42, 58, 115, 123–24
De Ecclesiastica Potestate (Giles of Rome), 227
De finibus malorum (Cicero), 108n14
de Maistre, Joseph, 177
democracy: alternatives to, 3–4; monarchy and, 64; tyranny and, 41, 63
D'Entrèves, Alessandro, 207
De officiis (Cicero), 102
De Regimine Principum (Aquinas), 11
De Regno (Aquinas): audience and aim of, 13–14, 16–17, 26; in canon, 253–54; as collection of fragments, 12–13; controversy surrounding, 11–12; dating of, 12; genre of, 15–16; as neglected text, 5–6; ordering of, 99–100; as practical work, 6–8; as *speculum principum*, 7–8, 13–16, 24–27, 54, 57–58, 70, 78–79, 86, 88, 144, 162–63, 197; structure of, 195–201; *Summa vs.*, 9; teaching of, 195–201; textual traditions surrounding, 10–12
De re militari (Vegetius), 201
de Tocqueville, Alexis, 214–15, 218
Deuteronomy, Book of, 111
Dionysius of Syracuse, 126
Donatism, 71–72, 118
Dondaine, H.-F., 9–12, 28n11, 42n43, 61, 87, 99–100, 101n6, 141, 143n55, 163, 169n20, 197
dualism, 1, 175, 207, 209–11, 219, 228, 235–36, 238, 240, 242–45, 247, 251, 254
Dyson, R. W., 56

Ecclesiastes, Book of, 29, 46
Échard, J., 10, 12
Education of a Christian Prince (Erasmus), 24
Ephesians, Epistle to, 121
Erasmus, Desiderius, 24
eschatology, 216–17, 226, 255, 258
Eschmann, I. Th., 9–10, 12–13, 13n30, 14–15, 30n14, 31, 33, 36, 41, 42n43, 48, 81, 87, 101n6, 134n46, 141, 143–44, 156, 157n9, 163, 170, 185n39, 192, 205
Ezekiel, Book of, 39–40, 52, 110

Fall of Man, 1, 70, 73, 134, 147, 149, 195–97, 199–200, 212–13, 217
Figgis, N., 248
Finnis, John, 16, 92–93, 151
Foucault, Michel, 26–27, 155–56
France, 179, 181–82
Frederick II, Emperor, 56
free man, 37–47, 106–7, 109, 111, 155

Garnett, Richard W., 221, 242, 245–46
Gelasianism, 1–2, 207–9, 217–18, 228–32, 235–50, 254
Genesis, Book of, 158
Giles of Rome, 221, 226–29, 231–32, 253–54
Gilson, Étienne, 171, 175–76, 193
glory, 101–3, 106, 201
God: creation and, 47, 136n47, 151–52, 187–88; government of, 26–27; law and, 189–91; monarchy and, 87, 97, 108–19, 121, 137; political naturalism and, 192; in *prooemium*, 27; sovereignty of, 91–92, 193–94; tyranny and, 63–64, 90–91, 109–10
government: in Augustine, 66; of Christ, 169–70; community and, 42–43; of God *vs.* humans, 26–27; of multitude, 37–38, 50; of nature, 152–57
Griesbach, Marc F., 207, 222, 225

Habermas, Jürgen, 4
happiness, 71–72, 113–14, 116
Henry VI, Emperor, 56
Hittinger, Russell, 49
Hobbes, Thomas, 130, 172, 239, 250n76
honor, 101–2, 106
Horwitz, Paul, 241n58
hypocrisy, 103–4
institutionalism, teleological, 217–18
Islam, 44

Jesus Christ: beatitude and, 164; government of, 169–70; law and, 174; monarchy and, 110–11; priesthood and, 174; salvation and, 71, 200
Job, Book of, 67, 131

Index 271

John of Paris, 180–81, 181n35, 221–26, 228–29, 231–32, 253–54
Jordan, Mark, 15, 17

Keys, Mary M., 16–17, 61
king. *See* monarchy
Kraynak, Robert, 17–18, 55, 171, 215, 217
Kraynak Dilemma, 18
Kries, Douglas, 179–80

law, 26–27, 98, 122, 129, 137, 165, 173–75, 177–79, 186–87, 189–91
Levy, Jacob T., 232–34, 236, 238, 240, 246–47, 249–50, 250n76, 252
liberalism, 3–4, 208–9, 211, 232–53
Locke, John, 91, 236–237

Machiavelli, Niccolò, 15, 24, 159, 239
Manent, Pierre, 255
Maritain, Jacques, 116, 147, 220, 250
marriage, 65–66
Marsilius of Padua, 224
McCoy, Charles N. R., 181n35, 222n20, 226–27
Metamorphoses of the City (Manent), 255
metaphysics, 31, 46, 63–64, 145, 154, 156, 225, 227, 243, 245
monarchy, 32, 61–62; "appeal to heaven" and, 86–93; in Augustine, 114–15, 118–19; as burdensome, 101; Christ and, 110–11; corruption and, 81–82; creation and, 187–88; in Giles of Rome, 227–28; glory and, 101–2, 201; God and, 87, 97, 108–19, 121, 137; Hebrews and, 76–77; honor and, 101–2; limitations of, 95–96; magnanimity of, 100–8, 135–36, 199; as office, 184–93; political authority and, 32, 99, 111; political naturalism and, 50–53; as prevailing ideology of time, 55–56; Rome and, 74–78, 128; as term, 58–59; between tyranny and, 74–79
monism, 209, 219, 234, 238, 251
Moses, 159–60, 174
Muñiz-Fraticelli, Victor, 232, 241, 243

Murray, John Courtney, 3, 175, 193, 206, 209, 221n20, 242

naturalism, political, 2, 73, 119, 146–47, 200, 212–13, 219–20; in Aristotle, 33, 95, 147–48; Cicero and, 43; Fall and, 134; God and, 192; monarchy and, 50–53; political authority and, 27–37; religion and, 180–81; revelation and, 210; virtue and, 189–90
Nederman, Cary, 17, 33, 35, 43–44, 73, 146–47, 201
Neuhaus, Richard John, 3–4
Nichols, Mary, 224
Nicomachean Ethics (Aristotle), 48, 104–5, 131n44, 136n47

Oakley, Francis, 31, 55–56, 208
oligarchy, 79–81
On Royal and Papal Power (John of Paris), 222
1 Corinthians, 191
1 Kings, 87n27
1 Peter, 89
1 Samuel, 86–87, 87n27, 121
O'Rahilly, A., 10

Paine, Thomas, 234
Paul, 67–68, 109, 216
pedagogy, political, 2, 96, 142, 166–67, 182–83, 213, 216–19, 228–29, 235–50
Peter, 110–11
Peterson, Erik, 183
Phaedo (Plato), 108n14
Pinckaers, Servais, 131n44, 142
Plato, 5, 51n54, 108n14, 158
pluralism, 22, 150, 219, 232–33, 232n37, 234–35, 240–50
Politics (Aristotle), 9, 12, 32, 41, 57, 65–66, 85, 131, 202
polyarchy, 77, 80, 82–83, 85, 89
priesthood, 111, 170–74, 176–77, 223–26
Prince, The (Machiavelli), 15, 24, 159
Proverbs, Book of, 68
prudence, 49, 96, 104, 154–57, 218

Psalms, Book of, 90, 115
Ptolemy of Lucca, 11

Quidort, Jean. *See* John of Paris

rationalism, 224–25, 232–33, 232n37, 233–40, 245
Rationalism, Pluralism, and Freedom (Levy), 232–33
Rawls, John, 234
redemption, 195–97, 199–200, 217
Republic (Plato), 51n54
revelation, 17, 60, 97, 112–13, 116–17, 140–41, 163–84, 196, 210, 217
Roguet, Claude, 14, 197
Romans, Epistle to, 109
Rousseau, Jean-Jacques, 161–62, 173
Rowland, Tracey, 259–60
Rule of St. Benedict, 111n18

Sallust, 75–76, 78, 103
Schmitt, Carl, 196
Schragger, Richard C., 245
Schwartzmann, Micah, 245
Scriptum Super Libros Sententiarum (Aquinas). *See Commentary on the "Sentences"* (Aquinas)
Simpson, Peter, 84–85
Social Contract (Rousseau), 161–62, 173
sociality, 28–30
Sokolowski, Robert, 210
Solomon, 29–30, 46, 68
speculum principum, 7–8, 13–16, 24–27, 54, 57–58, 70, 78–79, 86, 88, 144, 162–63, 197
Spinoza, Baruch, 177
Summa Theologica (Aquinas), 5–6, 9, 42, 88; apostates in, 205; coercion in, 205; creation in, 199–200; free men in, 39; law in, 26–27, 175, 191; *minister Dei* in, 111; political naturalism in, 35, 43; religion in, 180; revelation in, 167; temperance in, 155; theological virtues in, 168; tyrannicide in, 92
Symposium (Plato), 108n14

Taylor, Charles, 252
theocracy, 2, 72, 112, 118, 140–41, 209–12, 225
Tierney, Brian, 251
Trump, Donald, 3
tyrannicide, 16, 92–93, 130–31
tyranny, 61–62; in Aristotle, 84–85; in Augustine, 65; caprice of, 62–73; civil religion and, 211; common *vs.* private and, 63; damnation and, 134–38; defined, 126–27; family and, 67–68; fear and, 130; God and, 63–64, 90–91, 109–10; injustice of, 63–64; long-term effects of, 136–37; marriage and, 65–66; material losses of, 167; metaphysics and, 63–64; mild, 122–23; between monarchy and, 74–79; oligarchy and, 80–81; political authority and, 89–90, 136; preservation of, 79–86; pride and, 135–36; rationalism and, 233; types of, 83–84; virtue and, 65–67

Vegetius, 201

Whig Thomism, 3, 220
William of Moerbeke, 12, 48
Wyllie, Robert, 92

Zachariah, 123

~

The Christian Structure of Politics: On the "De Regno" of Thomas Aquinas was designed in Garamond and composed by Kachergis Book Design of Pittsboro, North Carolina. It was printed on 55-pound Natural Offset and bound by Maple Press of York, Pennsylvania.

www.ingramcontent.com/pod-product-compliance
Lightning Source LLC
Chambersburg PA
CBHW020317010526
44107CB00054B/1876